CONSCIENCE IN EARLY MODERN
ENGLISH LITERATURE

Conscience in Early Modern English Literature describes how poetry, theology, and politics intersect in the early modern conscience. In the wake of the Reformation, theologians attempt to understand how the faculty works, poets attempt to capture the experience of being in its grip, and revolutionaries attempt to assert its authority for political action. The result, Abraham Stoll argues, is a dynamic scene of conscience in England, thick with the energies of salvation and subjectivity, and influential in the public sphere of Civil War politics. Stoll explores how Shakespeare, Spenser, Herbert, and Milton stage the inward experience of conscience. He links these poetic scenes to Luther, Calvin, and English Reformation theology. He also demonstrates how they shape the public discourses of conscience in such places as the toleration debates, among Levellers, and in the prose of Hobbes and Milton. In the literature of the early modern conscience, Protestant subjectivity evolves toward the political subject of modern liberalism.

ABRAHAM STOLL is Professor of English at the University of San Diego. He is editing a new edition of *Paradise Lost*. He is author of *Milton and Monotheism* and has edited the five-volume edition of Edmund Spenser's *The Faerie Queene*.

CONSCIENCE IN EARLY MODERN ENGLISH LITERATURE

ABRAHAM STOLL

University of San Diego

CAMBRIDGE UNIVERSITY PRESS

CAMBRIDGE
UNIVERSITY PRESS

University Printing House, Cambridge CB2 8BS, United Kingdom

One Liberty Plaza, 20th Floor, New York, NY 10006, USA

477 Williamstown Road, Port Melbourne, VIC 3207, Australia

4843/24, 2nd Floor, Ansari Road, Daryaganj, Delhi – 110002, India

79 Anson Road, #06-04/06, Singapore 079906

Cambridge University Press is part of the University of Cambridge.

It furthers the University's mission by disseminating knowledge in the pursuit of education, learning, and research at the highest international levels of excellence.

www.cambridge.org
Information on this title: www.cambridge.org/9781108418737
DOI: 10.1017/9781108291309

First published 2017

Printed in the United Kingdom by Clays, St Ives plc.

A catalog record for this publication is available from the British Library.

ISBN 978-1-108-41873-7 Hardback

For Gary Stoll
For Louise Stoll

Contents

Acknowledgments

The research for this book was done at the British Library, the Folger Library, the Bailey/Howe Library of the University of Vermont, and Copley Library at the University of San Diego (USD). I thank their librarians and staff. The work has been supported by the Folger Library, and by several grants from USD, including a University Professorship.

Parts of the Introduction and Chapter 1 appeared earlier in "Thus Conscience," *Exemplaria* 24:1–2 (2012), 62–77. Parts of Chapter 2 appeared in "Spenser's Allegorical Conscience," *Modern Philology* 111:2 (2013), 181–204. Parts of Chapter 3 appeared in "*Macbeth*'s Equivocal Conscience," in *Macbeth: New Critical Essays*, ed. Nicholas Moschovakis (New York: Routledge, 2008). I thank each of these publishers for permission to include material here.

My interest in the early modern conscience began in a graduate seminar at Princeton, led by Victoria Kahn. In the years since, I have benefited from sharing ideas with Oliver Arnold, the late Rich DuRocher, Denise Gigante, Joseph Jeon, Carol Kaske, John Leonard, Catherine Gimelli Martin, Ted Miller, Nick Moschovakis, Cynthia Nazarian, Turner Nevitt, Nigel Smith, Richard Strier, Andrew Wadoski, and Joseph Wittreich. Most influential has been Paul Strohm's seminar on conscience at the Folger Institute, which afforded me the opportunity to study with the several participants of the seminar, and to benefit from Paul's ongoing guidance. I would like to thank all of these scholars, as well as the two anonymous readers at Cambridge University Press, and Ray Ryan, Edgar Mendez, and Abirami Ulaganathan. This is also the right moment to acknowledge my appreciation for my colleagues at USD – too many to name, but including Cindy Caywood, Noelle Norton, Fred Robinson, and Stefan Vander Elst.

Author's Note

All Biblical citations are from the King James Version, unless otherwise noted. All quotations of Shakespeare are from *The Riverside Shakespeare*, 2nd edition, eds. G. B. Evans, *et al.* (Boston: Houghton Mifflin, 1997). All quotations of Spenser's poetry are from *The Faerie Queene*, 5 vols., gen. ed. Abraham Stoll (Indianapolis: Hackett Publishing, 2006–7). All quotations of Milton's poetry are from *Paradise Lost*, ed. Alastair Fowler (London: Longman, 1992) and *Complete Shorter Poems*, ed. John Carey (London: Longman, 1990). This poetry is cited parenthetically.

Abbreviations

ATC	Alexander Hume, *Ane Treatise of Conscience* (Edinburgh, 1594). STC 13943.
CPC	William Ames, *Conscience with the Power and Cases Thereof* (London, 1643). Wing A2995A.
CPW	*The Complete Prose Works of John Milton*, gen. ed. Don M. Wolfe, 8 vols. (New Haven, CT: Yale University Press, 1953–82).
DC	William Perkins, *A Discourse of Conscience* (London, 1596). STC 19696.
DS	Christopher St. German, *Doctor and Student*, eds. T. F. T. Plucknett and J. L. Barton (London: Selden Society, 1974).
DV	Thomas Aquinas, *Quaestiones Disputatae de Veritate*, trans. James V. McGlynn as *Truth* (Chicago, IL: Regnery, 1953), 3 vols.
Inst.	John Calvin, *The Institution of Christian Religion*, trans. Thomas Norton (London, 1578). STC 4418.
Lev.	Thomas Hobbes, *Leviathan*, ed. Richard Tuck (Cambridge: Cambridge University Press, 1997).
LW	*Luther's Works*, gen. eds. Jaroslav Pelikan, Helmut T. Lehman, Joel W. Lundeen, 55 vols. (Saint Louis, MO: Concordia, Philadelphia, PA: Fortress Press, 1958–86).
OC	John Woolton, *Of the Conscience* (London, 1574). STC 25978.
OED	*The Oxford English Dictionary Online*, 2nd and 3rd editions.
ST	Thomas Aquinas, *Summa Theologiae*, trans. Timothy Suttor, 60 vols. (New York: Blackfriars, 1970), Latin and English.

Introduction: Thus Conscience

Scenes from Shakespeare

In early modern discussions of conscience, today's reader will find a seemingly endless recourse to metaphor. Time and again, and with notable creativity, writers leave literal language behind in their attempt to capture the workings of conscience. The most common metaphor is pricking, as conscience is said to, in Alexander Hume's words, "torment man with terribil pricks, with fearfull terrors, and intollerable paine" (*ATC* 21). And there are the related images of stings, thorns, and stabs, creating a wounded conscience, so that William Perkins says that "he that goes on to sinne against his conscience, stabbes and wounds it often in the same place" (*DC* Epistle). Also prevalent is the witness, taken from Romans 2:15, where the gentiles have "the work of the law written in their hearts, their conscience also bearing witness." So it becomes proverbial to say that conscience "is in steede of a thousande witnesses," as John Woolton has it (*OC* A1v). Or, in Joseph Hall's exponential description, "I can doe nothing without a million of witnesses: the conscience is as a thousand witnesses; and God is as a thousand consciences."[1] Stranger is the metaphor of the worm: "the worme of conscience that never dieth, which wil in a lingering maner waste the conscience" (*DC* 167).[2] The worm, and the conscience itself, tend to gnaw and bite repeatedly, a metaphor captured in "remorse," which literally means biting again or intensely: "The gude Conscience will remord and bite: that is to say, it

---

[1] Hall, *Meditations and Vows*, 366–7. Also see Tilley, *A Dictionary of the Proverbs*, s.v. "conscience."

[2] See *Richard 3*: "The worm of conscience still begnaw thy soul!" I.iii.221, or *Much Ado About Nothing*: "Don Worm (his conscience)," V.ii.84. The metaphor comes from Isaiah 66.24, and is associated with conscience by Philip the Chancellor, *Summa de bono*, in Potts, *Conscience in Medieval Philosophy*, 106.

will oftimes call to remembrance the sinnes which man has committed, and will accuse, and prick him with an inward pain thairfor" (*ATC* 22).[3]

Contemporary speech feels thin, even impoverished, in comparison. William Perkins, in the single text *A Discourse of Conscience* (1596), describes the faculty as an arbitrator, a notary, the master of a prison, a little god within, a little hell within, a continual feast, a guide on a pilgrimage, a book, the Lord's sergeant, a paradise upon earth, the human eye, and a ship (*DC* 5, 8, 9, 10, 161, 89, 90, 154, 165, 166, 171, 173). Such flights of metaphor suggest a concerted effort at description. But they also suggest, since the theorists keep trying, that these descriptions consistently fall short. Perkins gives concerted attention in *A Discourse* to conveying what conscience is and how it feels to be within its operations. He is meticulous and systematic, employing a vocabulary rich with terminology inherited from scholastic theology. But theological categories and literal language somehow fail to capture what is really happening. Conscience is felt to escape existing understandings, and so Perkins, and his many contemporaries, turn to the dynamic and imaginative realms of figurative language. The theologian must increasingly reach for the tools of poetry.

If theology turns toward the poetic, then early modern poetry meets it halfway. Look at the detail supplied by Richard III as he finds himself in the grip of conscience. Shakespeare stockpiles metaphors in a remarkable effort to capture how it is with Richard:

> My conscience hath a thousand several tongues,
> And every tongue brings in a several tale,
> And every tale condemns me for a villain.
> (V.iii.193–5)

Prying open the metaphor of a thousand witnesses, Richard finds a thousand tongues, each with its own damning story. Then, expanding into another common metaphoric association with courts and trials, these witnesses go on to form a clamorous courtroom session:

> Perjury, perjury, in the highest degree;
> Murther, stern murther, in the direst degree;
> All several sins, all us'd in each degree,
> Throng to the bar, crying all, "Guilty! guilty!"
> (V.iii.196–9)

---

[3] The metaphor received a Middle English translation as "ayenbite," as in the fourteenth-century confessional text, Dan Michel's *Ayenbite of Inwyt*.

The metaphors would have felt very familiar to Shakespeare's audience, although Richard's desperation mutates them into a poetic scene that is overcrowded and overwhelming. To be in the grip of conscience at this moment is much more than a neat movement from vehicle to tenor. It is to be immersed in a space filled with shouts and insistent accusations, teeming with repeated words and repeated rhymes, at risk of the sudden appearance of grotesquely multiplying tongues and tales and sins. Shakespeare is reinvigorating central but commonplace figures, lodging conscience within the textures of a most dynamic poetics. And the very moving effect is that the poetry begins to capture a psychological dimension – what it feels like for Richard to experience conscience.

The intensity of the poetry pushes toward dramatization, presenting conscience as if in real time. Such a scene of conscience, one actually taking place in Richard's experience and before the audience's eyes, is first rehearsed in Richard's dream, as one by one the ghosts of his victims appear to condemn him (V.iii.118–76).[4] When Richard wakes, the play shifts from the ghostly tableau to soliloquy, but the overriding quality is still one of acting out a case of conscience in the moment:

> Soft, I did but dream.
> O coward conscience, how dost thou afflict me!
> The lights burn blue. It is now dead midnight.
> Cold fearful drops stand on my trembling flesh.
> What do I fear? Myself? There's none else by.
> Richard loves Richard, that is, I am I.
> Is there a murtherer here? No. Yes, I am.
> Then fly. What, from myself? Great reason why–
> Lest I revenge. What, myself upon myself?
> Alack, I love myself. Wherefore? For any good
> That I myself have done unto myself?
> O, no! Alas, I rather hate myself
> For hateful deeds committed by myself.
> I am a villain; yet I lie, I am not.
> Fool, of thyself speak well; fool, do not flatter:
> My conscience hath a thousand several tongues . . .
> (V.iii.178–93)

Repeatedly, the poetry hinges around the strangeness of Richard's entering into relations with himself – he fears, loves, and hates himself, and

---

[4] This is a scene of interest to the theorist of conscience John Woolton, who discusses the historical Richard's dream as revealing the compunctions of conscience, *OC* F1r.

contemplates the absurd possibility of flying from himself. Most of these lines are broken by commanding caesurae that each mark a turn, and often two turns, of thought, as in, "Then fly. What, from myself? Great reason why." These turns richly attract our attention because they are moments of thinking, internal debates that are actually performed on stage. In a drama of self-reflection, the turns split and double the speaking voice, creating a play between two Richards who meet each other on either side of each caesura. More dialogue than soliloquy, the faculty unfolds in real time. The audience hears and feels the back and forth and back again of the scene of conscience when Richard laments, "I am a villain; yet I lie, I am not./ Fool, of thyself speak well; fool, do not flatter."

In *The Merchant of Venice*, two years later, a cowardly conscience again takes the stage, and again it is a scene dramatized in real time. As Launcelot Gobbo considers leaving the service of Shylock, the problem takes the form of a debate:

> Certainly my conscience will serve me to run from this Jew my master. The fiend is at mine elbow and tempts me, saying to me, "Gobbo, Launcelot Gobbo, good Launcelot," or "good Gobbo," or "good Launcelot Gobbo, use your legs, take the start, run away." My conscience says, "No; take heed, honest Launcelot, take heed, honest Gobbo," or, as aforesaid, "honest Launcelot Gobbo, do not run, scorn running with thy heels."
>
> (II.ii.1–9)

The debate continues at length, and by the end Launcelot decides to take the fiend's advice and run. Once again we are watching a character as he is experiencing conscience, but this time in a psychomachia that sets the faculty at a distance. It is an argument between two personifications, the Fiend and Conscience, which are clearly rhetorical figures. We are not invited into an overwhelming poetic experience, as in the confrontation of self with self performed by Richard, but instead see conscience working as a figural set piece, and so we view it as if from the outside.

This sense of distance fits the comic mood of the play. The clownish Launcelot reports a very stupid debate, in which the experience of conscience is like listening to Dogberry or Elbow:

> Well the most courageous fiend bids me pack. "*Fia!*" says the fiend; "away!" says the fiend; "for the heavens, rouse up a brave mind," says the fiend, "and run." Well, my conscience, hanging about the neck of my heart, says very wisely to me, "My honest friend Launcelot, being an honest man's son" – or rather an honest woman's son, for, indeed, my father did something smack, something grow to, he had a kind of

taste – well, my conscience says "Launcelot, bouge not." "Bouge," says the fiend. "Bouge not," says my conscience.

(II.ii.13–20)

Conscience here has none of the theological rigor, high rationality, or frightening power that we might expect of it. It is non-serious, hanging catachrestically on the heart's neck, and spoiling for a fight like a tavern brawler – "Bouge"; "Bouge not." This clownish conscience is funny because Launcelot's unmistakable voice pokes through the personifications. He calls them conscience and fiend, but they sure sound like Launcelot, which undermines the rhetorical effect of the personification. If no distinction can be made between Launcelot Gobbo, the fiend, and conscience, then the debate itself is a mere figure of speech, even a clownish view of the conscience and the self.

Launcelot's psychomachia would be familiar to Elizabethans from several interludes, including *The Conflict of Conscience* (1581), or from the prominent personification of Conscience in *Piers Plowman*. But this is a tradition which Shakespeare's Richard, and later Hamlet, was in the process of making obsolete. Coming from Launcelot, the psychomachia feels blatantly fictional, like an archaic approach that a current thinker might hardly believe in. Richard's conscience has a challenging freshness about it, a sense that the poetry is exploring new and modern terrain as it attempts to set up a view of the inside of Richard's thoughts. But the clown presents conscience, to use the phrase again, as if from the outside. And this external approach is tinged with a sense of irony that marks it as a comic and backward conception, an old-fashioned story that can no longer persuade. Not surprisingly, this comic conscience loses the case:

> Certainly the Jew is the very devil incarnation, and, in my conscience, my conscience is but a kind of hard conscience, to offer to counsel me to stay with the Jew. The fiend gives the more friendly counsel: I will run, fiend; my heels are at your commandment; I will run.
>
> (II.ii.27–32)

In this closing moment, as conscience fails, the faculty undergoes a kind of disintegration. It falls away from the coherence of the allegorical voice, toward Richard's inward struggle. When Launcelot says that "in my conscience, my conscience is but a kind of hard conscience," the voice of conscience itself becomes the object of an ethical calculation.

The personified Conscience that has been debating with the fiend is submitted to the judgment of another thing, also called conscience. What is this new conscience? It is something more fundamental than the personified Conscience, and seems to possess more authority, clinching the argument for running. And it is recognizably psychological, functioning by a certain kind of reflexivity: "in my conscience, my conscience is . . ." shows the faculty reflecting back on itself, much as Richard's does. The poetry pushes past the rhetorical figure, past voice and debate, and brings us to a faculty which finds authenticity in deep inwardness.

In this way, Shakespeare reaches toward a conscience that is both more important than before, and more inchoate. It rules the day, but it also escapes articulation, knowable not by personification or voice, but only by the one word "conscience." With both Launcelot and Richard, conscience recedes from the scene's ability to capture it in language. Richard's turns of thought perform a self-reflection that fascinates. But thoughts are proverbially quicker than action, and the pace of Richard's turns are perpetually incommensurate with what they are meant to represent. So as the caesura breaks the poetic line, it also marks how we do not quite get at the real workings of conscience. Such inwardness and self-reflection must resist the more external dramatic structures of personification and soliloquy – in fact, these structures' failures are what tell us that inwardness is there. Similarly, when Launcelot's voice pokes through the personification, the ridiculousness of the rhetorical figure points to a more authentic, inward conscience. A disintegrating conscience is knowable by our failure to capture it in language.

But if language fails to capture conscience perfectly, the theater very successfully dramatizes the failure. These scenes insist upon a conscience that escapes our ability to conceive and portray, and Shakespeare insists on putting the whole mess on stage. The faculty is the center of attention, but simultaneously resistant to that attention, slipping away while making a show of slipping away. So we know conscience not as a completed trope or a closed system, but as an imperfect and ongoing experience. As an incomplete process, as an experience, it has an inchoate structure which must be enacted rather than described or summarized. So Shakespeare's scenes of conscience dramatize the faculty in real time.

Real-time staging is given greatest scope in *Hamlet*, which has at its center a play performed in pursuit of conscience. "The play's the thing," Hamlet decides, "Wherein I'll catch the conscience of the King" (II.ii.604–5). And he is right: the *Murder of Gonzago* does activate the King's conscience, so that his experience of watching theater is also the experience of undergoing the pangs of a guilty conscience. Of course, Hamlet's play still cannot fully capture conscience, which must be enacted in a larger tableau. The King watches the play, while at the same time Hamlet watches the King, while at the same time the audience watches Hamlet – so what is really staged is the workings of conscience together with the ineluctably reflective effort of observing those work-ings. After the play, Hamlet feels certain that he has observed Claudius's guilt. But the King's inability to pray suggests that his conscience, how-ever caught out by the play, remains ineffective. The King's conscience recedes from Hamlet's understanding, and from ours. The tableau, as with Richard and Launcelot, is of a faculty that is central but inaccessibly inward, and that is experienced as a self-conscious effort to study and understand that inwardness.

Dramatizing such a conscience is arguably the goal of the entirety of *Hamlet*, in which the word appears no less than eight times. It is at the center of the play's most famous problem, whether Hamlet will take action or delay. The Ghost's commands are initially delivered as a prob-lem of conscience:

> But howsomever thou pursues this act,
> Taint not thy mind, nor let thy soul contrive
> Against thy mother aught. Leave her to heaven,
> And to those thorns that in her bosom lodge
> To prick and sting her.
>
> (I.v.85–8)

Picking up on the common metaphor of the prick in the heart, the Ghost is telling Hamlet not to engage in the business of his mother's conscience. The command to avenge, but not "taint" his own mind, in contrast, is an order for Hamlet to proceed in such a way as to keep his own conscience clean. But the problem is that, for most of the play, and preeminently in the third soliloquy, conscience makes Hamlet not the avenger his father demands, but a coward:

> Thus conscience does make cowards of us all.
> And thus the native hue of resolution
> Is sicklied o'er with the pale cast of thought.
>
> (III.i.82–4)

Hamlet avoids a tainted mind only at the expense of the pale cast of thought. His inaction issues from the ongoing experience of his own uncertain conscience.

As with Richard's coward conscience, Hamlet's is self-reflective. "Thus" in "Thus conscience" points back to what Hamlet has just been thinking, framing what has come before as example. So we come to understand that in Hamlet's iconic musings in the "To be or not to be" soliloquy, we have actually been observing, on stage and in real time, the workings of his conscience. Moreover, "thus" marks the beginning of a commentary on what has just been said, and so is a reflexive turn, as Hamlet thinks about his previous conscientious thoughts. Appropriately for Shakespeare's most self-aware character, Hamlet's conscience works by means of a thinking about conscience – as a consciousness of conscience. Indeed, Hamlet's "Thus conscience" has presented a crux to generations of readers, who have disagreed over whether to read "conscience" as the moral faculty, or as mere awareness.[5] In early modern English the word conveys both the modern sense of "the moral conscience," and what modernity calls "consciousness." With the two meanings blending regularly in the period, deciding between them, as editors sometimes do, is to miss the most interesting part of the poetry, that conscience here is indistinguishable from the inner landscapes of Hamlet's mind.

The Theorists of Conscience

With this complexity, Hamlet's "Thus conscience" carries Shakespeare well into the realm of religious speculation, to a point where, in the effort to capture the dynamic experience of conscience, early modern poetry and theology make common cause. Indeed, William Perkins's key theorization of conscience reads as a theological counterpart to both Hamlet's and Richard's soliloquies. Attempting, in the opening pages of *A Discourse of Conscience*, to capture how it feels to be an individual in the throes of conscience, Perkins conceives of the faculty in notably dramatic and reflexive terms.

In the first chapter, "What conscience is," Perkins pays particular attention to the etymology of the word, which, as Aquinas and many others had noticed, combines the Latin "con" with "scire," implying a knowing with some other. Perkins asserts that the *knowing with* takes place between the individual and God: "God knowes perfectly all the doings of man, though they be never so hid and concealed: and man by a gifte given him of God, knows togither with God, the same things

---

[5] Belsey, "The Case of Hamlet's Conscience," 127–48. Hannah Arendt sees the same double meaning in Shakespeare's Richard III, *The Life of the Mind*, 189–90.

of himselfe: and this gift is named Conscience" (*DC* 5). The faculty becomes the location in which takes place the Reformation ideal of private relations with the divine, marking the centrality of conscience to Protestant theology. Further, the shared knowledge is in a dynamic present tense. Conscience is not a static or complete insight, but specifically knowledge which is in the process of being shared and worked out as an ongoing experience.

While Perkins's conscience is a *knowing with* God, it is also lodged in the inner life of the individual, who "knows togither with God, the same things of himselfe." So conscience also becomes a knowledge about oneself. Perkins clearly does not dismiss God, but as he proceeds in his opening description, it is self-knowledge which dominates. Describing how conscience "beares witnes of our secret thoughts" (*DC* 6), he returns to the etymology. The process turns inward, and soon conscience emerges, in a remarkable passage, as synonymous with the process of self-reflection:

> For there must be two actions of the understanding, the one is simple, which barely conceiveth or thinketh this or that: the other is a *reflecting* or doubling of the former, whereby a man conceives and thinkes with himselfe what he thinks. And this action properly pertaines to the conscience. The minde thinks a thought, now conscience goes beyond the minde, and knowes what the minde thinks: so as if a man would go about to hide his sinnefull thoughts from God, his conscience as an other person within him, shall discover all. By meanes of this second action conscience may beare witnes even of thoughts, and from hence also it seemes to borrow his name, because conscience is a *science* or knowledge ioyned with an other knowledge: for by it I conceive and know what I know.
>
> (*DC* 6–7)

This description of the functioning of conscience posits a shifting and dynamic faculty, built out of the instantaneous movements of thinking, and of thinking about thinking. Conscience becomes a "reflecting" – a metaphor which captures the sudden multiplying of images which mirrors initiate. Compared to the static and structural conceptions of the scholastics, which will be discussed in Chapter 1, Perkins's reflexive conscience represents a profound shift toward an active process, and one that, in its resistance to structure, escapes summary. When "a man conceives and thinkes with himselfe what he thinks," or when "The minde thinks a thought, now conscience goes beyond the minde, and knowes what the minde thinks," the faculty becomes very hard to pin down. Self-reflection makes for a flashing and quickly multiplying mental experience, like the strange turns of thought in Richard's conscience.

A reflection in a glass also creates self-knowledge, and conscience here becomes recognizably psychological, leaning forward toward modernity. When Perkins describes it as a "doubling," and then "as an other person within him," he draws near to the Freudian uncanny. And the sense of conscience as self-reflection is exactly what Judith Butler, writing about nineteenth-century theorists, has identified as an origin of modern subjectivity.[6] Perkins and the theorists of conscience, like *Hamlet*, anticipate such modernity; conscience offers an historically specific framework for understanding early modern subjectivity.

This is felt especially in the fact that "conscience" in early modern English, as seen with Hamlet's "Thus conscience," also means consciousness. In some instances, the word makes no reference to the moral faculty, as a modern reader would expect, but means merely inward knowledge or awareness. The *Oxford English Dictionary* gathers many examples, illustrating a long period in which both concepts, inner awareness and the moral faculty, existed in the single word, were often used interchangeably, and shaded into each other in subtle ways. So in one of the *OED*'s examples of conscience as consciousness, Thomas More can write in a letter to Cromwell of "the conscience of mine own true faithful hart and devocion." As More's awareness is of inward convictions, it can be felt to be rather near to the moral faculty, though it makes no direct claim on theological valences. Several times in the same letter, meanwhile, More uses "conscience" clearly in its moral sense, including the important claim that Henry "declared unto me that he wold in no wise that I shold other thing do or say therein, than upon that that I shold perceive myn awne conscience shold serve me, and that I shold fyrst loke unto God and after God unto hym."[7] The most interesting thing here is not so much the concepts' former cohabitation, since that is still to be found in Romance languages, but their separation over the course of the seventeenth century.[8] The breaking away of consciousness from conscience takes place gradually, but one can point to John Locke's *An Essay Concerning Human Understanding* as a key moment, when Locke articulates a concept of consciousness that is secular. In Locke's understanding, consciousness becomes a building block of human subjectivity, distinct

---

[6] "Conscience is the means by which a subject becomes an object for itself, reflecting on itself, establishing itself as reflective and reflexive." Butler, *The Psychic Life of Power*, 22.
[7] *OED*, s.v. "conscience," def. 7a. *Correspondence of More*, Letter 199, 495.
[8] For an etymological discussion of conscience and consciousness in several languages, see Engelberg, *The Unknown Distance*, 8–39.

from conscience, with the two words bearing the meanings that they do today.[9] This distinction tells us something about conscience earlier in the century: it is as if, during the seventeenth century, consciousness emerges from the theological faculty in a kind of birth into its own status as secular philosophical concept.

It seems that such a shift could issue only from an energetic and productive theology. And in fact, early modern England experienced a surge of interest in conscience, a concerted effort to theorize it. The first English treatise on conscience per se is John Woolton's *Of the Conscience* (1574). Woolton, Marian exile and eventual Bishop of Exeter, devotes a number of pages to defining and describing the faculty, although most of this text takes the more historical approach of recounting examples of heroes of conscience.[10] The Scottish poet Alexander Hume's quite original *Ane Treatise of Conscience* (1594) is more theoretical in its approach. It pays particular attention to the inner workings of conscience, and so draws near to the reflexive faculty of Perkins, as, for example, when he says that conscience "is a particular knawledg quhilk every man has of himself, and that onlie of thochtis, words and deids, quilik he hes committit, whether they be gude or euill" (*ATC* 9–10). It is not clear whether Hume and Perkins influenced each other, though Perkins likely read Woolton.[11] In any event, Perkins produced the most extensive body of work on conscience, originating in a popular series of lectures on conscience in Cambridge in the 1580s. His first publication devoted entirely to conscience was in 1592, *A Case of Conscience: The Greatest There Ever Was*, followed in 1596 by *A Discourse of Conscience*. The Cambridge lectures were edited posthumously into *The Whole Treatise of the Cases of Conscience* (1606). And after Perkins, English theology sustains its interest in theorizing and anatomizing conscience, in such works as Immanuel Bourne, *The Anatomie of Conscience* (1623), Ephraim Huit, *The Anatomy of Conscience* (1626), William Fenner, *A Treatise of Conscience* (1640),

---

[9] Locke, *An Essay*, II.xxvii.9, 335; also see Book II, Chapter 1, "Of Ideas in general and their Original." On Locke's philosophy of consciousness, see Thiel, *The Early Modern Subject*, 109–50. According to the *OED*, this sense of "consciousness" first appears in 1678, in Cudworth's *Intellectual System of the Universe*. *OED*, s.v. "consciousness," def. 2a. Cudworth, *The True Intellectual System*, 36. Thiel discusses Cudworth, *The Early Modern Subject*, 67–71.

[10] Woolton's text is largely a translation of Rivius, *De Conscientia Libri III*. A significant difference is that Woolton leaves out Rivius's celebration of Thomas More as a martyr for conscience, replacing it with the Protestant martyr James Hales, *OC* G4r–H1r.

[11] Perkins seems to be following Woolton when he divides the faculty of understanding into the "theorical" and the "practical," *DC* 2. This distinction goes back to Peter Martyr, Vermigli, *The Common Places*, III.v.8, 165.

William Ames, *Conscience with the Power and Cases Thereof* (1643), and Henry Hammond, *Of Conscience* (1644).

Perkins is celebrated by Ames as "The most grave Divine William Perkins (who onely of our Countreymen hath set forth a peculiar Treatise of Conscience)" – an exaggeration that marks his prominence within the discourse (*CPC* 2). His writings on conscience continued to be published throughout the seventeenth century in the complete *Works*. Perkins is celebrated as the father of English moral theology, and the foundation upon which Ames and Anglicans such as Robert Sanderson and Jeremy Taylor built an English casuistry.[12] Modern accounts generally view Perkins's work on conscience in light of the subsequent casuistry.[13] But his influence also extends to a generation of Calvinists and radical preachers, including Ames, as well as figures such as Thomas Goodwin, and Samuel Ward.[14] These Puritans are often less interested in solving practical cases than in theorizing a conscience that plays a role in ideal theological questions of inspiration and salvation. As will be argued in Chapter 4, this line of theological descent casts Perkins's work less as casuistry, with its focus on practical cases, and more as an effort to theorize conscience as a pivotal concept in the inner life of Christians, particularly their salvation. So this study refers to Perkins and Woolton and Hume and the others around them not as casuists, but as theorists of conscience. Recent literary accounts of the early modern conscience have tended to approach it as a function of casuistry.[15] But this is to allow the important but quite particular discourse of casuistry to obscure the earlier effort, on the part of Perkins and other theorists, to capture the workings of conscience itself.

Conscience must be theorized – understood, anatomized, described, and captured as an experience – because it has come to occupy such a central position in the theology of the Reformation. The theology of the whole person, in its fundamental move toward inwardness, relies significantly on conscience. The faculty is not just a means of determining right and wrong, but becomes a key to the movement from works to faith. It therefore becomes the ground on which Christian liberty is won, and so salvation attained. This inward theology of conscience is on display in the narrative of origin that Luther tells for the Reformation itself, the tower conversion,

---

[12] Keenan, "William Perkins and the Birth of British Casuistry."

[13] According to Thomas Merrill, Perkins "set a pattern for all later work in Protestant moral divinity." Perkins, *William Perkins*, xx.

[14] See Perkins, *The Work of William Perkins*, 9.

[15] Slights, *The Casuistical Tradition*. Gallagher, *Medusa's Gaze*. Brown, *Donne and the Politics of Conscience*. Sullivan, *Rhetoric of the Conscience*.

where the young Luther, while trying to fulfill his monastic vows, is gripped by a "fierce and troubled conscience." Then in a moment of conversion that sets him on the path to reformation, Luther finds Christian liberty in a conscience freed by his new conception of faith (*LW* 34:336–7).[16]

This protypically Protestant crisis of conscience, with the intimate experience of its prickings, of despair and self-reflection, and of the longed-for regeneration in faith, becomes a foundational narrative for some of the most important literary characters of the period, including Redcrosse Knight, Hamlet, Lady Macbeth, and Samson. These figures all enact, in real time, the workings of the faculty, as the poets take up the work of the theorists of conscience. Theology and poetry together conceive of the workings of conscience, and together capture how it feels to experience it firsthand. This is the early modern scene of conscience that will be the primary subject of this book. It is a poetic and theological scene, but also one with profound political stakes.

The Politics of Conscience

Even as Protestant theology sets about theorizing conscience, the faculty begins to take on a newly comprehensive political authority. In another of the Reformation's origins, the Diet of Worms, Luther concludes his resistance to Rome with "my conscience is captive to the Word of God. I cannot and I will not retract anything, since it is neither safe nor right to go against conscience. I cannot do otherwise, here I stand, may God help me, Amen" (*LW* 32.112–13). Luther asserts the authority of individual conscience over temporal power and law. His claim, and the claim of the Reformation itself, is for the right to resist the sovereignty of the Pope, of Canon Law, of ecclesiastical power, monastic vows, and much else, because conscience says so. Although an opponent of Luther, Thomas More takes a parallel position, that conscience authorizes him to resist the demands of his sovereign. In his letter from the Tower to his daughter, Margaret Roper, More describes feeling as if he has no good argument for his refusal to swear the oath in support of Henry's supremacy, other than conscience:

> I coulde againe answere nothinge thereto but only that I thought my self I might not well do so, because that in my conscience this was one of the cases, in which I was bounden that I shoulde not obey my prince, sith that

---

[16] Reflecting this original place of conscience, it is not uncommon for Protestantism to be described as a "religion of conscience." Holl, *What Did Luther Understand by Religion?* 48–62. Tillich, "A Conscience above Moralism," 50–1.

what so ever other folke thought in the matter (whose conscience and lear-
ninge I wolde not condempe nor take upon me to iudge) yet in my
conscience the trouth semed on the tother side.[17]

More's refusal to judge other people's consciences, humble as it is, force-
fully carves out the authority of individual conscience, which can bind
even more powerfully than the duty owed to one's prince. In such prominent confrontations, Luther against the Church or More against Henry,
the early modern conscience is erected as an exception to authority. It is
the means by which an individual is able to set him- or herself up against
law, both civil and ecclesiastical. In this vein, William Perkins places
conscience above law, which is an "improper binder" of conscience, and
which "doth not constraine conscience, but the outward man." So he
declares, "For body and goods and outward conversation I grant all: but a
subjection of conscience to mans laws, I deny" (*DC* 38–9, 47).

Although Perkins is a moderate member of the English church, the
revolutionary potential of such an assertion is clear. From Thomas More,
through Foxe's martyrs, and on through the Civil War, conscience is regularly deployed in England as a justification for resistance to law. Giving a
lasting voice to this kind of individual authority, John Milton insists
repeatedly that the faculty must be protected from powers that threaten to
become "forcers of conscience."[18] For Milton, and for most radicals of the
mid-seventeenth century, conscience is a protected site, the guarantee of
political and religious freedom, and that part of the individual that law cannot touch. Such a sovereign conscience has remained in modernity the priv-
ileged point at which individuals resist law, for example in Thoreau's "Civil
Disobedience," or when Martin Luther King submits that "an individual
who breaks a law that conscience tells him is unjust, and willingly accepts
the penalty by staying in jail to arouse the conscience of the community
over its injustice, is in reality expressing the very highest respect for law."[19]

And so the early modern conscience can persuasively be seen as a
forerunner of modern liberalism.[20] In the toleration debates that valorize

---

[17] *Correspondence of More*, Letter 200, 505.
[18] Cf. "On the New Forcers of Conscience Under the Long Parliament," as well as *Eikonoklastes*,
CPW III:488, and *Of Civil Power*, *CPW* VII:242.
[19] King, "Letter from a Birmingham Jail," 72. Henry David Thoreau: "Why has every man a conscience, then? I think that we should be men first, and subjects afterwards. It is not desirable to
cultivate a respect for the law, so much as for the right." *Walden and Civil Disobedience*, 236. On
modern conscientious objection and its relation to the early modern conscience, see Walzer,
Obligations, 120–45.
[20] E.g. Rawls, *Political Liberalism*, xxiv.

liberty of conscience, and in the revolutionary moment of the Civil War, conscience projects for the individual a newly powerful authority. In its strongest form, it makes the political subject sovereign. This means not only justifying the individual's authority, but also imbuing it with ideological confidence – forming a political subject that can become the foundation of such things as rights and contracts, and even revolution. The Puritan preacher Richard Sibbes, for example, readily anticipates the authority and energy of the modern liberal subject when he declares:

> Where the soule is convinced of the righteousnesse of Christ, there the conscience demands boldly: It is God that justifies, who shal condemne? It is Christ that is dead and risen againe and sits at the right hand of God; who shall lay anything to the charge of Gods chosen. So that a convinced conscience dares all creatures in Heaven and Earth, it works strongly and boldly.[21]

But the politics of conscience in the early modern period cannot be fully understood through analogy with Thoreau or King. Although in many places tending toward liberalism, it should not be aligned with any particular political ideology. Conscience does not take sides. Or rather in the period it takes all sides – not just the Levellers claim conscience, but also Hobbes, not just Milton but also Charles. So a whiggish story of the early modern conscience leading to Enlightenment will be incomplete. Robert Bolt may err in this way in *A Man for All Seasons*, making Thomas More look too much like the possessive individual of the author's own twentieth century.[22] When the historical More's conscience sets itself resolutely against Henry's royal authority, after all, it does so not in the name of liberal philosophical ideals, but in order to subject itself to the authority of the Catholic Church. He is not asserting the sovereignty of the individual conscience, so much as its subjection to one kind of law over another, the Church's over England's. This is neither individualistic nor liberalizing – and neither, on the other side, is Henry's frequent invocation of conscience in his attempts to win the Church's support for his divorce.[23]

The important point is that whatever conclusions are reached, when the early modern subject moves to take political action, that movement

---

[21] Sibbes, *The Saints Priviledge*, 507.

[22] John Guy argues against Bolt's depiction of More's "adamantine self." *Thomas More*, 199–200. Also see Cummings, "Conscience and the Law in Thomas More."

[23] See Henry's speech to the Lord Mayor and Aldermen, as reported by Edward Hall (*Chronicle*, 753–5). *English Historical Documents*, V:707–9. Cardinal Wolsey describes how Henry "has found his conscience somewhat burthened with his present marriage," *Letters and Papers* IV:ii.1634.

proceeds through, and is understood in terms of, conscience. Conscience names the process by which the individual becomes political, and is one of our best ways to study the political subject. So this book takes the opportunity to trace conscience from its inward scenes to its public and political discourses. This movement is reflected in the book's structure: the first half focuses on the theology and psychology of private conscience, concerned with salvation and consciousness. And its second half investigates what happens when this faculty is mapped onto the politics of reformation and revolution.

To give a brief outline of the book: the first half begins with a mainly theological chapter, which traces the way that the Protestant conscience falls away from scholastic structures, becoming the inchoate and reflexive faculty of the theorists of conscience. It then examines how such a faculty fits, and fails to fit, into representation, taking up in Chapter 2 the case of allegory in Spenser's *The Faerie Queene*. And in the third chapter it considers how, in the tragic mental landscapes of *Macbeth*, the destructured conscience resists conscious efforts to know it, tilting toward a modern subjectivity. The second half studies how the energies of these inward scenes find expression when communicated in the public sphere. Chapter 4 examines how conscience is put to use in the religious discourses of Protestant casuistry and Puritan preachers, discerning two fundamental kinds of public conscience, casuistic and antinomian. Chapter 5 traces this split in several domains of mid-century politics, in the toleration debates, among the Levellers, and in Hobbes's *Leviathan*. Chapter 6 turns to Milton, who as a theologian, political theorist, and poet brings together many of the most important elements of both the private destructured faculty and the public political faculty. Milton builds an expansive conscience that takes on some of the habits of modern liberalism.

Along the way, this study covers an array of adjacent topics, including the scholastic *synderesis*, the Lutheran theology of the whole person, despair, equity, disenchantment, toleration, social contract, and the liberal subject. But conscience sprawls so broadly across early modern England that not every avenue has been pursued – more, for example, could be said on Catholic casuistry, on natural law, on rational religion, and on Restoration versions of conscience; some of the best recent scholarship on conscience has done so.[24] This study finds its focus instead on

---

[24] Andrew, *Conscience and its Critics*. Strohm, *Conscience: A Very Short Introduction*. Braun and Vallance, *Contexts of Conscience*. Kahn, *Wayward Contracts*. Leites, *Conscience and Casuistry*. Slights, *The Casuistical Tradition*.

the inward scene of conscience, its theology and psychology, and on the political scene when it becomes public.

These scenes are of a conscience that has slipped away from practical structures, finding expression in poetic language, and in the unfolding energies of theater. In these modes, conscience becomes more vibrant and speaks to our experience, but also becomes less clear in cause and effect. So this book does not seek to make the strongest historical claims, that a change in conscience causes some change in the world, or that worldly events cause a change in the idea of the faculty. The early modern conscience does not create early modern subjectivity, but it does provide a uniquely detailed way to observe how subjectivity works. It does not cause revolution or modern liberalism, but it is a forum in which we can see them taking form. This less assertive kind of argument is appropriate to a study of literature, perhaps best suited to its fictions and poetics. It is also suited to an early modern conscience that, as it becomes increasingly important, becomes increasingly inchoate.

And so it is that Shakespeare can tell us much about the early modern conscience. *Hamlet*, in fact, stages an experience with conscience that anticipates the path of the faculty in the seventeenth century, as well as in this book's argument. The long-standing crux of the action, Hamlet's delay, depends upon conscience, and as the play unfolds we see on stage the reflexive, private faculty become a public and political force.

In the first three acts of the play, conscience makes a coward of Hamlet, leading to delay. Like Perkins's conscience, "whereby a man conceives and thinkes with himselfe what he thinks," Hamlet's conscience reflects on itself and catches him in a web of thought, and thought about thought, which, as the Romantics stressed, destroys action:

> Thus conscience does make cowards of us all,
> And thus the native hue of resolution
> Is sicklied o'er with the pale cast of thought,
> And enterprises of great pitch and moment
> With this regard their currents turn awry,
> And lose the name of action.
>
> (III.i.82–7)

The brooding, paralyzed Hamlet is continuous with the Hamlet caught in a cowardly conscience.[25]

---

[25] A. C. Bradley has argued against "the conscience theory" to explain Hamlet's delay. But Bradley does not recognize that his preferred theory of melancholy should really be counted as an aspect of Protestant conscience, as Chapter 2 shows. Bradley, *Shakespearean Tragedy*, 97–101.

Hamlet's inaction, however, famously comes to an end in Act Four, on the high seas. He returns to Denmark with the theology not of a hesitant subject, but of a bold political actor, able first to fight pirates and finally to kill a king. "The readiness is all" (V.ii.222) represents a pure expression of political energy, a spring ready to uncoil at a single touch. Meanwhile the belief that "there is Providence in the fall of a sparrow" (V.ii.220) gives theological shape to that politics, assuring Hamlet that he has the freedom to act, and that his political actions will coincide with the larger plot of divine justice. This remarkable confidence resembles that of the Puritan, Sibbes, when he declares that "a convinced conscience dares all creatures in Heaven and Earth."[26]

Hamlet does not find his vigor by rejecting conscience as cowardice – that is the method of Laertes, who prepares for political action by declaring, "To hell, allegiance! vows, to the blackest devil!/ Conscience and grace, to the profoundest pit!" (IV.v.132–3). Action for Laertes depends upon a thrusting aside of conscience and the providential structure that subtends it. In contrast, Hamlet arrives at a theology in which political action coincides with conscience. So he is at last certain of his action against the king: "is't not perfect conscience/ To quit him with this arm?" (V.ii.67). This is not a break from the conscience of the early acts, but rather a perfection of it. No longer sickly and pale or pricking and stinging, it has become complete and whole. The self-reflection of "Thus conscience" may appear cowardly and inert from the outside, but in Hamlet's soliloquies, in the movements of his thoughts and the force of his consciousness, there is a braveness of spirit and an undeniable psychic energy. When this energy is perfected and directed outward, it becomes a powerful kind of political action. In this way, Hamlet achieves a conscientious political action that is not a rejection of self-reflection, so much as a harnessing.

Such a decisive Hamlet may recall Carl Schmitt's detection of sovereignty in *Hamlet*, and his claim that it "falls within the first stage of the English revolution," by which he means that Hamlet anticipates the Hobbesian absolute sovereign.[27] But on the other hand, as Walter Benjamin's "*Trauerspiel* Hamlet" implies, he remains not a transcendent

---

[26] John Wilks sees Hamlet "resolving his inner discord" in perfect conscience, which becomes a rational component of public justice. *The Idea of Conscience*, 122–3.

[27] Schmitt, *Hamlet or Hecuba*, 62. Julia Reinhard Lupton describes Hamlet's new sense of purpose as "not a Christian conversion so much as a political-theological reorientation of the vertical sovereignty at Sinaii towards its horizontal axis in collective covenant." *Thinking With Shakespeare*, 89.

authority but a melancholy king and a martyr.[28] Indeed, the decisive
and sovereign Hamlet is ironized by the ambivalence of his "perfect conscience." The scriptural source is Hebrews 9:9, in which Paul describes
the inability to attain perfect conscience so long as one is ruled by Law.
Accordingly, "perfect conscience" is almost universally cited as a false
trust in works and human action, and so a failure to attain Christian liberty.[29] This ambivalence glosses Hamlet's assertion a few lines earlier, that
Rosencrantz and Guildenstern are "not near my conscience" (V.ii.58).
As part of his new theology, Hamlet is sure he knows the outlines of his
own conscience, and trusts that he can clearly tell that his schoolmates
are not near them. Any pricks the reader may feel at Hamlet's disregard
for Rosencrantz and Guildenstern hint at the violence and tyranny of a
too-certain conscience. Hamlet's inward drama of conscience in the first
half of the play becomes the ambivalent energy of his perfect conscience
in Act 5, a journey that can be glimpsed, perhaps, in the expression of
Manet's Hamlet on this book's cover.

Following a path similar to that in *Hamlet*, the destructured conscience
of Protestantism becomes the politically productive conscience of the
mid-seventeenth century, moving England through despair and Christian
liberty, reflexive consciousness and toleration, revolutionary action and
the precarious political subjectivity of liberalism. As a first reckoning
of these events, Chapter 1 details the emergence of the Protestant conscience out of its scholastic origins, describing a theological process in
which conscience falls away from structure.

[28] Benjamin, *The Origin of German Tragic Drama*, 137. On Schmitt's *Hamlet* and Benjamin, see
Weber, "Taking Exception to Decision" and Kahn, *The Future of Illusion*, 23–53.
[29] E.g. *ATC* 8; Hammond, *Of Conscience*, 7. Harold Skulsky sees the imperfection of Hamlet's conscience as an indication that he is the scourge of God, "Revenge, Honor and Conscience in
Hamlet," 86.

Destructuring: Aquinas, Luther, Perkins

As Shakespeare brings conscience on stage, unfolding the faculty in real time, we are invited to consider how it feels to be in its grip. This is to conceive of conscience as if from the inside – not as something that one might hear about from another, but as something that must be experienced by oneself and in oneself. The private experience of conscience, understood and described as if from the inside, is fundamental to Protestant thought, and to the theorists of conscience in early modern England, such as John Woolton, Alexander Hume, and William Perkins.

Such an inward and experiential approach sets the theorists of conscience apart from Renaissance casuists, who write extensively about cases of conscience, but very little about the faculty itself. Catholic manuals of casuistry can be long, and show a patient interest in complex and proliferating details. The Spanish casuist Martín de Azpilcueta (known as Navarrus) can write in *Enchiridion, sive manuale confessiorum, et poenitentium* over a thousand pages solving doubts that occur in confession, and resolving subtle concerns about sin and absolution. But he adds only a brief entry in a miscellany at the end to describe conscience.[1] Two of the most widely used manuals, the *Summa Angelica* and the *Summa Rosella*, devote merely a page each to a definition of conscience.[2] But they offer elaborate methods for interrogating penitents, for the point of the *summae* is to instruct the confessor on how to understand and pursue clarity in the consciences of other people.[3] The confessor must handle conscience with sophistication and care – but it is another's conscience, and so is conceived as if from the outside.

---

[1] de Azpilcueta, *Enchiridion*, 1037.
[2] Carletti, *Summa Angelica*, 83. Trovamala, *Summa Casuum Conscientiae*, 78. On the sophistication of the casuistic approach, see Jonsen and Toulmin, *The Abuse of Casuistry*.
[3] See Tentler, *Sin and Confession*, 31–9 and *passim*.

Perkins and the theorists of conscience, on the other hand, do not write for confessors, and do not aim at facilitating the sacrament of confession. Rather, within a Protestant practice that had abolished private confession, they write to the laity.[4] Their treatises are meant as direct pastoral care, to be read by the individual whose own conscience is at stake. So John Woolton encourages his reader: "I trust that the knowledge of Conscience, which hath bene secret and obscure, shall shewe hir selfe somewhat plainely to the eyes, and shall stirre up in men a marveylous love and desire of a sincere conscience" (*OC* b3v-b4r).[5] The animating assumption is that each Christian can benefit from a greater degree of self-consciousness about conscience. And so the faculty is handled in such a way as to inform and shape that lay reader's own private experience – to know conscience from the inside. Perkins, Woolton, and Hume describe what conscience is and how it functions, and, as in Shakespeare, how it feels to be in its grip. They methodically define parts and structures, and detail the faculty's operations and duties. They are also intimate, always bending conscience toward inwardness. Early in *A Discourse of Conscience* Perkins stresses the private nature of the Protestant conscience: "For as many men as there are, so many consciences there be: and every particular man hath his owne particular conscience" (*DC* 4).

To know conscience from the inside is also to know it incompletely, as a scientist must who observes a phenomenon from within its system. If conscience is a privately unfolding experience, then one cannot view it as if from the outside, as a completed structure. It is not readily defined and understood, but rather known in process, as experience. This is the reflexive conscience described in the Introduction. As both conscience and consciousness, Perkins's faculty becomes a "reflecting or doubling" of thought, so that "a man conceives and thinkes with himselfe what he thinks," becoming like "an other person within him." Conscience becomes a kind of drama between voices, as with Richard and Launcelot,

---

[4] In England, the 1552 *Book of Common Prayer* omitted reference to private confession, and the Thirty-Nine Articles did not count confession as a sacrament. Luther and most reformers valued voluntary and general confessions, but not private auricular confession resulting in absolution *ex opere operato*. See Tentler, *Sin and Confession*, 349–63; Rittgers, *The Reformation of the Keys*; Beckwith, *Shakespeare and the Grammar of Forgiveness*, 57–81.

[5] Thomas Pickering, who assembled William Perkins's unpublished writings for the posthumous *The Whole Treatise of the Cases of Conscience* (1606), lays out a number of the standard objections to Catholic confession, among them that priests are "absolute Iudges of the Conscience," and "authors and givers of remission of sinnes." Perkins's writings are necessary so that the penitent "may satisfie the iustice of God, for the temporall punishment of his sinnes committed." Perkins, *The Whole Treatise*, "The Epistle Dedicatorie." Also see Braun and Vallance, *Contexts of Conscience*, xiv.

or pure self-consciousness, as with Hamlet. The reflexive conscience is also an unstable experience, full of movement and without clearly marked divisions. Like opposing mirrors, it has an infinity within it, so that "The minde thinks a thought, now conscience goes beyond the minde, and knowes what the minde thinks," so that through conscience, Perkins says, "I conceive and know what I know" (*DC* 7). This is a process that resists completion, as the self-reflection makes for a flashing, turning, and endlessly multiplying mental experience.

Despite these differences between Protestant and Catholic conceptions of conscience, Perkins begins his treatise with Aquinas, and with an account of conscience that is derived from the scholastic tradition. So his reflexive faculty, and the theorists of conscience, must be understood as evolving out of this preceding discourse. The scholastic conception of conscience was primarily engaged in defining its parts, by distinguishing between anthropological categories such as power, habit, and act, and by describing conscience as structured by the important theological faculty of *synderesis*. Nearly all Catholic casuists follow such accounts, as the structured approach of the scholastics matches the sacramental project of the casuist, constructing a conscience which is knowable in another and as if from the outside. But Perkins and the theorists of conscience separate themselves from the structured conscience. This departure is initiated in the reformations of Luther and Calvin, who pull away from medieval conceptions as they locate conscience in the experiential and inward domain of the whole person.

This primarily theological chapter describes England's theorists of conscience as emerging from both influences, scholastic and Protestant. It moves from Aquinas's writings on conscience, through Luther's, to arrive at Perkins. Aquinas is concerned primarily with parsing and categorizing the conscience, and so portrays the faculty in highly organized terms, typical of the scholastic approach. Luther rejects such categories, pushing conscience away from Aquinas's carefully wrought structures, and so initiates a process I call "destructuring." Following Luther and Calvin, Perkins and the theorists arrive at a reformed conscience which has broken out of its received structures, becoming a more fluid, less definable experience.

But the fall from structure does not mean that conscience is of any less importance. On the contrary, conscience in Reformation theology becomes more central than ever, as the rejection of order and the increase in theological value happen together. This is not to claim that one causes the other – it is enough to see that they are intertwined. So for Perkins, and for early modern England, conscience becomes more important as it becomes more inchoate. The result is a conscience that matters more, and receives closer attention, even as it disintegrates. This dynamic leads to a conscience that, in its functioning, repeatedly asserts its own destructuring. So destructuring does not simply name a historical trend in which conscience pulls away from structure after the scholastics – this is the case, but only part of the argument. For as conscience follows this historical trajectory away from structure, it also finds in the process of destructuring such theologically creative energy, such authenticity, that the move toward imperfect forms, which is also a move away from works, itself becomes a standard and repeated quality of the experience. Destructuring, therefore, also names how conscience repeatedly enacts the move away from structure. How it becomes a faculty that again and again loses structure before our eyes, and in the moment.

Aquinas and the Scholastic Conscience

Moving back to the eve of the English Reformation reveals a very different conscience. Shortly before the Act of Supremacy, Christopher St. German provides in his *Doctor and Student* (1530) one of the most widely read accounts of conscience in England. Theorizing the legal concept of equity, St. German describes a conscience with a highly rational architecture, and little of the dynamics of Richard or Launcelot. Although St. German became an important reformer, this is the last great expression of the scholastic conscience in England, providing a window into the faculty before it was reconceived, via Luther and Calvin, by Perkins.

St. German begins with a concept which is entirely absent from our modern understanding of conscience, as well as from Perkins: the category of *synderesis*.[6] *Synderesis* is "a naturall power or motive force of the rational soule sette always in the hyghest parte thereof movynge and sterrynge it to good & abhorrynge evyll" (*DS* 81). It never sins or errs, and is a remnant of higher reason in humans after the fall, participating in the intelligence of angels, and never extinguished in anyone: "for Aungell is of a nature to understande without serchynge of reason: and to that nature man is Joyned by sinderesis the whiche sinderesis maye not holly be extyncted neyther in man ne yet in dampned soules" (*DS* 81). This perfect and idealized source of moral knowledge is the first part of a bipartite

---

[6] Alternately spelled "synteresis." I preserve each author's preference.

structure in conscience: following from *synderesis* is *conscientia*. This secondary part takes the general principles of *synderesis* and applies them to the particular situations of the world. So St. German has the *synderesis* providing the universal insight, "No evil is to be done," and then *conscientia* considers a particular case and judges, "This is evil," and so concludes, "This is not to be done" (*DS* 89). Unlike the undifferentiated conscience of today, then, the scholastic conscience has two fundamental parts, and functions by means of this movement from *synderesis* to *conscientia*.

With this bipartite structure, St. German is following a long scholastic tradition. *Synderesis* dates from Jerome, who, in a commentary on Ezekiel, first uses the term. Jerome describes what

> the Greeks call *synteresin*: that spark of conscience which was not even extinguished in the breast of Cain after he was turned out of Paradise, and by which we discern that we sin, when we are overcome by pleasures or frenzy and meanwhile are misled by an imitation of reason.[7]

The word is not biblical, appearing only in Jerome's allegorical commentary on the throne-chariot. The unclear origins of *synderesis*, which possibly developed out of the Greek *syneidesis*, do not prevent this small reference from initiating a wide scholastic conversation, in which *synderesis* proves central to most scholastic accounts of conscience.[8]

St. German's descriptions turn out to be typical. *Synderesis* comes to be associated with the higher forms of reason, which, as Philip the Chancellor says, are "part of the original righteousness of man's powers, which Adam had in the state of innocence, which remained as a little light leading him to God."[9] This remnant of prelapsarian knowledge is often described as a "storehouse" which preserves that knowledge and cannot be extinguished and cannot err.[10] It is natural, and like prelapsarian understanding, is located in higher reason. And, as in Jerome's "spark of conscience," *synderesis* initiates the process of conscientious thought, as a faculty prior to conscience itself.

Thomas Aquinas makes *synderesis* central to conscience in both the *Summa Theologiae* and *Quaestiones Disputatae de Veritate*, synthesizing

---

[7] Jerome, *Commentary on Ezekiel*, I.7, in Potts, *Conscience in Medieval Philosophy*, 79. Potts translates the major passages of the scholastic conscience; for a more expansive but untranslated anthology, see Lottin, *Psychologie et morale*.

[8] On the origins of *synderesis*, see Delhaye, *The Christian Conscience*, 105–10.

[9] *Summa De Bono*, in Potts, *Conscience in Medieval Philosophy*, 100.

[10] For the storehouse metaphor, see Suarez, *De Anima*, III: 752; Vermigli, *The Common Places*, III.v.8, 165. Jeremy Taylor calls it a "repository," *Ductor Dubitantium*, I: 10.

many of the medieval discussions. The Thomist summaries in turn become influential accounts for later casuists and theologians.[11] Aquinas will be taken here as the foundation for St. German's *Doctor and Student*, and as representative of the pre-Reformation conscience.[12] *Synderesis*, in Aquinas, offers humans access to a rarefied level of moral knowledge. In the anthropology of the *Summa*, it is the culmination of intellectual power and the center of higher reason, based on "naturally sure principles" (*ST* Ia.79.12, XI: 189). In the more expansive treatment in *De Veritate*, it is also that part of the human soul which "attains to that which is proper to angelic nature." And it is "a natural habit of first principles of action, which are the universal principles of the natural law" (*DV* Q.16, Art.1, II: 304). Aquinas describes two more important characteristics of *synderesis*, both of which are common to scholastic conceptions. First, it cannot err or sin: "there must be some permanent principle which has unwavering integrity, in reference to which all human works are examined, so that that permanent principle will resist all evil and assent to all good. This is synderesis, whose task it is to warn against evil and incline to good. Therefore, we agree that there can be no error in it" (*DV* Q.16, Art.2, II: 310).[13] And second, *synderesis* can never be fully extinguished. Even among the despairing, and even in Cain, it remains universal and permanent. Aquinas admits particular circumstances in which it is rendered ineffective by the will, but these are only particular circumstances: "For the force of concupiscence, or of another passion, so absorbs reason that in choice the universal judgment of synderesis is not applied to the particular act. But this does not destroy synderesis altogether but only in some respect. Hence, absolutely speaking, we concede that synderesis is never destroyed" (*DV* Q.16, Art.3, II: 312–13).[14]

As a repository of absolute knowledge, *synderesis* anchors the bipartite structure of the Thomist conscience. It provides universal moral direction, and then *conscientia* applies those universals to the particular

---

[11] For the influence of Aquinas among casuists, see de Azpilcueta, *Enchiridion*, 1037; Carletti, *Summa Angelica*, 83; Azor, *Institutionum*, II: 81. For a Thomist statement of *synderesis*, see Antoninus, *Summa*, I.iii.9.

[12] One important source for *Doctor and Student* is the *Summa Angelica*, which, like many examples of casuistry, describes a Thomist conscience of *synderesis* and *conscientia*. Carletti, *Summa Angelica*, 83. St. German's chapter "What Sinderesis Is" is a close summary of the anonymous Thomist tract *De Natura et Qualitate Conscientiae*. This was printed in Gerson, *Opera*, but is listed as not of genuine authorship, I:3r.

[13] Also see Philip the Chancellor, *Summa de bono*, in Potts, *Conscience in Medieval Philosophy*, 102–5.

[14] Also see Bonaventure, *Commentary on Peter Lombard's "Books of Judgements"* in Potts, *Conscience in Medieval Philosophy*, 117–21.

situations of real life: "through conscience the knowledge of synderesis and of higher and lower reason are applied to the examination of a particular act" (*DV* Q.17, Art.2, II: 324). This bifurcation can be seen as a strategy to deal with the vexing problem of the erring conscience. While *synderesis* is incorruptible, *conscientia*, being subject to the vicissitudes of lower reason, can wander and make mistakes in such things as an understanding of justice, or in logical reasoning from a premise, as St. German summarizes:

> conscience takes a lower place and is conjoined rather to the simple or lower reason, and is then called a dictate of reason. And so conscyence taken in this sense is not always in itself right but may somtyme erre and somtyme not erre. This is because it has to deal with particular things by means of knowledge or research in which there is often chance of error.
>
> (*DS* 89)[15]

The bipartite structure contains error by limiting it to *conscientia*, thereby preserving a part of the process, *synderesis*, which is free from change and sin. This is a structural solution: it creates a locus of impeccability which can be named and deployed to authorize the overall process of conscience. The two-part structure transfers error down from *synderesis* to *conscientia*, carving out a place of perfection within conscience – an ideal location in which there are no errors or uncertain shifts.

Synderesis offers such stability to the conscience that the overall process is represented as functioning according to the purely logical structure of the syllogism. *Synderesis* supplies the major premise and *conscientia* the minor:

> Thus the act of conscience is the result of a kind of particular syllogism. For example, if the judgment of synderesis expresses this statement: "I must not do anything which is forbidden by the law of God," and if the knowledge of higher reason presents this minor premise: "Sexual intercourse with this woman is forbidden by the law of God," the application of conscience will be made by concluding: "I must abstain from this intercourse."
>
> (*DV* Q.17, Art.2, II: 324)

To the modern ear, syllogism sounds like an unlikely way for conscience to function. We may expect the faculty to proceed in more associative ways, and with less logical precision. It should be acknowledged that the syllogism may not be entirely literal. Nevertheless, it is one of the scholastics' most common representations of the workings of conscience,

---

[15] On the erring conscience, see *DV*, Q.17, Art.2, II:322–6.

and so frames the faculty as operating in rational and highly structured terms.[16] So St. German, while, like Aquinas, discussing the erring conscience, also places *synderesis* at the origin of a syllogism:

> All these matters can be more clearly understood by the example of some doctors who frame a sort of syllogism about conscience, of which sinderesis propounds the major thus: "No evil is to be done". . . But inferior reason sometimes forms under this major, a minor premise by descending to some particular case of fact, thus: "This is evil." Now if conscience (according to the second description described above) conjoining to reason itself assents to this minor premise, it may err, or it may not err. In the end, conscience draws from these two premises the conclusion thus: "This is not to be done."
>
> (*DS* 89)

The syllogism usually appears within a discussion of the erring conscience, as reassurance that the conscience, which otherwise may be prone to any number of complexities and doubts and errors, in fact unfolds in an organized and reliable manner. The impeccable *synderesis* anchors the scholastic conscience, and the syllogism assures that it can only drift a short distance from that locus of certainty.

The syllogistic conscience feels like a typically scholastic rendering of anthropology in organized and rational terms, what Timothy Potts describes as the "medieval preoccupation with psychological topology."[17] But this should not lead us to dismiss it as mere style. Rather, the syllogism is at the center of the scholastic effort to give structure to the conscience. The scholastic debate is similarly concerned with identifying and naming categories within the conscience, and these categories work to solidify the syllogism, so that both construct an orderly faculty. The biggest issue is how to locate the bipartite structure among the faculties of the soul. Scholastics regularly ask whether *synderesis* is a power (*potentia*) or a habit (*habitus*), and then whether *conscientia* is a habit or an act (*actus*). Thomists and casuists rehearse the same debate almost invariably. Aquinas devotes both chapters on conscience in the *Summa* entirely to it, and the beginnings of the two chapters of *De Veritate*, concluding that *synderesis* is a habit, and *conscientia* is an act (*ST* Ia., Q.79, Art.12–13; *DV* Q.16, Art.1, Q.17, Art.1). The distinction between power and habit (also translated as "disposition") is subtle and often effaced in discussions

---

[16] See Bonaventure, in Potts, *Conscience in Medieval Philosophy*, 120; Antoninus, *Summa*, I.iii.10.

[17] Potts, *Conscience in Medieval Philosophy*, 9.

of *synderesis*, habit being deeply intertwined with power.[18] The more important distinction is made with *conscientia*, which as an act is located in a far less stable position than either habit or power.

In his discussion of the intellectual powers in the *Summa*, Aquinas distinguishes between power and act through the distinction between a perfect and an imperfect understanding. The human soul

> arrives at an understanding of reality discursively, by a process, pro and con. And it has but an imperfect understanding, both in that it does not understand everything and in that what it does understand it comes to understand through an unfolding process, passing from potential to actual understanding.
>
> (*ST* Ia, Q.79, Art. 4, XI: 159)

Imperfect, non-finished understanding is what can err, and is what comprises the act, rather than the power, of understanding. Imperfection is aligned with movement, the need for the understanding to go through the back and forth of discursive thought. Similarly, in *De Veritate*, higher reason is described as perfect because without movement: "And that which is at rest and that which is moved are like perfect and imperfect" (*DV* Q.15, Art.1, II: 274). *Conscientia*, as an act, turns out to be full of the movements of imperfect reason, as Aquinas stresses when he describes its multiple manifestations in human activity: "it is said to witness, to bind, to incite, and also to accuse, to torment, or to rebuke. And all these depend on applying some of our knowledge to what we are doing" (*ST* Ia., Q.79, Art.13, XI: 193). This activity, full of movement and based in the imperfections of the practical world, explains how *conscientia* is susceptible to error. But the act of *conscientia* issues from the power or habit of *synderesis*, which does have the stasis of perfect and higher reason: "An act, though not permanent in itself, abides permanently in its cause, which is the power or habit it proceeds from. Now though the habits which inform conscience are many, nevertheless they all take effect through one chief habit, the grasp of principles called synderesis" (*ST* Ia., Q.79, Art.13, XI: 193–5).

---

[18] Aquinas argues that *synderesis* is a habit, but also plays down the issue: "the name synderesis designates a natural habit simply, one similar to the habit of principles, or it means some power of reason with such a habit. And whatever it is it makes little difference, for it raises a doubt only about the meaning of the name." *DV* Q.16, Art.1, II:304. Similarly, Philip the Chancellor calls *synderesis* a "dispositional potentiality," and concludes "if anyone asks whether it is a potentiality or a disposition, the right answer lies in taking something in between." Potts, *Conscience in Medieval Philosophy*, 97.

More could be said about the distinctions between power, habit, and act, which become complex.[19] But the very effort to name the two parts of conscience is worth observing in itself. It is the struggle to fit the workings of conscience into a more defined set of terms, and into language. In the scholastic conception, conscience can be described because it is understood to be something that has a recognizable structure. And the naming of the parts of that structure, such as *conscientia* as an act, solidifies that structure. Further, the project of naming is predicated by sanguine assumptions about language's ability to capture the workings of conscience. Scholastic descriptions pass on these assumptions, so that Aquinas's careful investigation of the proper category for the parts of conscience in effect asserts that conscience functions in recognizable and nameable structures.

The nameability of conscience, the sense that its functioning can be captured in language, is expressed most fully in what follows from *synderesis*, the syllogism. The progression from major to minor to conclusion cuts out many of the associative and indirect paths that we might assume an inward faculty such as the conscience would take. Rather than psychological complexity, the syllogism posits a direct and logical way of working, through transparent language. Aquinas's "I must not do anything which is forbidden by the law of God . . . Sexual intercourse with this woman is forbidden by the law of God . . . I must abstain from this intercourse" presents the syllogism not as a partial or inadequate representation of conscience, but as a totalizing summary. The syllogism provides the sanguine assurance that we know how conscience works. It offers a perfect language about conscience, just as *synderesis* structures a perfect knowledge within conscience.

Luther

But the perfect and nameable conscience of the scholastics disintegrates in the Reformation. Perkins, in all his extensive writings about conscience, never uses *synderesis*, and by the seventeenth century, the word is scarce.[20] Our modern unfamiliarity with *synderesis* can be traced to the emergence of Protestant theology, and to Luther himself. Luther moves away from the scholastic conception in his early years, and then drops *synderesis*

---

[19] On the distinctions surrounding *habitus*, see *ST*, Ia2a, Q.49–54 and Anthony Kennny's Introduction to vol. 22 of the Blackfriars edition.

[20] Greene, "Synderesis." The *OED* lists no quotations after 1651.

altogether in his two main works on conscience. Conscience is, of course, absolutely central to Luther – but it becomes a conscience which, like our modern faculty, does not have a part that is called, or performs the offices of, the *synderesis*. As a result, the workings of conscience veer away from the order of the syllogism, and the faculty is understood in terms that resist structure. This destructuring has everything to do with Luther's basic theological shift from works to faith, so that the disappearance of the *synderesis* and the destructuring of the faculty are part of the separation from Catholic theology, and central to the emerging Protestant conscience.

In Luther's early works can be traced a turn away from the *synderesis* of Aquinas and the scholastics, as Steven Ozment and Michael Baylor have shown.[21] Luther uses *synderesis* in fairly orthodox ways in his *Dictata super psalterium* (1513–16) and the sermon *De propria sapientia et voluntate* (1514). In the latter, he uses recognizably orthodox vocabulary, calling *synderesis* a natural remnant from before the fall, inextinguishable, and a spark for Grace.[22] But in the *Lectures on Romans* (1515–16), *synderesis* shifts from a locus of reliable certitude to something that is significantly less effective. *Synderesis* is so limited that it has no effect on salvation. This sets the stage for a conscience fully separated from the bipartite structure.

Early in the lectures, Luther makes use of the *synderesis* in typically scholastic terms. In the scholion to Romans 1:20, while discussing why gentiles are culpable for their idolatry, he explains that they are without excuse because they knew by *synderesis* to worship a supreme God:

> They knew the invisible things of God, His eternal power and divinity. This major premise of the practical syllogism, this theological synderesis, is in all men and cannot be obscured. But in the minor premise they erred when they said and claimed: "Now this one," this is, Jupiter or any other who is like this image, "is of this type, etc." This is where the error began and produced idolatry.
>
> (*LW* 25:157–8)[23]

---

[21] Ozment, *Homo Spiritualis*, 184–216. Baylor, *Action and Person*, 119–56. The following discussion of the early Luther is largely derived from these studies.

[22] "Nam ista Synteresis in voluntate humana in perpetuum manet, quod velit salvari, bene beateque vivere, nolit et odiat damnari, sicut et rationis Synteresis inextinguibiliter deprecatur ad optima, ad vera, recta, iusta. Haec enim Synteresis est conservatio, reliquiae, residuum, superstes portio naturae in corruptione et vitio perditae ac velut fomes, semen et materia resuscitandae et restaurandae eius per gratiam." *D. Martin Luthers Werke*, I:32.

[23] The Concordia translation has "insight of the conscience" rather than *synderesis*, which is in the Latin: "hec syntheresis theologica est inobscurabilis in omnibus." *D. Martin Luthers Werke*, 56:177.

Synderesis is impeccable and leads to a conscience which functions according to the logic of syllogism. It is only in the minor premise, usually associated with *conscientia*, that error creeps in, leading the gentiles to the false conclusion that is idolatry. Luther's commitment to this customary account is qualified, however, by his introduction to the passage. He prefaces the argument by saying that he will "present for my fellow spectators a playlet (*modicum ludere*) according to my understanding and then await either their approval or their criticism" (*LW* 25:157).[24] If it is a bit of theater, then *synderesis* and syllogism are not literally structuring conscience. They become a performance to be clapped for or not, and believed or not. Luther's theatrical framing suggests that the language of his argument is not meant to signify in a totalizing way. The syllogism is mimetic, or a figure of speech, not the mechanics of conscience as it really works. Even as he makes use of a scholastic *synderesis*, we can sense a caution about it.[25]

Luther's wariness centers on righteousness.[26] In the scholion to Romans 4:7, he argues against the sacrament of confession, which instills too much confidence in the merely human ability to overcome sin. This is both an underestimation of sin, and an overestimation of human behavior, or righteousness, and the latter is associated with *synderesis*:

> All of these monstrosities have come from the fact that they did not know what sin is nor forgiveness. For they reduced sin to some very minute activity of the soul, and the same was true of righteousness. For they said that since the will has this synteresis, "it is inclined," albeit weakly, "toward the good." And this minute motion toward God (which many can perform by nature) they imagine to be an act of loving God above all things!
>
> (*LW* 25:262)

In Luther's understanding, we are not capable of comprehending and moving significantly toward the good by means of our own faculties, because of our fallen nature: "Therefore we are all born in iniquity, that is, in unrighteousness, and we die in it, and we are righteous only by the imputation of a merciful God through faith in His Word" (*LW* 25: 274-5). Imputed Grace implies that there cannot be a meaningful role in

---

[24] *Ibid.*, 56:176.

[25] Baylor's discussion of *synderesis* and syllogism in this passage registers a number of further qualifications to the scholastic tradition. *Action and Person*, 137–43.

[26] On Luther's critique of righteousness as the theological center of *Lectures on Romans*, see Rupp, *The Righteousness of God*, 160–4. Luther also mentions *synderesis* in the scholion to Romans 3:10, "None is righteous," *LW* 25:222.

salvation for righteousness: after the fall, there simply is not a sufficient spark in the human mind. *Synderesis*, which is that spark, and which for the scholastics holds out the promise of righteousness, inclines toward God only weakly. The scholastic conception of *synderesis* exaggerates the human capacity for righteousness, aligning conscience with angelic or prelapsarian knowledge, and the perfect language of the syllogism. But for Luther, *synderesis* is only a minute motion.

In this passage can also be seen the importance of Luther's fundamental revision of human will. He is arguing against a *synderesis* that is aligned with will, and that therefore supplies not just an epistemological clarity about the good, but also the inclination toward it, driving humans toward salvation. The question of the relation of *synderesis* to will is a long-standing scholastic disagreement. The Franciscan position is expressed by Bonaventure, that "*synderesis* simultaneously embraces reason and will."[27] Aquinas, in contrast, rejects the alignment when he explicitly locates *synderesis* among the Intellectual Powers, or higher reason, rather than among the Appetitive Powers, which include sensuality, will, and free will (*ST* Ia., Q.80–3).[28] Jean Gerson extends Bonaventure's position by making *synderesis* a key part of his valorization of human affect in his *Mystical Theology*. For Gerson, *synderesis* is an "affective power," the highest among will and sensitive appetite, which takes on an "inclination to the good."[29] According to Ozment, Luther's turn away from *synderesis* evolves in part as a rejection of Gerson's volitional *synderesis*, with its potential to lead fallen humans toward salvation.[30] Luther's challenge to the efficaciousness of the human will goes with a weak *synderesis*. This anticipates the close association of conscience with the emerging predestinarian anthropology of Calvinism. And the resistance to will highlights how Luther limits the motivating strength of *synderesis*, which undermines the functioning of the syllogistic conscience. The syllogism is not a transparent representation of the bipartite functioning of *synderesis* and *conscientia*, but merely a bit of theater, meant to capture a far less ideal understanding, harnessed to a far less clear will. Suspicious

---

[27] Bonaventure, *Commentary*, II.39.2, in Potts, *Conscience in Medieval Philosophy*, 116. Also see Langston, *Conscience and Other Virtues*, 21–37; Oberman, *The Harvest of Medieval Theology*, 65–7.

[28] See McInerny, *Ethica Thomistica*, 108–11.

[29] Gerson, *On Mystical Theology*, in *Early Works*, 279.

[30] Ozment, *Homo Spiritualis*, 62–83. Baylor, however, argues for Gabriel Biel as a more important influence than Gerson, *Action and Person*, 161–8.

of will and the efficacy of works, Luther enacts, in Ozment's words, "the suffocation of the *synteresis* as a significant soteriological resource."[31]

And so, according to Baylor, in the period 1517–19 "Luther came to discard the *synteresis* altogether from his conception of conscience."[32] Over the next several years, Luther develops his primary statements on conscience, making the faculty central to his theology. But it is a reformed conscience, without the bipartite structure of the scholastics. Loosened from such structure, conscience instead is enmeshed in the new problem of works versus faith, and takes as its object the whole person. Shortly after the *Lectures on Romans*, Luther continues to brood on the problem of righteousness, and in 1518 experiences the iconic crisis known as the tower conversion. This is, in Luther's telling, the true origin of his new theology, and the role conscience plays at the origin marks the centrality of the faculty to the Reformation itself:

> I had indeed been captivated with an extraordinary ardor for understanding Paul in the Epistle to the Romans. But up til then it was not the cold blood about the heart, but a single word in Chapter 1 [:17], "In it the righteousness of God is revealed," that had stood in my way. For I hated that word "righteousness of God," which, according to the use and custom of all the teachers, I had been taught to understand philosophically regarding the formal or active righteousness, as they called it, with which God is righteous and punishes the unrighteous sinner.
>
> Though I lived as a monk without reproach, I felt that I was a sinner before God with an extremely disturbed conscience. I could not believe that he was placated by my satisfaction. I did not love, yes, I hated the righteous God who punishes sinners, and secretly, if not blasphemously, certainly murmuring greatly, I was angry with God, "As if, indeed, it is not enough that miserable sinners, eternally lost through original sin, are crushed by every kind of calamity by the law of the decalogue, without having God add pain to pain by the gospel and also by the gospel threatening us with his righteousness and wrath!" Thus I raged with a fierce and troubled conscience.
>
> (*LW* 34:336–7)

Here can be recognized the familiar Lutheran angst, as well as a vexed conscience that feels quite modern. Without the assurance of *synderesis*, without its access to perfect knowledge and its promise of the motivating structure of a syllogism, conscience has become "disturbed," "fierce," and

---

[31] Ozment, *Homo Spiritualis*, 199.
[32] Baylor, *Action and Person*, 177.

"troubled." It is still energetic – but without an identifiable vector for that energy. Quite unlike the smooth functioning of a syllogism, it takes on a theatrical quality, unfolding in real time like the consciences of Richard or Hamlet, or like the conscience Luther calls a "playlet."

The source of Luther's troubled conscience turns out to be its damaging relationship to works. Monks, with their vows and strict lives, exemplify the Church's belief in works. But it does not seem right that God would be placated this way – once again, Luther is dissatisfied with the orthodox confidence that human action can establish righteousness. So Luther finds himself chafing against life in the monastery, against the decalogue, and even against God Himself. Then, in the concluding step of the conversion, Luther experiences the realization that true righteousness comes from faith, not works:

> There I began to understand that the righteousness of God is that by which the righteous lives by a gift of God, namely by faith. And this is the meaning: the righteousness of God is revealed by the gospel, namely the passive righteousness with which merciful God justifies us by faith, as it is written, "He who through faith is righteous shall live." Here I felt that I was altogether born again and had entered paradise itself through open gates.
>
> (LW 34:337)

Having rejected the older conscience's entanglement with works, Luther has imagined a new kind of conscience. It is a conscience that has broken free from works, and, in the realization of faith, has found salvation.

The renovation that conscience undergoes in the tower animates Luther's most extensive theorization of conscience, *The Judgment of Martin Luther on Monastic Vows* (1521), as well as *A Sermon on the Three Kinds of Good Life for the Instruction of Consciences*, both of which are written in the year of the Diet of Worms. The treatise *On Monastic Vows* is addressed specifically to "people tortured under the tyranny of conscience and sin" – monks, the argument goes, who fall under such tyranny because their monastic vows, over such things as celibacy and poverty, have focused their attention on works (LW 44:251). Luther argues that the monastic vow "is in itself a most dangerous thing" (LW 44:252), because it represents a presumptuous overvaluation of works and a blasphemous pride in the efficacy of human action in attaining salvation. And in the monastery, conscience itself is perverted by this obsessive focus on works: "How many penances are there, how many chainings of the body how many punishments, how many sorrows for those who do not attain this ungodliness? What a burdened conscience they have when they have not observed their rule!" (*LW* 44:293–4). As is common in Luther's theology, such a commitment to works is associated with the Law: in the tower, Luther the monk feels "crushed" by the decalogue; here he declares that monastic vows "ensnare the conscience and hold it captive to the bondage of the law" (*LW* 44:304).

Conscience has become a problem for Luther, a place of suffering and bondage, in which one is ensnared by works. But just as Luther is born again into faith in the tower, so in *On Monastic Vows* he imagines a conscience liberated from works. This renewed conscience, purified by faith, is aligned with Christian liberty: "Christian or evangelical freedom, then, is a freedom of conscience which liberates the conscience from works" (*LW* 44: 298). Conscience becomes the keystone of salvation, and salvation depends upon a conscience freed from works.

In *A Sermon on the Three Kinds of Good Life for the Instruction of Consciences*, Luther traces the same progression with the aid of a spatial conceit, likening conscience to the architecture of a church. First is the conscience of the churchyard. There ceremonies and sacraments are like the vows of the monastery – they trick Christians into believing they are righteous. In the churchyard, one "makes things which matter little if at all into strict matters of conscience, but has a very free and easy conscience in things of great importance on which everything depends. People who do this are all Atrienses Sancti, churchyard saints" (*LW* 44:238). The sermon then moves from the churchyard to the nave, an intermediate place of "teaching, works, and concepts of conscience which are really good," such as humility and love, rather than food and clothing (*LW* 44:239). But Luther is quick to point out that many "drag their dead works in with them" to the nave, turning good works into sins because they "maintain a pious posture not of their own desire, but because they fear disgrace, punishment, or hell" (*LW* 44:240). Conscience once again acts as a corrupting force, because its orientation toward works, and its promise of effective human action, lead even those people in the nave to become falsely righteous.

Then Luther describes the sanctuary, "the holy of holies," which holds out the promise of a properly functioning conscience. Here, as in the tower conversion and *On Monastic Vows*, conscience is not problematically engaged with works, but rather has freed itself: "Such a heart is holy for the sake of holiness and righteousness alone and does everything with joy. Look! Here is really sound doctrine! This shows what a conscience is and what good works are!" (*LW* 44:241–2). Having rejected the older conscience's entanglement with works, Luther imagines a newborn conscience, purified by faith, able to receive the Holy Spirit, and aligned with Christian liberty.

Like the tower conversion, neither the sermon nor the treatise on vows ever mentions *synderesis*. They also eschew the scholastic tendency to name and categorize: while Aquinas spends the majority of his time considering whether *synderesis* and *conscientia* are powers or habits or acts, Luther is uninterested. Conscience, for Luther, does not have discernible and nameable parts, and so does not have the characteristics of structure. As the bipartite structure of *synderesis* and *conscientia* collapses into the single term "conscience," the faculty loses a spatial and temporal conception, so that it is no longer felt to function first in one part, and then in the next part. What takes the place of such a structured functioning is something undifferentiated and inchoate – conscience as a kind of black box that admits no searching and only disorganized description.

This inchoate conscience emerges as a feature of the basic Protestant move from works to faith. Works are themselves clearly organized structures, as Luther stresses in the *Sermon on the Three Kinds of Good Life*, when he explains that they "are bound up with time and place" and that for churchyard saints "holiness is circumscribed by their five sense and their bodily existence" (*LW* 44:235, 238). All of the ceremonies, vestments, and food are easily known and practiced, whereas the good works of the nave, such as humility and meekness, "are not bound up with food and clothing, or with place, time, or person" (*LW* 44:239). Without works, the conscience must operate among concepts and actions that are less organized. And the difficulty of inhabiting such a conscience of faith is obvious to Luther. Although he pictures the possibility of the good conscience which he associates with the nave, he admits that "Such gladness, love, joy, and willingness are not found in the heart of any man on earth" (*LW* 44:240) – this relationship to conscience is not naturally available to us, just as *synderesis* cannot effectively lead to the Holy of Holies.

So Luther's theology depends upon a conscience that devolves from structure. The disappearance of *synderesis* reforms Aquinas's structured conscience in order to break free from works. But this is not so much a reformation as a de-formation, or what I am calling a destructuring of conscience. Structure is left behind, and with it any means of clear differentiation within the faculty. And so also lost is any straightforward way to describe its parts and functioning. Luther's conscience coalesces into a black box. This is a transformation of considerable historical import, beginning with its proximity to the Diet or Worms.[33] But it is not a one-time movement – not simply an historical shift, but a shift that also must take place within each person. Luther's monk fettered by vows, or his "churchyard saint," must find a way from a conscience devoted to works to one freed by faith. So must each believer, for whom salvation itself depends upon faith, and so depends upon a conscience that can leave behind works. Destructuring must take place within each person's conscience, and so is a phenomenon which must occur over and over again. And even within each person, destructuring is not likely to be a single event leading directly to salvation, but rather an experience which does not readily succeed, and so demands repeat performances.

For Luther, in fact, a neatly operating conscience, one that works efficaciously and so need not repeat itself, is a suspect thing. For such a conscience is surely attaching itself to works, and so becomes a kind of trap that prevents the essential Protestant move to the freedom of faith. Randall Zachman, reading broadly in Luther's writing, argues that conscience itself is associated with the flesh, and is "oriented toward sensible and visible things," like the monk's vows.[34] Conscience, in Zachman's argument, actually becomes a temptation, tempting us to dwell on our bad works, and to imagine God as the righteous judge of the Law rather than the merciful deliverer of the Gospel. Conscience

> is certain that it already knows who God is and how God is to be worshiped; it portrays to itself a God who is pleased by works of the law. When the Word tells the conscience that God wishes to be worshiped by faith alone and not by works, reason and conscience reject the Word as an outright lie and falsehood.[35]

Finding in works a more certain and structured set of terms, conscience veers toward them, and tempts us to do the same. The move to faith and a free conscience, then, first requires a breaking of the faculty's certainty. The Law and the neat functioning of conscience must be left behind. And so the possibility of a more authentic conscience is bound up in

---

[33] In *On Monastic Vows* Luther argues that the renewed conscience is congruent with the Reformation itself: "Here you see the entire canon law as well as the dominion of the pope condemned as being against Christ, because they do nothing else but ensnare consciences in their own works and take them away from Christ, after having first destroyed their freedom." *LW* 44:300.

[34] Zachman, *The Assurance of Faith*, 21.

[35] *Ibid.*, 38.

uncertainty – the fierce and troubled conscience of the tower itself is a marker of the possibility of a regenerate conscience.[36]

For this reason the reformed conscience is one that, in its functioning, must assert its own destructuring. Again, destructuring does not simply name a unidirectional trend in which conscience pulls away from structure after the scholastics. It also names how conscience repeatedly enacts the move away from structure, in a process of continual destructuring. So it becomes a thing not explained so much as experienced, and not described so much as dramatized. This is the force of Luther's suggestion that the syllogism be considered a "playlet," and it is the theology behind Shakespeare's staging of conscience in real time. Dramatic language does not assert the faculty's structural completeness, but rather admits imperfections: the audience experiences the scene subjectively, and in the moment. These imperfections are the very point of the reformed conscience, which takes the move away from structure to be a move toward salvation.

The psychological complexity of such an inchoate conscience coincides with the emergence of the theology of the whole person, as Michael Baylor asserts:

> Luther has established a new object for the working of the conscience: its judgments are not just about actions – "What is to be done or is not to be done, or what has been done well or done badly," as he put it in his more traditional definition – it also judges about the agent who performs these actions, the individual or person as a whole.[37]

The turn from works is also the turn from the structured conscience: "In order to develop a view of the conscience which depicted the conscience as concerning itself, on the highest level, with the person as a whole rather than just his particular actions, Luther was forced to discard the *synteresis* as the ontological base and, in this sense, determinant of conscience."[38] Without *synderesis* and the scholastic syllogism, without the orderly and linear movement from major to minor, the inchoate conscience lurches associatively from thought to thought, and from despair to sudden conversion and rebirth. Conscience has become more like the human mind than a logical proof. Destructuring, as it leads to the Reformed focus on the whole person, brings conscience into close

---

[36] Rupp also associates conscience with Luther's *anfechtung*, or temptation, *The Righteousness of God*, 105–15.
[37] Baylor, *Action and Person*, 201.
[38] *Ibid.*, 202.

contact with early modern subjectivity. It makes possible Hamlet's lament, "Thus conscience does make cowards of us all," in which conscience is inextricable from consciousness. And it leads to a parallel expression among the theorists of conscience, such as William Perkins in *A Discourse of Conscience*, who begin to describe the inchoate faculty as an experience of self-reflection. And so this chapter arrives back where it began, with the destructured and reflexive conscience of early modern England.

Perkins and the Theorists of Conscience

For England's theorists of conscience, the faculty is cut loose from the anchor of *synderesis*. Woolton does describe *synderesis* in fairly orthodox terms, including its role as a storehouse of knowledge and the major premise of a syllogism (*OC* B4v–C3v). But then he adds an important caveat, saying that he has used the traditional distinction between *synderesis* and *conscientia* only for convenience. In fact, "most certayne it is that these things differ not in mans mind, if you respect their substance and essence: being in deede mingled and confused one with another: onely for instruction sake, they are separate in thought and cogitation" (*OC* C4v). *Synderesis* is descriptive but not a true account of conscience, which is a more confused and unstructured part of the mind. Alexander Hume ignores *synderesis* altogether. And Perkins never uses the word in any of his writings. *A Discourse of Conscience* is strongly influenced by Aquinas, and describes the inner workings of conscience in ways that recall the scholastic tradition. Chapter 1 is titled "What conscience is," just as Aquinas asks "Quid conscientia sit?" in the *Summa*. But when Perkins begins with conscience in this manner, he is skipping over what for Aquinas is the more primary inquiry, "Quid synderesis sit?" Following Luther, Perkins has cut out the bipartite structure, building a "conscience" which is fundamentally different from the *conscientia* that results from *synderesis*.

In answering what this conscience is, Perkins remains engaged with the scholastic approach. So when he retheorizes conscience without *synderesis*, he explains himself by means of the scholastic vocabulary. After placing conscience within the understanding, as Aquinas does, Perkins rejects Aquinas's argument that conscience is an act. Aquinas, as we have seen, posits *synderesis* as a "natural habit," which is a naturally occurring, unchanging disposition to know and comprehend universal principles. And he then posits *conscientia* as an act, which issues from the habit of *synderesis*. But Perkins specifically disagrees with Aquinas on this matter, as he elevates conscience from act to something like a habit:

> Againe I say that conscience is a part of the minde or understanding, to shew that conscience is not a bare knowledge or iudgement of the understanding (as men commonly write) but a naturall power, facultie, or created qualitie from whence knowledge and iudgement proceede as effects. This the Scriptures confirme in that they ascribe sundrie workes and actions to conscience, as accusing, excusing, comforting, terrifying. Which actions could not thence proceede, if conscience were no more but an action or act of the minde. Indeed I grant, it may be taken for a certen actuall knowledge, which is the effect thereof: but to speake properly, this knowledge must proceede of a power in the soul, the propertie whereof is to take the principles and conclusions of the minde and applie them, etc. by applying either to accuse or excuse. This is the ground of all, and this I take to be conscience.
> (*DC* 3)

The parenthetical "as men commonly write" includes a gloss pointing to Aquinas's discussion of conscience in the *Summa*, as well as to two later Thomists, Antoninus and Domingo Bañez. Aquinas's key argument for *conscientia*'s being an act is that it is said by Scripture to do the actions of accusing, excusing, etc., which Perkins repeats.[39] But for Perkins this demonstrates that conscience is not itself a mere action, but rather something prior to action, which then leads to accusing and excusing as effects. Instead of an act, conscience for Perkins is "a naturall power, facultie, or created qualitie." The first is presumably equivalent to Aquinas's *potentia*, which houses *synderesis*. What Perkins calls a faculty or created quality is very like what Aquinas calls habit, a permanently existing part of the power. For Perkins conscience is not an act but is either a habit or a power.

This is not a merely semantic difference: Perkins is moving conscience up the hierarchy of scholastic categories, giving it more permanence and prestige. Acts only come into being when a habit is actualized in practice, and so they are discursive and can err. When Perkins makes conscience a habit or power, he asserts a more reliable and solid conception of conscience than Aquinas has for *conscientia*. In elevating conscience, Perkins adds to it the characteristics of *synderesis*. Still needing to anchor the conscience with universal ideals, he gives it the task of supplying the "principles and conclusions" which once belonged to *synderesis*. While in Aquinas it is the *synderesis* which cannot be lost, now conscience takes on

---

[39] *ST*, Ia.79.13, XI: 193. Aquinas and Perkins refer to Romans 2:15.

that status. Perkins makes the permanence of the conscience unmistakable, saying it bears witness continually,

> not for a minut, or a day, or a moneth, or a yeare, but for ever: when a man dies conscience dieth not; when the bodie is rotting in the grave, conscience liveth and is safe and sound: and when we shall rise againe, conscience shall come with us to the barre of God's iudgement, either to accuse or excuse us before God.
>
> (*DC* 8)

Elevated from act to power or habit, conscience takes on the immutability of *synderesis*, and becomes eternal. In effect, *synderesis* is folded into the conscience, so that what Aquinas calls *synderesis* and *conscientia* are now both within what Perkins calls "conscience."[40]

In *A Discourse of Conscience*, Perkins depends on Aquinas and the scholastic tradition. But, following the less systematic innovations of Luther and Calvin, he quite deliberately removes conscience from its two-part structure. The categories matter less to Perkins than they do to Aquinas – conscience is not an act, but he seems uninterested in deciding if it is a habit or a power. And without *synderesis*, the ability to think of conscience functioning as a structured process becomes impossible. Perkins's destructured conscience instead takes on a more psychological cast. In place of *synderesis*, Perkins offers a far more inchoate term: "mind."

Still looking at the above argument against conscience as an act, it can be seen that Perkins first locates the faculty in "a part of the minde or understanding," taking the traditional scholastic part of the soul, understanding, and adding a new locus, the mind. He goes on to say that what conscience does is "to take the principles and conclusions of the minde and applie them," so that it is the mind which provides the universal knowledge traditionally associated with *synderesis*. The substitution of mind for *synderesis* becomes clear later in *A Discourse* when he describes the "manner" in which conscience judges, which is still in the form of a practical syllogism. Whereas in the scholastic conception *synderesis* provides the major term to initiate the syllogism, with Perkins it is the mind:

> *Every murderer is cursed*, saith the minde:
> *Thou art a murderer*, saith conscience assisted by memory.
> ergo, *Thou art accursed*, saith conscience, and so giveth her sentence.
>
> (*DC* 84)

---

[40] Immanuel Bourne credits Perkins and Alexander Hume with this shift away from Aquinas, *Anatomie of Conscience*, 7–8.

Here Perkins describes the mind exactly as *synderesis* has been described: "The mind is the storehouse and keeper of all manner of rules and principles. It may be compared to a booke of law, in which are set down the penall statutes of the lande. The duty of it is to preferre and present to the conscience rules of divine law whereby it is to give judgement" (*DC* 84). The mind is a less technical term, with a far less precise signification – Perkins never explains it, nor is the Latin *mens* used in a precise way by Aquinas. Whereas *synderesis* reifies a part of the conscience and assures a locus of impeccability, mind diffuses conscience, making it harder to discern a structure in its functioning, and harder to locate where the faculty is reliable and where not.[41]

As Perkins continues to describe what conscience is, he primarily discusses thought and the intellectual experiences of the mind. And his account bends strongly toward what a modern would recognize as the shifting and self-reflective qualities of consciousness. He details various kinds of knowledge, and distinguishes conscience by its reflexivity: "To be certen what an other man hath saide or done, is commonly called knowledge: but for a man to be certen what he himselfe hath done or saide, that is conscience" (*DC* 4). Conscience enables self-consciousness. And then conscience seems to become consciousness itself – it becomes identical with the elusive mental process of reflection and human consciousness:

> For there must be two actions of the understanding, the one is simple, which barely conceiveth or thinketh this or that: the other is a reflecting or doubling of the former, whereby a man conceives and thinkes with himselfe what he thinks. And this action properly pertaines to the conscience. The minde thinks a thought, now conscience goes beyond the minde, and knowes what the minde thinks: so as if a man would go about to hide his sinnefull thoughts from God, his conscience as an other person within him, shall discover all. By meanes of this second action conscience may beare witnes even of thoughts, and from hence also it seemes to borrow his name, because conscience is a science or knowledge ioyned with an other knowledge: for by it I conceive and know what I know.
>
> (*DC* 7)[42]

<hr />

[41] This matches Luther's approach, according to Ozment: "We find that Luther employs other terms, and without the precision which would permit us to speak of anthropological 'categories' in parallel, if not in synonmy, with anima. He speaks, for example, of 'my mind or spirit' (mens mea vel spiritu). Or 'spirit or soul' (spiritus vel anima), and of 'my heart, conscience or soul' (cor meum, conscientia mea vel anima). These parallels indicate that spiritus, mens, cor, and conscientia are not independent parts of the soul for Luther." *Homo Spiritualis*, 94.

[42] Elsewhere Perkins writes: "There be in man two kinds of cogitations, or as one may say reasons: the first is a single cogitation, whereby a man simply thinketh, or knoweth, or iudgeth this or

With "two actions" comes the possibility of a two-part process. But in place of the neat distinction between *synderesis* and *conscientia* is the murky difference between the mind's thought and the conscience's knowledge of that thought. When "a man conceives and thinkes with himselfe what he thinks," his reflections quickly multiply toward infinity, like the reflections between two mirrors. It is a marvelous puzzle to decide where *thought* ends and *thought about thought* begins.

The sheer movement of Perkins's conscience marks how far it has come from the scholastic structure of *synderesis*, which for Aquinas attains perfect understanding in that it is static and unchanging. The kinetics of self-reflection, moreover, efface any clear origin to anchor the process, or clear endpoint to conclude it. In this destructuring conscience there is an active sense of pursuing moral truth, rather than simply receiving it. And there is also the sense of pursuing a thing which ever recedes from us, like the reflection in a glass. Conscience is no longer understood as a completed and totalizing faculty, but rather as an unfolding experience, a mental drama that repeatedly escapes completion and perfect comprehension. This is a destructuring not simply for the historical shift away from *synderesis*, but because the energy of self-reflection enacts and reenacts the loss of structure. Conscience becomes the experience of pursuing an understanding that infinitely recedes from the structures of language and thought. Such imperfection cannot be summarized, but must be won anew for each person, and in successive moments of each person's life.

Perkins's reflexive conscience crystallizes the tendencies of his fellow theorists. John Woolton explicitly rejects the scholastics, "who with great curiositie of definitions and devisions, have altogether darkened rather then lightened this matter" (B3r). Separating conscience from the bipartite structure of *synderesis* and *conscientia*, Woolton simultaneously submits it to the careful searching of the lay reader, in the hope that his theorization "shall stirre up in men a marveylous love and desire of a sincere conscience" (B3v–B4r). The inchoate conscience becomes the occasion for theorization and investigation, a "stirring" that brings forth the possibility of a regenerate Protestant conscience. For Alexander Hume, who never mentions *synderesis*, conscience is intensely reflexive, "As gif wee wald say, the knawledg quhilk man hes inwartly with himselfe, of all his actiounis, wordis, and cogitations" (*ATC* 13).

---

that: and this is properly called the mind: The other is a reflex cogitation or reason, whereby a man iudgeth that he knoweth or thinketh this or that; and it is commonly called *Conscience*." *A Treatise of Man's Imagination*, 54.

This theoretical turn is central to what R. T. Kendall describes as the "experimental predestinarian tradition" of English Calvinism. Without assurance of permanent Grace, the believer must constantly search within him or herself, in order to seek faith and the promise of election. Inward experimentation is based on a constant intellectual testing, and a pursuit of knowledge about the self, what Kendall calls the "reflex act."[43] He introduces the term while referring to the key passage in *A Discourse of Conscience*, in which Perkins describes the doubling of the reflective conscience, and he makes Perkins the central figure of experimental predestinarian tradition.[44] Moreover, in Kendall's view Perkins's use of the syllogism as a way of understanding conscience, destructured in comparison to its scholastic predecessor, becomes the primary means of attaining experimental knowledge. It is how one turns inward, "drawing a conclusion by reflecting upon oneself."[45] This experimental effort to understand faith and to seek election depends especially on the conscience: "The will to believe in and of itself cannot deliver the immediate assurance but the conscience can do it, by reflecting upon itself."[46]

If conscience has become enmeshed in the thorny problem of election, the most proximate impetus is Calvin. *The Institutes of the Christian Religion* view conscience almost entirely through the lens of salvation. Calvin never describes the parts of conscience and its functioning, and nowhere mentions *synderesis*. Relative to Luther, he intensifies the personal stakes with a rigorously soteriological and predestinarian focus. For Calvin, a good conscience serves as an assurance of salvation: "It is an assurednes that maketh the conscience quiete and cherefull before God, without which the conscience must of necessity be vexed, and in a maner torne in peeces with troublesome trembling" (*Inst.* III.ii.16, 225). There is a feeling of quiet and cheerfulness that comes over the free conscience, a kind of comfort that contrasts with the vexation of an unregenerate conscience. So the fundamental question whether one is elect or reprobate can be referred to an examination of conscience, whether it is vexed or quiet. Of course the elect are few; most are reprobate, who

> go not thus farre forwarde with the children of God, that after the throwing downe of their flesh they be renued and florish againe in the

---

[43] Kendall, *Calvin and English Calvinism*, 57.

[44] Kendall also includes Richard Sibbes, Thomas Hooker, and William Ames, among others.

[45] Kendall, *Calvin and English Calvinism*, 8. Perkins's frequent reliance on the syllogism is also a characteristic of his Ramism. See McKim, "The Functions of Ramism in William Perkins' Theology."

[46] *Ibid.*, 63.

> inward man, but amazed with the first terrour do lie still in desperation: yet it serveth to shewe forth the equitie of Gods judgement, that their consciences be tossed with such wayes.
>
> (*Inst.* II.vii.9, 136)

Nevertheless, the careful examination of conscience, even as it is bound up in the pricks and stings of despair, is necessary to the possibility of salvation. It serves as a gateway, an ordeal that turns the sinner toward God's Grace:

> For conscience can not beare the burden of iniquitie, but that by and by the iudgement of God is present before it: and the iudgement of God can not be felte, but that it striketh into us a dreadfull horrour of death. And likewise being constrained with proofs of her owne weakenesse, it can not choose but by and by fall into despeire of her own strength. Both these affections do engendre humility & abatement of courage. So at length it commeth to passe, that man made afraide with feling of eternal death, which he seeth to hang over him by the deserving of his owne unright-eousnesse, turneth him selfe to the only mercy of God.
>
> (*Inst.* II.viii.3, 141)

So the theorists of conscience devote considerable attention to the problem of how to know whether one is saved, and to the pastoral task of helping believers examine their own consciences, with the goal of discerning election. Perkins's first treatise on the conscience is *A Case of Conscience: The Greatest There Ever Was: How a Man May Know Whether He Be the Child of God or No* (1592), which is addressed to those "much troubled with feare, that they are not Gods children."[47] Having theorized what conscience is, the second half of *A Discourse* is dedicated to the role of the faculty in salvation. Perkins speaks primarily in comforting tones about the regnerate conscience and its "certain persuasion" of election, hailing the turning point as the "reformation of conscience," which is "when it doth cease to accuse and terrifie, and begins to excuse and tes-tifie unto us by the holy Ghost, that we are the children of God" (*DC* 163). Woolton and Hume do the same. And many more treatises emerge, dedicated to the particular task of comforting afflicted consciences and protecting them from despair. Among these are one by Perkins's men-tor at Cambridge, Richard Greenham's *A Most Sweet Comfort for an Afflicted Conscience* (published posthumously in 1598), Robert Linaker's

---

[47] Perkins, *A Case of Conscience*, 2.

A Comfortable Treatise for the Reliefe of Such as Are Afflicted in Conscience (1595), and Robert Bolton's *Instructions for a Right Comforting Afflicted Consciences* (1631).

Not surprisingly, among English Calvinists the examination of conscience is mostly about comforting the afflicted – self-reflection tends to break down into torment and despair, such as Luther experiences in the tower. Perkins in *A Discourse* describes how "when a man sinnes against his conscience, as much as in him lieth, he plungeth himselfe into the gulfe of desperation" (*DC* Epistle). This despair, "whereby a man through the vehement and constant accusation of his conscience, comes to be out of all hope of the pardon of his sinnes," leads many to attempt to "hang or drowne them selves, or to cutt their owne throats" (*DC* 88). Hume is especially graphic, as conscience is liable "to torment man with terribil prickis, with fearfull terrors, and intollerable paine," and the reprobate caught in such suffering "heaps sinne upon sin, quhairby his *conscience* is mair and mair wounded, and his paine thereafter incraeased: Quhil at the last, hee fallis in utter despair; and ather puts violent hands in himselfe, as Iudas did; or else is perpetually tormented with the worme of his *conscience*, as Cain was" (*ATC* 21, 44).

The despairing conscience, with all of its overwhelming torment, is one key consequence of the destructuring of the faculty. It is a product of the move away from the certainty and structure of *synderesis* and syllogism, to the experience of pricking and wounding and, as Calvin describes it, being "tossed with such wayes." Here is another way to recognize how the Protestant conscience becomes increasingly important as it becomes increasingly inchoate, slipping into the disorder of despair even as it takes on the greatest of Christian stakes, salvation. The effort to move beyond despair into the experience of a peaceful and regenerate conscience, then, can be seen as an effort to perfect the inchoate, to put back together the pieces of what has been destructured. The next chapter will study how Spenser attempts such a restructuring. In *The Faerie Queene* conscience emerges as an energetic theological and political force, one that Spenser attempts to organize, not entirely successfully, in the highly structured mode of allegory.

2

Spenser's Allegorical Conscience

Conscience seems to lend itself to allegorical personification. It regularly finds expression as a voice or a person, often with striking personality. Pinocchio's cricket is a modern example. George Herbert's "Conscience" gives us a similarly annoying "Pratler." Launcelot Gobbo's Conscience is a more amiable character, but just as conversational. The notion of an interlocutor is in Paul's metaphor of the conscience "also bearing witness" (Romans 2:15). Kant says that "For all duties a human being's conscience will, accordingly, have to think of someone other than himself . . . . This other may be an actual person or a merely ideal person that reason creates for itself."[1] The conception is familiar and widespread, and the impetus for it must lie in conscience itself – something about how it works in us tends to call forth the idea of another person talking.

So Conscience often shows up personified. He is one of the most sustained figures in *Piers Plowman*: first a knight who resists the King by refusing to marry Lady Mede, then a host of a banquet, where he clashes with Clergy, and lastly a focus for the poem's close, when Conscience declares himself a pilgrim seeking Piers.[2] Several Tudor interludes give conscience personhood, such as *The World and the Child* (1522), *A Newe Interlude of Impacyente Poverte* (1560), and *The Conflict of Conscience* (1581). And as the Elizabethan theater scene warms up, Robert Wilson brings Lady Conscience onto the stage in the *Three Ladies of London*

---

[1] Kant, *The Metaphysics of Morals*, 189.

[2] Langland, *Piers Plowman*, Passus 3–4, 13, 19–20 (B text). Judith Anderson sees the role of pilgrim as initiating a move away from pure personification: "In Conscience's decision to part with Clergy lies a birth of conscious choice and a transformation from Conscience as fixed concept, to a pilgrim, a figure who changes in and through time." *The Growth of a Personal Voice*, 91. Among medieval poems also see the anonymous *The Assembly of Gods*, where Conscience sits with Synderesys, lines 934–7; Jean Gerson, *Treatise Against The Romance of the Rose*, in *Early Works*, 378.

(1584), and its sequel, *The Three Lords and Three Ladies of London* (1590).[3] These personifications give conscience coherence. They supply the faculty with a materiality that organizes its relationship to the world, allowing it to communicate and assert itself. And they represent the inward experience of conscience in the structured terms of body and character. Running quite counter to the Protestant destructuring of the faculty, allegory organizes the inchoate conscience. The popular representational mode of an allegorical conscience carries the promise of a faculty that is whole, and that can be imagined and discussed in ways that seem complete.

Leaning toward the archaic and the allegorical, Spenser could be expected to follow this tradition in *The Faerie Queene*. Yet there is no character in the poem that presents a personified Conscience. The faculty never takes on a body, nor does it materialize in the allegory as a geographical feature, such as a house or a fountain. It never finds expression in a pageant or coherent episode. There is no Conscience – conscience, however, proves to be of deep importance. Not the figure but the word appears four times in Book 1, playing a crucial role in the despair and subsequent salvation of Redcrosse Knight. And it appears at two important junctures in Book 5, significantly shaping the justice enacted by Artegall, Talus, and Britomart.[4] In these moments *The Faerie Queene* develops for conscience an oblique relationship to allegory.

It helps to recognize that Spenserian allegory is a spectrum of possibilities, from bare personifications to rounded characters, and from fully extended metaphors to passing glimmers. Allegory figures forth in many ways in *The Faerie Queene*, varying in clarity and structure, and in the directness with which it signifies. As this chapter shows, conscience appears in surprising and uncanny parts of this spectrum. It appears in the highly organizing allegory of the House of Holiness, and it appears in a parodic moment of disarrayed personification, in the figure of Talus. While a personified Conscience might organize the inchoate Protestant conscience, Spenser's allegorical conscience falls away from such structuring. Cracks in Spenser's allegory form around conscience, unsettling representation while destructuring the faculty. *The Faerie Queene* moves our gaze from a structured conscience, seen as if from the outside, to an obscuring and unreliable faculty that is experienced as if from the inside.

---

[3] Wilson's play is taken as a source for *Merchant of Venice*, so Lady Conscience may be read as the kind of personification that Shakespeare is parodying with Launcelot Gobbo. For more on personification and conscience, see Escobedo, *Volition's Face*, Chapter 3.

[4] The other two appearances are isolated and less significant: I.xii.30.5 and III.vi.10.2.

Despaire and Holinesse

Spenser first brings conscience into *The Faerie Queene* in the Despaire episode. After Despaire's rhetorical assault, at the key moment when Redcrosse sinks into desperation, we are told that

> The knight was much enmoved with his speach,
> That as a swords point through his hart did perse,
> And in his conscience made a secret breach.
>
> (I.ix.48.1–3)

And in the next stanza the knight is seen "to waver weake and fraile,/ Whiles trembling horror did his conscience daunt" (49.3–4). Despaire has been recalling Redcrosse's many misdeeds from Book 1, reminding him, for example, of his stay in Orgoglio's prison: "Witnes the dungeon deepe, wherein of late/ Thy life shutt up, for death so oft did call" (45.5–6). Despaire acts as an integral part of Redcrosse's conscience, even taking on the metaphoric role of the witness. Despaire goes on to dredge up Redcrosse's most shameful moment, reminding him how he left Una for Duessa (46.6–9). Redcrosse never admitted that he had wronged Una, much less apologized. But while the infidelity remains unspoken, it has left its trace somewhere within him, and returns as the voice of Despaire. This is simultaneously the voice of conscience, for it is this speech that "as a swords point through his hart did perse," enacting another common metaphor for conscience, that of pricking. And it is this speech that "in his conscience made a secret breach."

These are the first two appearances of the word "conscience" in *The Faerie Queene*, and they match the early modern practice of pairing it with despair. Despaire speaks for, and functions as, Redcrosse's conscience. In doing so, Spenser is in a certain sense continuing the personifying tradition. The Cave of Despaire is probably the episode in *The Faerie Queene* most aligned with psychomachia and the medieval allegorical tradition, so that conscience appears in a familiar setting.[5] Yet any body or voice of conscience is subsumed by Despaire. Despaire talks; conscience, more concept than person, does not. It is no coincidence that Despaire disperses and overshadows conscience, dominating the poetic scene. In accounts of the despairing conscience, such domination – and destructuring – are primary symptoms.

---

[5] See Snyder, "The Left Hand of God"; Carpenter, "Spenser's Cave of Despair."

Theologically, despair's hold on conscience has to do with the interrelated problems of works and assurance. For Luther and Calvin conscience often becomes a temptation, focusing too insistently on the Law and on works such as vows and sacraments. According to Calvin, this orientation to Law creates an overactive sense of sin and retribution, pulling one into a false understanding of God as righteously focused on works:

> there be tentations which both infinite in number, and diverse in kinde, do oftentimes with great sodaine violence assaile us. But specially our owne conscience oppressed with heavy burden of sinnes lying upon it, doth sometime lament and grone with it selfe, and sometime accuseth it selfe sometime secretly murmureth, and sometime is openly troubled. Whether therefore adversities do shewe an apparance of the wrath of God, or the conscience doth finde in it selfe any proufe or matter of his wrath, from thense unbeliefe doth take weapons and engines to vanquishe faith withall.
>
> (*Inst.* II.iii.20, 227)[6]

Conscience tempts us to consider ourselves convicted by God's righteousness, and so to lose faith and begin to despair. Calvin sees a way out of this trap for the elect, who escape despair precisely because the Law does not bind their consciences.[7] The problem, though, is in the assurance of election. The children of God can escape the Law – but in the real world, and in a theology of double predestination, few were certain of salvation.[8] Sensitive to this problem, in *A Discourse of Conscience*, Perkins describes the regenerate conscience as coinciding with freedom from the Law and its works (*DC* 98–9) and certainty of election (*DC* 107–9). It is against exactly this kind of comfort that Despaire argues.

In the episode, Redcrosse is mired in the experience of a conscience obsessed with works and sin. The confrontation with Despaire begins

---

[6] Randall Zachman argues concerning both Luther and Calvin, "The conscience, given its relationship to the law, and its judgment that renders us either condemned or acquitted *coram deo*, simply cannot picture God in any other way than as a righteous judge who hates sinners but who rewards those who are righteous according to works of the law." *The Assurance of Faith*, 35–6.

[7] "(W)hereas the lawe hath toward the faithful a power to exhorte, not such a power as may binde their consciences with curse, but suche as with often calling on, may shake of sluggishnesse and pinche imperfection to awake it . . . it be no more unto them that which it was before, that is, that it do no more, by making afraide and confounding their consciences, damne and destroie them." *Inst.* II.vii.14, 138.

[8] As John Stachniewski explains, "Anyone's faith might be common or temporary or – another Calvinist idea – an unconscious pretence (e.g. *Inst.* III.ii.10; III.ii.12). Moreover, since grace was supposed to arrive with irresistible force, uncertainty as to whether one was an authentic recipient had alarming implications." *The Persecutory Imagination*, 20.

with the kind of condemning justice that Luther and Calvin associate with bondage to the Law. Speaking of Terwin, Despaire says:

> What Justice ever other judgement taught,
> But he should dye, who merites not to live?
> None els to death this man despayring drive,
> But his owne guiltie mind deserving death.
> Is then unjust to each his dew to give?
> (38.3–7)

Just as Luther, in the tower, knows a "righteous God who punishes sinners," so Redcrosse is tempted to picture an unmerciful kind of divine justice. Justice, judgment, and guilt echo throughout Despaire's words, as Redcrosse becomes caught up in a skewed perspective on God, one that overemphasizes the Law and works, to the detriment of mercy. When Despaire turns to Redcrosse's own case, he lays the groundwork by asserting the insurmountability of sin: "The lenger life, I wote the greater sin/ The greater sin, the greater punishment" (43.1–2). He then invites Redcrosse to conceive of justice as a scale, in which his misdeeds – his works – cannot be counterbalanced:

> Thou wretched man, of death has greatest need,
> If in true ballaunce thou wilt weigh thy state:
> For never knight, that dared warlike deed,
> More luckless dissaventures did amate.
> (45.1–4)

God's justice, according to Despaire, is based on a strict measurement of Redcrosse's "dissaventures." And he returns repeatedly to the image of the righteously judging God: "Is not he just, that all this doth behold/ From highest heven, and beares an equall eie?" and "Is not his law, Let every sinner die" (47.1–2; 5). This is the speech which pierces and daunts Redcrosse's conscience.

Redcrosse only beats back his Protestant despair when Una reminds him what the conscience too often forgets, that God is merciful, and that the Gospel ushers in a freedom from the Law:

> In heavenly mercies has thou not a part?
> Why shouldst thou then despeire, that chosen art?
> Where justice growes there grows eke greter grace,
> The which doth quench the brond of hellish smart.
> (53.4–7)

Redcrosse is seemingly among the elect, and through Grace should be capable of attaining a free conscience.[9] Grace specifically quenches the "fiery darts" of Ephesians 6, painful weapons that are often associated with the pricks and stings of conscience.[10] Una's intervention averts Redcrosse's suicide, and gets him from the cave of Despaire into the House of Holinesse. There, under Fidelia's tutelage, he makes spectacular progress: "The faithfull knight now grew in litle space,/ By hearing her, and by her sisters lore,/ To such perfection of all hevenly grace" (x.21.1–3). But Una and Fidelia do not liberate Redcrosse so easily. For in the course of this very same stanza loathing of mortal life suddenly transforms back into despair:

> That wretched world he gan for to abhore,
> And mortal life gan loath, as thing forlore,
> Greevd with remembrance of his wicked wayes,
> And prickt with anguish of his sinnes so sore,
> That he desirde, to end his wretched dayes
> So much the dart of sinfull guilt the soule dismayes.
>
> (x.21.4–9)

This stanza has been read as a progressive part of the knight's regeneration. But Redcrosse has clearly retreated back into the cave of Despaire: dismayed by the memory of sin, he dwells on works and considers suicide. The dart of guilt, and the way that anguish pricks Redcrosse, reveal that conscience is once again causing despair.

Such backsliding is a frequent object of attention in the project of comforting consciences. Alexander Hume describes the great sensitivity of a wounded conscience, as the smallest thoughts or memories can send it into despair, and then just as suddenly back into comfort:

> For like as the wound of the body wil be sa sair, that the patient can scarselie suffer any thing to touch it: Even so, the woundit *conscience* is sa waik that the lest unseemly word, wrang luke, or wavering thocht quhilk man can use, wil hurt and trouble it, and make it to remord. Finally, when the oppressed *conscience* gets any blenk of comfort, or release of his paine, he wil spring for joye, and think that he sal never again be moved with sik perturbation: Bot as sone as the Lord turnis away his face, newe trouble and doubtings wil arrise again, as though he had never received comfort.
>
> (*ATC* 46–7)

---

[9] See Doerksen, "'All the Good is God's.'"
[10] *ATC* 127; Bright, *A Treatise of Melancholy*, 193.

In the oscillation between despair and the sense of election, the key experience is in the sudden movement between perturbation and comfort, between oppression and release. This reflects the frequent descriptions of the despairing conscience as roiled, or as Perkins describes it, as "a *perturbation* or disquietnes of the whole man: whereby all the powers and faculties of the whole man are forth of order" (*DC* 88–9). Meanwhile the free conscience is quiet and orderly, so that Hume's despairing Christian will "spring for joye" to be, at least temporarily, free of perturbation, and free of the disorderly mode of despair.

After Redcrosse backslides there is a palpable spring for joy when Speranza shows up with the decisive means of assurance:

> But wise *Speranza* gave him comfort sweet,
>   And taught him how to take assured hold
>   Upon her silver anchor, as was meet;
>   Els had his sinnes so great, and manifold
>   Made him forget all, that *Fidelia* told.
>   (22.1–5)

Fidelia's lore was not enough. But the anchor of hope pulls Redcrosse from the despairing conviction of a righteous God.

At this turning point, the poetry itself produces the experience of discovering a free conscience, a jumping for joy at the move from perturbation into order. This is one of Spenser's most emblematic moments, when allegory figures forth with sharp clarity. The anchor of hope is familiar from Hebrews 6:19–20, and the picture itself graces the title page of the 1596 *Faerie Queene*. With the emblem fresh in the reader's mind, allegory functions immediately and resolutely. Just as an anchor provides stability in a tossing ocean, so hope provides succor from the perturbations of despair. The allegorical emblem signifies with equal stability, anchoring the poem, on the level of representation, amidst the disruptions of despair, and so initiating the process of curing Redcrosse's conscience.

For the cure is a highly orderly allegorical process. In the next stanza comes the personification Patience, a leach summoned because he has "great insight/ In that disease of grieved conscience" (23.7–8). He goes to work with a team of surgeons, and after an allegorized medical regimen, Redcrosse is brought back to Una, "Who joyous of his cured conscience,/ Him dearely kist" (29.3). These are the next two appearances of "conscience" in *The Faerie Queene*, and they reveal how the cure for Redcrosse's despairing conscience, and his ultimate progression into the free conscience of the elect, coincide with that kind of Spenserian allegory which is most organized and most structured. The cure is lasting, as Book 1 tells a redemptive tale of conscience. But this optimism is possible only with the poem's shift to the most orderly end of the spectrum of allegory.

The House of Holinesse can be seen as a reordering of a poetic landscape that had fallen into serious disarray. The allegorical cure soothes an unstable and overwrought imagination in Redcrosse, as well as in the poem itself. Distempered thought and confused mental landscapes are in fact hallmarks of the despairing conscience. The pricks of conscience are painful, and usher in a disordering of the mind, which perceives the world as full of incongruities and fearful shocks – what Perkins calls "perturbation," and his mentor Richard Greenham calls "hurly burlyes." According to Greenham, the wounded conscience

> breeds such hurly burlyes in him, that when it is day he wisheth for night; when it is night he would have it day, his meat doth not norish him; his dreames are fearefull to him, his sleepe oftimes forsaketh him; If he speaketh, he is little eased, if he keepeth silence, hee boileth in disquietnes of heart; the light doth not comfort him, the darkenes doth terify him.[11]

The world assaults body and mind with discomforts, as the bites and pricks of conscience are projected onto the sensory world, with its food and sounds and lights. Dreams also terrify, as they break down the border between imagination and reality. Hume describes how a wounded conscience will cause "uglie dreams," and how upon waking the sufferer will feel as if in a waking nightmare: "Yea it wil appeare to himselfe, that al the creatures of God are animate, as it were, and conspired against him" (ATC 42–3). The superstitious sense of an animist world marks the unbounded intrusion of the supernatural into the sufferer's mental experience – everything is alive and suddenly coming at him. This paranoia and distempered imagination often lead observers to think that someone experiencing a despairing conscience is "either to be furious, lunatick, or fantastick; either els to have taken sum apprehension, melancholie, or vaine conceit" (ATC 36).

As Hume indicates, these perturbations lead many to confuse conscience with melancholy. The two must be carefully distinguished, Perkins says, "for many hold that they are all one."[12] In a chapter devoted to distinguishing the two, Hume explains that "the trouble of the spirit

---

[11] Greenham, *Paramythion*, 11.
[12] Perkins, *The Whole Treatise*, 194.

wil oftimes redound to the bodie," so that a wounded conscience can cause melancholy (*ATC* 35). Timothy Bright, in *A Treatise of Melancholy* (1586), explains in more medical detail that the afflicted conscience is "so beset with infinite feares and distrust, that it easilie wasteth the pure spirit, congeleth the lively bloud," and so turns into melancholy. And then melancholy can in turn exacerbate conscience:

> This increaseth the terrour of the afflicted minde, doubling the feare and discouragement, and shutteth up the meanes of consolation, which is after another sort to by conveyed to the minde, then the way which the temptation taketh to breed distrust of Gods mercy and pardon.[13]

There is a kind of feedback loop, in which the symptoms of melancholy and conscience blend, forming an intractably feverish and intemperate state of mind. The despairing conscience loses the ability to sort reality from imagination and matter from spirit. The world turns animist and transforms into a startling landscape that is disrupted and out of natural order.

Just such a neurotic and distempered state infects the Despaire episode. Despaire's cave is "Darke, dolefull, dreary, like a greedy grave," and has all the trappings of Halloween:

> On top whereof ay dwelt the ghastly Owle,
> Shrieking his balefull note, which ever drave
> Far from that haunt all other chearefull fowle;
> And all about it wandring ghostes did wayle and howle.
>
> (ix.33.6–9)

This is followed by an even more precipitous slide into a shattered and disorderly world:

> And all about old stockes and stubs of trees,
>   Whereon nor fruit, nor leafe was ever seene,
>   Did hang upon the ragged rocky knees;
>   On which had many wretches hanged beene,
>   Whose carcases were scattred on the greene
> And throwne about the cliffs.
>
> (34.1-6)

Dominating the scene are the broken structures of trees, bearing the strange fruit of human carcases. Hanged and broken bodies are scattered

---

[13] Bright, *A Treatise of Melancholy*, 195–6. Cf. Douglas Trevor's distinction between neo-Platonic and Galenic versions of melancholy, and his readings of Despaire and the House of Holinesse, *The Poetics of Melancholy*, 1–24, 47–60.

and thrown about. Like the bodies, the trees also hang, onto a geographical feature described as "ragged rocky knees." Standing for a part of the
cliffs, these knees bring alive the inanimate world, in keeping with the
corpses, ghosts, and ghastly owls that fill out the scene. Just as Hume
warns, it is as if "al the creatures of God are animate."

The knees also place at the vanishing point of this tableau, amidst the
stubs of trees and violently shortened lives, the disrupted poetic figure of
catachresis. Catachresis, or *abusio*, puts words in the wrong place, often
grotesquely inserting body parts, like the leg of a table. As abuse, it has
been read as the figure for the breakdown of figural language itself.[14] So
the ragged rocky knees disorganize even poetic form. Denied the coherence of personification in *The Faerie Queene*, conscience is first relegated
to the metaphors of pricks and darts. It then slides from a metaphoric
to a catachrestic mode, as the resistance to the body of personification
becomes the abusive appearance of body parts. Falling away from organizing poetic figures, conscience is present in the poetry only obliquely, as
the body parts that surround Despaire figure forth the undoing of both
bodily integrity and poetic form. Despair dwells in the deforming of
Spenser's allegorical personification.

Indeed, the cave of Despaire is in every way deformed, as Trevisan puts
it when he describes how he, "Dismayd with that deformed dismall sight,/
Fledd fast away" (30.4–5). And deformation is precisely what undoes
Redcrosse when he first suffers the pangs of conscience. Despaire's speech

> in his conscience made a secrete breach,
> Well knowing true all, that he did reherse,
> And to his fresh remembraunce did reverse,
> The ugly vew of his deformed crimes,
> That all his manly powres it did disperse
> As he were charmed with inchaunted rimes,
> That oftentimes he quakt, and fainted oftentimes.
> (48.3–9)

The deformed sight of Despaire's cave becomes in Redcrosse's conscience the deformed view of his own sins. The landscape imprints itself
on Redcrosse's mind, as the breaking apart of form moves from the

---

[14] "For catachresis is less a matter of the relation between literal and figurative, proper and trans-
ferred, senses than it is a question of naming, marking, putting a word and imposing a sense where
there is neither word nor sense. In other words, as much as catachresis is a figure (because it is a
transfer of sense), it is also – supplementarily – a mere marker, a place-holder; it has nothing to do
with sense; it only stands in the place of a lack." Warminski, *Readings in Interpretation*, lv.

physical world to the life of the mind. Or vice versa: Redcrosse cannot tell where the deformed outward world ends and his deformed inward experience begins. What follows is the quaking and fainting of the perturbed state of despair.

Critics have usually focused on the powerful rhetoric of Despaire, despite the fact that it often veers into illogic.[15] Even chopped logic proves persuasive through the deforming lens of the despairing conscience. So Redcrosse is not cured through rebuttal and argumentation, but through a clearing up of disorder. A new lens, a more formal landscape, a more structured and orderly experience is required. The possibility of such a cure is announced by Una when she reveals that Redcrosse is among the elect. But his backsliding is only conquered, and the cure only effected, when the House of Holinesse reorders the poetic landscape that had fallen into disarray. Stabilized by the anchor of hope, the House of Holinesse reasserts allegory, and so rescues Redcrosse from the destructured conscience of despair.

The House of Holinesse is the first of Spenser's great allegorical houses, a prominent part of the spectrum of Spenserian allegory in which every architectural element and every inhabitant, like an extended emblem, figures forth clear allegorical meaning. Patience is brought in, and it is clear that the tide has begun to turn, for he "had great insight/ In that disease of grieved conscience,/ And well could cure the same" (23.7–9). Next come Amendment, Penaunce, Remorse, and Repentance, forming a regimen that is a clear success for Redcrosse:

> Whom thus recover'd by wise *Patience*,
>   And trew *Repentaunce*, they to *Una* brought;
>   Who joyous of his cured conscience,
>   Him dearely kist, and fayrely eke besought
>   Himselfe to chearish, and consuming thought
>   To put away out of his carefull brest.
>   (29.1–6)

Unlike the shattered experience of despair, conscience now unfolds as a clearly labeled, highly structured experience.

The allegorical personifications, moreover, reassert a bodily integrity that had been compromised in despair. For Patience cures Redcrosse's "disease of grieved conscience" with rigorous medical treatment: he "gan apply relief,/ Of salves and med'cines, which had passing prief" (24.4–5).

---

[15] Sirluck, "A Note on the Rhetoric"; Skulsky, "Spenser's Despair Episode."

Redcrosse's inwardness and sin are figured as body, full of infection, marrow, and skin (10.25). And the cure involves such medical interventions as surgery: "ever as superfluous flesh did rott/ *Ammendment* readies till at hand did wayt,/ To pluck it out with pincers fyrie whott" (26.6–8). Finally, *Repentance* "used to embay/ His blamefull body in salt water sore/ The filthy blottes of sin to wash away" (27.5–8) – a bath Lady Macbeth could use. Not only does each personification form a coherent body capable of acting in expression of its personified idea, but each personification also contributes to a cure that is itself a cleansing and perfecting of a damaged body. The bodily integrity of this holistic therapy, in comparison to the ghosts and catachrestic body parts of despair, enacts the allegorical reordering of Redcrosse's conscience.

Such a medical regimen contradicts the common wisdom of the theorists of conscience. In response to the intertwining of conscience and melancholy, they regularly assert that conscience cannot be cured by a physician. Perkins explains that

> [s]orow that comes by melancholly ariseth onely of that humour annoying the body, but this other sorrow ariseth of a mans sinnes for which his conscience accuseth him. Melancholly may be cured by physicke; this sorrow can not be cured by any thing but the blood of Christ.
>
> (*DC* 87)

Melancholy is merely bodily, and far less important than conscience, with its spiritual stakes. Even the physician Bright agrees: "no medicine, no purgations, no cordiall, no tryacle or balme are able to assure the afflicted soule and trembling heart, now panting under the terrors of God."[16]

But Spenser's allegory, by recasting conscience in physiological terms, returns it to the possibility of a cure. The coherence of bodies and persons in allegorical personification provide a form and structure – for the patient and the surgeons as well as for the reader – within which the medical regimen can work. While the deformed conscience offers nothing to work on, and few clear steps to take, the allegory of the medical cure offers a set of purposive actions, and an orderly course. The language of medical cure is not uncommon among the theorists of conscience, but it is just metaphor, evoking a set of actions that recede beyond literal description. Spenserian allegory, in contrast, in its totalizing form in the House of Holinesse, proves sovereign.

---

[16] Bright, *A Treatise of Melancholy*, 189. Also see *ATC* 37.

This formalist religious practice surely contributes to the common perception that the House of Holinesse feels Catholic. Carol Kaske sees the "Catholic coloring of almost everything" in the House of Holinesse.[17] This is not a claim for recusancy, but for lingering predilections, or what Darryl Gless calls "common mental reflexes" that kept Catholic ways of thinking present in England and in Spenser's poem.[18] Even Perkins admits as much when, in a treatise on imagination, he reflects on "Iustification and salvation by workes; which opinion every man brings with him from his mothers wombe."[19] As much as reformed theology asserts faith, works continue to exert a seemingly innate pull. What particularly lingers for Protestants vexed by despair is the need for a formal means of repentance and absolution, an *ordo salutis*. The sacrament of confession very conveniently materializes absolution. As Thomas Tentler observes, "the formulas that exalt the power of the keys and emphasize the automatic efficacy of a sacrament – 'from the work worked' – are nothing more than ways to make grace sensible and comfort accessible"; the priest is able to say, "in the indicative mood," *ego te absolvo*.[20]

This is precisely what Calvin mocks as simplistic: "when they seeme to have throughly wounded the heartes, they heale the bitternesse with a light sprinkeling of ceremonies" (*Inst.* III.iv.1, 252). Instead, the regenerate conscience depends, Perkins says, on "a speciall faith," which creates "a large and plentiful perswasion of the pardon of mans owne sinnes" (*DC* 114). Sacraments can only confirm, not create the persuasion:

> Now it may be demanded how a bodily element, as bread, wine, water, should be able to confirme a perswasion of our adoption that is in the conscience. *Answ.* The element in the sacrament is an outward seale or instrument to confirme faith not as a medicine restores and confirmes health, whether we thinke on it or not, whether we sleepe or wake, and that by his owne inherent vertue, but by reasoning in syllogisme made by the good conscience.
>
> (*DC* 141–2)

Perkins specifically rejects the medical analogy, because it implies an operative effect for the sacrament.[21] "Perswasion," which is the key to the

[17] Spenser, *The Faerie Queene*, "Introduction," I:xxiii–xxiv.

[18] Gless, *Interpretation and Theology*, 13. Virgil Whitaker sees frequent remnants of Catholicism in Spenser's religion, *The Religious Basis*, 54–6.

[19] Perkins, *A Treatise of Man's Imagination*, 133.

[20] Tentler, *Sin and Confession*, 297, 281.

[21] On the common use of the medical metaphor to describe the sacrament of confession, see Thayer, "Judge and Doctor."

regenerate conscience, can only come from the experimental and reflexive work of the conscience. That is to say, regeneration is thrown back on the inchoate and destructured conscience, the very place that breeds the disordered landscape of despair.[22]

The emergence of clear allegory in the House of Holinesse, then, can be seen as a return of an *ordo salutis*, restructuring the formlessness of Protestant repentance. Personification puts a person back in the scene of conscience, filling the gap left by the priest, and the medical cure reinstates the efficacy of sacraments. The leach Patience, in fact, begins with confession: "Who coming to that sowle-diseased knight,/ Could hardly him intreat, to tell his grief" (24.1–2). And he proceeds to absolution: he "gan apply relief,/ Of salves and med'cines, which had passing prief,/ And there to added wordes of wondrous might/ By which to ease he him recured brief" (24.4–7). However, for Protestant Spenser the *ordo salutis* must be incomplete.[23] The enigmatic "wordes of wondrous might" hint at the priestly formula, *ego te absolvo*, but this is rather too magical, and so Redcrosse's corruption remains "Not purg'd nor heald" by the words (25.2–3). Allegory draws close to the sacrament, and then swerves back to figural medicine.

If not Catholic per se, the moment certainly feels archaic, as Spenser returns to the poetics of psychomachia and the medieval tradition of personification found in Langland and others. In Book 1 Spenser brings Redcrosse backward in time, from the psychological complexities of Protestant despair to the clarity of a medieval-tinged conscience. In a deft blend of early modernity and archaism, conscience is both informed by Protestant theology and couched in the poetics of psychomachia. In such a settlement, Spenser's allegory proves to be a strong organizing force, containing and curing the conscience, and thereby representing it in redemptive terms. And so in Book 1 we find a pattern not just of destructuring, but also of restructuring – a response to the inchoate conscience that seeks to rebuild the possibility of order in the faculty. Just as Hamlet ultimately locates his "perfect conscience," Redcrosse achieves a "cured conscience,"

---

[22] Sarah Beckwith describes the psychological complexity that results from the abandonment of auricular confession in terms that are very close to the despairing conscience: "Self-scrutiny that has lost its pastoral context in the specter of popish abuse is subject to relentlessly circular intensifications, restless anxieties of uncertainty, cravings for an impossible assurance. The religious subject begins to be gripped by an interminable problem of knowledge." *Shakespeare and the Grammar of Forgiveness*, 45.

[23] John King reads the House of Holinesse as fundamentally Protestant, *Spenser's Poetry*, 58–65. Also see Hume, *Edmund Spenser*, 96–101.

expressing a theological hopefulness, and a sanguine conclusion about the workings of the faculty. In the second major engagement in *The Faerie Queene*, however, in the political landscape of Book 5, Spenser engages with conscience in a way that is far less assured. In the Legend of Justice, the destructured conscience proves inassimilable to the allegory, and so resists restructuring. Incurable and dangerously disorderly, conscience is parodied, and must finally be removed from Spenser's political thought.

Equity and Justice

Conscience in Book 5 is fractured by a parodic undoing of personification. This, the second important engagement with conscience in *The Faerie Queene*, hinges on an exceedingly strange moment in Canto 6, when Talus suddenly develops an inner life. After Artegall has been captured by Radigund, Talus hastens to tell Britomart. She asks where his master is, but Talus surprisingly becomes reticent:

> The yron man, albe he wanted sence
> And sorrowes feeling, yet with conscience
> Of his ill newes, did inly chill and quake,
> And stood still mute, as one in great suspence,
> As if that by his silence he would make
> Her rather reade his meaning, then him self it spake.
> (V.vi.9.4–9)

Of all unlikely figures, it is the iron man that displays a conscience. Everywhere else, Talus presses relentlessly forward with his flail, with no care for argument or subtlety. But here he hesitates, and we catch a glimpse of inwardness and personality.

It is a contradictory inwardness: Talus lacks "sence/ And sorrowes feeling," but he still appears to "inly chill and quake." The contradiction is accentuated by Talus's robotic essence. He is "Immoveable, resistlesse, without end" (i.12.7), and not at all likely to doubt or delay. There is a purity and simplicity about such a machine, so that Angus Fletcher calls Talus a "perfect allegorical agent," using him to exemplify the way that personifications take on a daemonic single-mindedness.[24] As a perfect allegorical figure, he is driven by a single purpose, like fanatic

---

[24] Fletcher, *Allegory*, 55. Fletcher describes personifications as "daemonic" because "obsessed with only one idea," 40. Steven Knapp uses the word "fanatic" to describe such allegorical personifications, *Personification and the Sublime*, 83.

personifications such as Envie, who envies herself (V.xii.31), or Disdayne who "did disdayne/ To be so cald" (II.vii.41). So Talus's conscience becomes a moment of deep incongruity in the representation, similar to the moment when the relatively rounded character of Malbecco descends so far into jealousy that he actually becomes "Gealosy" (III.x.60). As occasionally happens in the wide spectrum of Spenser's allegorical figures, the novelistic qualities of character clash with the flat and mechanical elements of personification. As with Malbecco, or Amoret in the Maske of Cupid, Spenser brings personification into sudden contact with character, creating an ontological confusion in representation, rather like the effect of Sin and Death in *Paradise Lost*.

As in the cave of Despaire, conscience surfaces where allegory crumbles. But while the House of Holinesse reassembles the orderly poetics of allegorical personification, here in Book 5 there is no cure. The sanguine approach of Book 1 gives way to a conscience that seems to be a dangerously unreliable construct. Once destructured, it remains at odds with the symbolic economy. In the larger landscape of the Legend of Justice, and in Spenser's conservative politics, conscience eventually has no place.

The first appearance of the word "conscience" in Book 5 makes clear that the faculty is central to how the poem will think about justice. Artegall is educated by the perfect embodiment of justice, Astraea. And she trains him to make his judgments by means of the dictates of conscience:

> There she him taught to weigh both right and wrong
> In equall balance with due recompence,
> And equitie to measure along,
> According to the line of conscience,
> When so it needs with rigour to dispence.
>
> (i.7.1–5)

As the core of Astraea's curriculum, conscience promises to shape all of Artegall's subsequent actions as the knight of justice. The "line of conscience" suggests that the faculty provides an orderly and precise distinction between right and wrong.[25] If Artegall makes his judgments according to this idealized line, there is the hope that the justice of Astraea can be reproduced on earth.

But conscience enters into the Legend of Justice alongside a mediating term. Not only must Artegall determine the line between right and

---

[25] See Nohrnberg, *The Analogy of* The Faerie Queene, 385–6.

wrong, he must also measure equity. An important legal concept in early modern England, equity theorizes how conscience meshes with common law. It tends to efface the clarity of the line between right and wrong: in its classical sense, equity serves to expand justice beyond a strict reading of the particulars of the law. According to Aristotle in *The Nicomachean Ethics*, since law must be universal, and lawmakers cannot foresee every particular case, we rely on equity as "a rectification of law where law is defective because of its generality."[26] This can mean reading for the spirit rather than the letter of the law, and it necessarily implies a movement inward, to intentions. In *The Art of Rhetoric*, Aristotle says that equity must look "not to the letter of the law but to the intention of the legislator; not to the action itself, but to the moral purpose."[27]

By depending on intentions and moral purposes, equity begins to move justice toward the realm of conscience, a movement which is substantiated in early modern England's most influential account of equity, a text that has already been discussed for its use of *synderesis*, Christopher St. German's *Doctor and Student*. St. German's project is to bring conscience to bear upon English common law, essentially making a space in the law for the judgments of conscience:

> The present dialogue shows what are the principles or grounds of the laws of England, and how conscience ought in many cases to be formed in accordance with those same principles and grounds. It likewise discusses briefly the question of when English law ought to be rejected or not on account of conscience.
>
> *(DS 3)*

St. German follows Aristotle's understanding that equity corrects for the generality of law, and anchors that departure in the authority of conscience. When the general law does not satisfy the justice of the particular case, equity demands that the judge's conscience step in to make a judgment that can potentially depart from the letter of the law. So that if one is without remedy in Common Law, "yet he maye be holpen *in equity* by a sub pena & so he may in many other cases where conscyence servyth for hym" (*DS* 79).[28]

---

[26] Aristotle, *The Nicomachean Ethics*, V.x.6.
[27] Aristotle, *The Art of Rhetoric*, I.xiii.17.
[28] For comprehensive accounts of equity, see Fortier, *The Culture of Equity*; Majeske, *Equity in English Renaissance Literature*. For equity in Book 5, see Zurcher, *Spenser's Legal Language*, 123–52.

As that moment when conscience directs a judge to depart from the strictness of the law, equity often takes on a less technical sense of mere mercy. St. German first defines equity as a justice "that consideryth all the pertyculer cyrcumstaunces of the dede the whiche also is temperyed with the swetnes of mercye" (*DS* 95). Such mercy is directly connected to equity's departure from exact readings of the law:

> And therefore to folowe the wordes of the lawe were in some case both agaynst Iustyce & the common welth: wherefore in some cases it is good and even necessary to leve the wordis of the law & to folowe that reason and Justyce requyreth & to that intent equytie is ordeyned, that is to say to tempre and myttygate the rygoure of the lawe
>
> (*DS* 97)[29]

This is exactly Astraea's teaching, which calls for equity and conscience "When so it needs with rigour to dispence." Spenser may have become familiar with these legal ideas when he held office in the Irish Court of Chancery.[30] Because it offers a point of contact between the inwardness of the individual conscience and the external world of the justice system, equity appropriately enters into *The Faerie Queene* as we move from the private holiness of Redcrosse to the public justice of Artegall.

The poem's attempt to construct justice through conscience and equity frequently gravitates toward the question of mercy, which eventually receives a direct personification in the figure of Mercilla. But Book 5 is famously cruel, and clearly struggles with, rather than simply celebrating, the idea of mercy. Even in Astraea's tutelage there is real doubt whether Artegall's justice is to be considered equitable, and so whether it is to be read as ideally conscientious. The ambiguity of the last clause in Astraea's teaching, "When so it needs with rigour to dispence," calls into question any assumption that, because he is the knight of justice, Artegall's actions are necessarily just. In one reading of "dispence," Artegall will pursue equity and conscience by means of administering, i.e. dispensing, rigor. But in a contrary reading, equity and conscience are only in play when Artegall forebears dealing out, i.e. dispenses with, the infliction

---

[29] William Perkins's treatise on equity pays less attention to legal arguments, and foregrounds an understanding of equity as "moderation of minde," a virtue that leads to irenic and tolerant dealings between people. *Hepieikeia*, A1r.

[30] From 1581 to 1588, Spenser served either as Registrar or Clerk of Faculties in the Irish Chancery. Maley, *A Spenser Chronology*, 18. It is possible that the office was merely a sinecure, but Andrew Hadfield speculates that it "had a profound effect on his conception of the law and his literary imagination." *Edmund Spenser*, 176–7.

of rigorous punishment. With equity a close synonym of mercy, we are invited to acknowledge the commonly held reaction to Book 5, that Artegall's justice is far too violent and far too rigorous.[31] Artegall, after all, needs Guyon to remind him to control his anger against Braggadochio: "Sir knight, it would dishonour bee/ To you, that are our judge of equity,/ To wreake your wrath on such a carle as hee" (iii.36.6–8). Particularly with its echoes of England's brutality toward the Irish, Book 5 is often read either as unconscionable colonialist propaganda, or as a negative representation of justice that can elicit sympathy for the Irish. Either way, Artegall strays dramatically from Astraea's training, and seems to forget equity and conscience altogether amidst the carnage.

As Artegall veers away from conscience, Talus's influence is increasingly felt. The robot is the lead agent of violence, and becomes an expression of justice without equity or conscience. In the first occurrence of Talus's unrestrained violence, Munera arouses pity in Artegall, who then pushes himself away from his instinctive mercy. His turn from mercy is a turn to Talus: "Yet for no pitty would he change the course/ Of Justice, which in *Talus* hand did lye;/ Who rudely hayld her forth without remorse" (ii.26.1–3). Talus has no remorse – literally "the biting" of conscience – but instead drives Munera out of her castle and cuts off her hands and feet.[32] And throughout Book 5, Talus metes out excessive punishment with his iron flaile, tending to leave "heapes" of dead and wounded across the fairy landscape. These are moments when rigor has obviously not been dispensed with. In full obedience to law and the rigorous course of justice, Talus lives up to his mythological source. Talus likely derives from the brass figure Talos, who made the rounds of the villages of Crete, carrying the laws inscribed on tablets. A metal guardian of the written law, Talos represents the strict adherence to law – the very opposite of equity.[33] As Talus's actions fill the early cantos of Book 5, justice appears to be proceeding without the influence of equity and conscience.

If Artegall and Talus combine to form a pitiless justice in the opening cantos, we learn why in Canto 7, in Isis Church. There it is revealed that Britomart, rather than Artegall, is the figure in which Spenser allegorizes equity. The allegory is suggested when Isis is said to "shade/ That part

---

[31] On Artegall's failures as the knight of justice, see Anderson, "'Nor Man It Is'"; Fowler, "The Failure of Moral Philosophy."

[32] The absence of conscience in this scene can also be felt through literary allusion. Munera is said to descend from Lady Meed in *Piers Plowman* Passus 3–4, where Lady Meed's marriage to Conscience is considered but roundly rejected. Spenser, *The Works*, V:172.

[33] *Ibid.*, V:165–7.

of Justice, which is Equity" (vii.3.3–4), and then, in both waking devotion and prophetic dream, Britomart is repeatedly identified with Isis. Ultimately, the priest instructs Britomart that the crocodile in her dream is Artegall, and that she must subdue his violence, for "clemence oft in things amis,/ Restraines those sterne behests, and cruell doomes of his" (vii.22.8–9).[34] Compared with Astraea's straightforward instruction, this is a more oblique origin for equity. But the delicate virtue of equity, with its inwardness and readiness to depart from the clear letter of the law, perhaps springs more appropriately from a dreamscape. It certainly sticks better to Britomart, who in the following episode embraces her role as bringer of equity, conscientiously restraining Talus's sternness and rigor.

In their first adventure together, it becomes clear that Britomart will control Talus in ways that Artegall never has. Facing Radigund's warriors, Talus is typically ready to inflict excessive pain:

> There then a piteous slaughter did begin
> For all that ever came within his reach,
> He with his yron flale did thresh so thin,
> That he no worke at all left for the leach:
> Like to an hideous storme, which nothing may empeach.
>
> (vii.35.5–9)

Talus's violence is graphic even by the standards of Book 5, and the feeling that nothing can "impeach" Talus – which means hinder, but also carries the moral shadings of accuse or censure – elicits the suspicion that his violence has become unconscionable. So Britomart calls Talus off:

> And now by this the noble Conqueresse
> Her selfe came in, her glory to partake;
> Where though revengefull vow she did professe,
> Yet when she saw the heapes, which he did make,
> Of slaughtred carkasses, her heart did quake
> For very ruth, which did it almost rive,
> That she his fury willed him to slake.
>
> (vii.36.1–7)

At first Britomart wants to fight. But the sight of the "heapes" Talus has made causes a crisis of conscience. Specifically, the inward struggle of a quaking heart asserts its authority over a vow: conscience allows for a

---

[34] On Britomart as equity, see Aptekar, *Icons of Justice*, 54–57; Majeske, *Equity in English Renaissance*, 97–108.

departure from a strict interpretation of obligation. Talus is called off, and equity finally asserts itself in the workings of the Legend of Justice.

That a nearly broken heart should be at the center of this momentous shift marks the importance of Britomart's inwardness. For equity moves our gaze inward, as Joel Altman stresses: "Equity mitigates the law by examining the internality of an action – the defendant's motives and background, the circumstances attending the act – and also the interiority of the law itself, by referring to the intentions of the legislator."[35] Equity injects subjective experience into legal judgment, making justice depend upon inwardness. So Lorna Hutson argues that equity creates its own particular psychological positioning, or "principle of interpretation" that follows intent rather than the letter of the law.[36] This involves hypothesizing the intention of others, an intellectual practice which takes place within "an absence of certain knowledge," and which creates the distortions of incomplete or conflicting motives and a double voice.[37]

The vagaries of inwardness, both the psychological complexity of motives and the impossibility of knowing inwardness with certainty, insert into equity an area of disturbing imprecision. So the private conscience becomes a source of anxiety for theorists of equity, who are concerned that, in departing from the letter of the law, equity may yield to antinomianism. John Selden famously captures this fear in his *Table Talk*:

> Equity is A Roguish thing, for Law wee have a measure, know what to trust too. Equity is according to the conscience of him that is Chancellor, and as that is larger or narrower soe is equity. Tis all one as if they should make the Standard the measure wee call A foot, to be the Chancellors foot; what an uncertain measure would this be; One Chancellor has a long foot another A short foot a third an indifferent foot; tis the same thing in the Chancellors Conscience.[38]

This risk was not lost on St. German, who is careful to argue that equity does not function outside of law. "Lawes covet to be rewlyd by equyte," he says, implying that equity is the perfecting of law, an improvement of what is already there rather than a departure (*DS* 95). The laws of God and nature serve to harmonize conscience and law.[39]

[35] Altman, "Justice and Equity," 414.
[36] Hutson, "Not the King's Two Bodies," 171. Also see Wilson, "*Hamlet*: Equity, Intention, Performance."
[37] Hutson, "The 'Double Voice,'" 151.
[38] Selden, *Table Talk*, 43.
[39] See especially *DS* Chapter 19. John Guy, explains that "Within St. German's framework, the universal laws of God and Nature were shown to be rationally antecedent to, and harmoniously

Concern over the radical force of equity, however, seems to grow over the course of the sixteenth century, as the courts of Chancery gain power. Edward Hake's *Epieikeia*, written probably in the 1580s, begins with the concern that some might think that "Equity and the Common lawe weare distincte things and dissevered the one from the other."[40] Hake responds at length, arguing that equity is "the sowle and spyrit of the lawe" – equity does not undermine law but rather fulfills it.[41] Hake works to contain what Selden fears, that equity gives too much authority to the individual conscience. So he explains how the Chancellor "must order his conscience," and points directly to the chapters in *Doctor and Student* in which St. German explains the bipartite conscience. Carefully arguing against the idea that conscience will render equity unruly, he recounts the functioning of *synderesis* and *conscientia* in a syllogism.[42] With conscience positioned precisely where the inward life of the individual meets the political world, an orderliness in one sphere implies an orderliness in the other. The destructured conscience becomes a political problem.[43]

Lorna Hutson's description of the mental work of equity, as operating in "an absence of certain knowledge," and as making room for contradiction, contrasts strongly with the logic of noncontradiction that underlies the syllogism. The very subjective quality of equitable thought does not conform to such structured and linear representations of conscience, but rather slips into distortions of time and a "double voice." Such a destabilizing faculty draws near to William Perkins's reflexive conscience, with its doubling of thought, or to the intemperate psychology of despair experienced by Redcrosse Knight. And it matches the inwardness which most characterizes Britomart. Many critics have viewed Britomart as one of Spenser's most fully realized figures.[44] This is particularly evident in her entrance into Book 5, where, seemingly stood up by Artegall, Britomart

---

coexistent with, native English common law (the law of man) and good conscience (equity) despite the fact that conscience, as derived from natural reason and moral calculation, might nevertheless speak directly contrary to individual rules of common law in specific instances." *Politics, Law and Counsel*, 102. Also see Cormack, *A Power to Do Justice*, 105.

[40] Hake, *Epieikeia*, 5. Hake's manuscript was presented to James I, but left unpublished until the twentieth century.

[41] *Ibid.*, 28.

[42] *Ibid.*, 130–1.

[43] Hake is aware of the emerging theorists of conscience: alongside St. German he cites Rivius's *De Conscientia*, which John Woolton translates. On Hake, see Klinck, *Conscience, Equity and the Court of Chancery*, 100–6.

[44] "She is less simply a metaphor and more simply herself than are the heroes of earlier books" says Judith Anderson, "Britomart," 114. Also see Gregerson, *The Reformation of the Subject*, 9–47; Eggert, *Showing Like a Queen*, 22–50.

is molested by a "misdoubtfull mynde" (vi.3.8) and a "troubled mynd" (vi.4.5), and reels through a deeply psychological display of emotional conflict, jealousy, and complaint, enacting the inward experience of equitable thought.[45]

Equity arrives at a critical moment, for after Artegall's capture, justice in Faerieland is left to Talus. The robot has never shown mercy, and the scales seem poised to tip even further toward extreme rigor. Moreover, like a judge, Talus is forced to take over deliberation and decision-making, for which he seems spectacularly unsuited. As a mere extension of Artegall's will, Talus has never had to stage an internal debate. But when Artegall is taken by the Amazons, Talus is met with the need for his own moral compass. He must do the inward work of conscientious thought to determine a just course of action. When Artegall is captured, Talus is still in the field, where he has left such destruction that "th'heapes of those, which he did wound and slay,/ Besides the rest dismayd, might not be nombred" (v.19.6–7). He is so dominant with his iron flail "That they were fayne to let him scape away," (v.19.3). Yet surprisingly, despite this dominance, Talus makes no effort to free Artegall: "Yet all that while he would not once assay,/ To reskew his owne Lord, but thought it just t'obay" (v.19.6, 8–9). No longer merely a figure of action, Talus is now also a figure of thought. He is forced to think about justice, and in this initial moment of judicial reasoning, leaves Artegall enthralled.

At issue here is a vow. Artegall has agreed to Radigund's conditions, "That if I vanquishe him, he shall obay/ My law, and ever to my lore be bound" (4.49.2–3). To be bound is to have an obligation, which is the language of vows and conscience. Talus's "thought" leads him to the position that the vow continues to bind exactly. But this is certainly not a clear decision. St. German's first example of equity involves the dissolving of a vow, in which a man has vowed not to eat white meat, but can find no other to eat, and equity allows him to make an exception (*DS* 97). Casuists and theorists regularly ask under what conditions a vow is binding. Perkins says that an oath does not bind "When it is against the word of God, and tends to the maintenance of sinne," which is arguably the case with Artegall when he is placed in sexualized thrall, and must obey the pagan "law" and "lore" of the Amazons.[46] Conservatively, Talus

---

[45] Hutson aligns equitable thought particularly with the spurned women of Ovid's *Heroides*. "The 'Double Voice,'" 143–51. Britomart perfectly fits the Ovidian model.

[46] Perkins, *Whole Treatise*, 395, and on oaths in general, 379–99. Also see Spurr, "'The Strongest Bond of Conscience.'"

does not allow equity to override the vow. But this case provides in Talus a glimmer of inward debate, as he does not simply obey, but "thought it just t'obay."

The next time we see Talus this glimmer expands, as the poem stages an awakening of conscience in the robot that thrusts him out of the role of mechanically perfect allegory, and into a world of inwardness and equitable thought. Here is the second occurrence of the word "conscience" in Book 5, as Talus comes to find Britomart, but hesitates to reveal what has happened to Artegall:

> Even in the dore him meeting, she begun;
>   "And where is he thy Lord, and how far hence?
>   Declare at once; and hath he lost or wun?"
> The yron man, albe he wanted sence
> And sorrowes feeling, yet with conscience
> Of his ill newes, did inly chill and quake,
> And stood still mute, as one in great suspence,
> As if that by his silence he would make
> Her rather reade his meaning, then him self it spake.
>
>   (vi.9)

The poetry reminds us that Talus is an iron man, and that he lacks sense and feeling. But very strangely, he also has a conscience. In the plainest paraphrase, conscience could just mean "awareness," as it often does in the early modern period, so that Talus is aware of how badly his news will be taken. But even this level of awareness in the robot implies empathy, and the kind of thinking into another's intentions that is associated with equity. Moreover, conscience leads him to experience an inward reaction, as he "inly" chills and quakes. Talus's conscience opens up a space of inner awareness, shading subtly into both the moral faculty and what we now call consciousness. So Talus surprisingly enters into the self-reflective space that William Perkins describes, or that a few years later Shakespeare captures in Hamlet's "Thus conscience does make cowards of us all." His silence in turn calls forth a searching in Britomart, who must try to "reade his meaning." Talus, like Hamlet, has that within which passeth show.

Deciding the right thing to do is not easy in this, Talus's second moment of decision-making. Britomart is presumably bound just as much as he to honor Artegall's vow. And there is the awkwardness that anyone would feel in this situation. So, Talus incongruously, and I would suggest parodically, takes a turn as Hamlet. In the throes of the self-reflective, early modern conscience, Talus experiences a ballooning inwardness, which, as in *Hamlet*, creates the experience of early modern subjectivity. Britomart insists that Talus speak, and he finally reaches some kind of resolution to his vexed conscience:

> To whom he thus at length. "The tidings sad,
> That I would hide, will needs, I see, be rad.
> My Lord, your love, by hard mishap doth lie
> In wretched bondage wofully bestad."
>
> (vi.10.4–7)

These are Talus's first words in the poem, and they emerge in a mumbled speech, with halting meter. With three caesurae in his first full line, it is as if Talus cannot get the jaw muscles working; like the Tin Woodman, he needs oil. This is wonderfully comic. And it is also a rich moment in Spenser's allegory: Talus's difficulty in speaking traces a burgeoning inwardness, as finding movement in frozen jaws figures forth the discovery of language. And as words make their way from somewhere inside Talus, they express a richly human psychology in the mechanical man.

Talus's new subjectivity is matched by even greater gusts of emotion in Britomart, who runs to her room and falls into four stanzas of "monefull plaint" (12.1). Finally calm, she returns to get the whole story. And remarkably, when Talus begins to speak, he has himself acquired the vocabulary of complaint: "'Ah wellaway' (sayd then the yron man,)" (16.1). Even in her spirited fits of woe, Britomart is given no direct discourse or exclamations. The dynamic and personal "wellaway" is reserved for the iron man, whose inner life of feeling seems to be expanding precipitously. As with his conscience and humorously creaking jaws, "wellaway" jars the poetry to the point of parody.

The crisis within Talus becomes a crisis in the allegory of *The Faerie Queene*. Standard psychomachia would make Talus a mere extension of Artegall, and a mechanical expression of his Justice. Talus's suddenly fulsome inner life, however, creates another site of thought, a doubling that undermines the psychomachic relationship. The robot coming to life as a whole person itself makes for an uncanny scene, like the rocky knees of the Despaire episode. So in place of the legible poetics of perfect allegorical agency emerges a mode of representation that looks more like the distempered imagination associated with despair. Under the pressure of its destructuring, conscience has become difficult to understand, and so breaks in on the clarity of allegory. Personification flirts with subjectivity, projecting the shattered imagination of the early modern conscience onto the poem itself.

The spectacle of Talus setting aside his flail to give scope to conscience, only to devolve further into effeminate lament, is, from a certain perspective, just silly. The scene feels parodic, although it is hard to say exactly how the parody should read. Either Talus is held up to scorn for being a rigorous justicer, or conscience itself is parodied. Which of these pertains depends upon how we read the justice of Book 5 as a whole – whether we see it as a meditation that critiques the English colonial regime as lacking in equity and conscience, or whether we see it as constructing a colonialist justice that has no mercy for the Irish. In either case, Talus's moment of inwardness positions conscience at cross purposes with the Legend of Justice, and as fundamentally unassimilable to the larger allegory.

This is a crisis that, as Book 1 shows, can be cured by a reconstitution of representation. Redcrosse's despairing conscience is healed by the reassertion of neatly functioning allegorical personification in the House of Holiness, and a similarly hopeful outcome appears to be in the offing in Book 5, when Britomart and Talus begin to strike a balance between conscience and justice. After "wellaway," Talus finds a more settled mode of speech: "he gan at large to her dilate/ The whole discourse of his captivance sad" (17.1–2). Britomart matches Talus's equilibrium by putting aside complaint and taking on a knight's duties: "But streight her selfe did dight, and armor don;/ And mounting to her steede, bad Talus guide her on" (19.8–9). Talus now seems to be *her* psychomachic expression, as Britomart assumes the office of the Knight of Justice. Overcoming its excessive inwardness, the poem returns to the quest, and to an economy of straightforward representation.

Optimistically, such allegory seems to include the newly developed inwardness of conscience in the practical duties of justice. Not only does Britomart fulfill her knightly duties with stunning efficiency, but she does so with a strong sense of conscience. Having dispatched Radigund, Britomart still finds a way for mercy to assert itself when "her heart did quake" at Talus's violence and she calls him off. The Legend of Justice seems to have attained the "equall balance" that Astraea originally taught, using "equitie to measure along,/ According to the line of conscience."

And yet, after this clear triumph of equity, Britomart famously repeals female rule and disappears from the poem. Equity has been identified with a specifically feminine approach to justice.[47] But Britomart herself

---

[47] Fortier, *Culture of Equity*, 138–45. Brian Lockey shows how the female rule of Spenser's Amazons contradicts natural law, suggesting that Britomart is here acting equitably, "Equitie to Measure."

buries the possibility of such equity when reigning as Princess over the Amazons,

> And changing all that forme of common weale,
> The liberty of women did repeale,
> Which they had long usurpt; and them restoring
> To mens subjection, did true Justice deale.
>
> (vii.42.4–7)

The reestablishment of the patriarchy, we are told, is true justice, suggesting that Britomart's equitable approach must undo itself by recognizing its own limits. Her uniquely feminine understanding of justice is precisely what tells her that Artegall, rather than she, should be responsible for justice. Justice ejects Britomart's equity, and she disappears. The poem instead follows Artegall's quest, reinstalling him as the Knight of Justice, and never mentioning Britomart again.

In this way the poem contains the complexities of conscientious thought, along with the subversive politics it can engender. Artegall rides on his quest again, with Talus at his side. As Book 5 shifts in the latter cantos to a highly masculinist historical allegory, Artegall betrays little that could be read as doubt or inwardness. Talus also seems to revert to the resistless iron man when he captures Malengin and "with his yron flayle/ Gan drive at him, with so huge might and maine,/ That al his bones, as small as sandy grayle/ He broke, and did his bowels disentrayle" (ix.19.2–5). At the same time, the poem picks up the pace of the larger allegory. Artegall resumes the forward drive of his quest, and such figures as Belgae, Burbon, and Irena make up some of the most transparently signifying allegories of the poem. If conscience and equity appear where allegorical personification unravels, in the latter cantos allegorical representation is reknit. But while the return of allegory becomes a means of curing Redcrosse's shattered conscience in Book 1, here its return constitutes an exclusion of conscience. The ascendant allegory of justice has no room for conscience, just as it elides Britomart.

Mercilla's court confirms the poem's retreat from Britomart's equitable order, which, like female rule, appears too liberal. The episode deploys a surge of strict allegorical personification, as court procedure is entrusted to Zele, Authority, Nobilitie, and many more such figures. Mercilla herself personifies what could be a synonym for equity, but what turns out to be a pointedly alternate articulation of justice. Pity was Artegall's major mistake against Radigund: when he has her down and unlaces her helmet, "his cruell minded hart/ Empierced was with pittifull regard" (v.13.1–2). In a version of misguided conscience, a pierced heart leads Artegall to spare Radigund, which then leads to his enthrallment. But in Mercilla's court no such mistake is made. The allegorical figure Pittie "with full tender hart" is said to plead for Duessa (ix.45.3). But this time Artegall "with constant firme intent" will not be swayed. As an external, allegorical figure, and one that never actually speaks in the poem, Pity exerts no inward grip upon him. With pity contained, Artegall can enforce a more rigorous justice. So too can Mercilla, who weeps for Duessa but countenances her execution. Once again equity calls for its own abandonment: being merciful requires the containment of mercy, just as being a conscientious leader requires the execution of Mary, Queen of Scots.[48]

Mercilla's version of mercy has little room for conscience, but is well suited to empire: Mercilla rules "From th'utmost brinke of the *Armericke* shore,/ Unto the margent of the *Molucas*" (x.3.6–7). As he leaves Mercilla's court and returns to his quest, Artegall's last adventures become similarly expansionist, allegorically figuring the conflicts in the Netherlands and Ireland, as he brings justice beyond the English borders. These are blood-soaked affairs, which call forth both rigor and pity, and so develop a justice that wavers between conscience and raw power.

In the Burbon episode Talus flails the mob "Like scattred chaff" (xi.47.9), and "ceassed not, till all their scattred crew/ Into the sea he drove quite from that soyle" (65.3–4). Artegall finally seems to feel some conscience and calls Talus off: "But *Artegall* seeing his cruell deed,/ Commaunded him from slaughter to recoyle" (xi.65.6–7). And the concluding episode of Book 5 starts off in a similarly conscientious fashion. Landing on Irena's island, Talus does the usual thing with Grantorto's armies:

> But *Talus* sternely did upon them set,
> And brusht, and battred them without remorse,
> That on the ground he left full many a corse;
> Ne any able was him to withstand,
> But he them overthrew both man and horse,
> That they lay scattred over all the land,
> As thicke as doth the seede after the sowers hand.
>   (xii.7.3–9)

In response, Artegall again restrains Talus: "Till *Artegall* him seeing so to rage,/ Willd him to stay" because "not for such slaughters sake/ He thether

---

[48] See Graziani, "Elizabeth at Isis Church"; Stump, "Isis Versus Mercilla."

came," (8.1–2, 7–8). This may be a cynical attempt on Spenser's part to distance Artegall from Talus's violence, and Lord Grey from the massacre of Smerwick. But even so, it is a moment, such as was often called forth by the violence of the English, when pity and conscience bid to assert themselves in the workings of justice. The poem holds out hope for a conscientious resolution to the plot, as well as to the problem of Ireland.

But pointedly, the equity does not last. After his victory over Grantorto, Artegall turns to the task of establishing "true Justice" in Irena's realm, which involves the immediate deployment of Talus:

> During which time, that he did there remaine,
>   His studie was true Justice how to deale,
>   And day and night employ'd his busie paine
>   How to reforme that ragged common-weale:
>   And that same yron man which could reveale
>   All hidden crimes, through all that realme he sent,
>   To search out those that usd to rob and steale,
>   Or did rebell gainst lawfull government;
> On whom he did inflict most grievous punishment.
>
> (xii.26)

Integral to this justice is sending Talus throughout the commonwealth. That Talus can reveal hidden crimes is not a testament to his psychological insight, which was abandoned with Britomart, but clearly references torture and inquisition, leading to "most grievous punishment."

Artegall and Talus are back to dispensing rigor on Irena's island because in Ireland there is no place for conscience, at least according to Irenius in *A View of The Present State of Ireland*. A central part of this text argues that English common law cannot be applied effectively in Ireland. Irenius makes this case by insisting that the Irish lack conscience. Perhaps drawing on his own perception in the Irish Courts of Chancery, Spenser has Irenius declare that the Irish will readily give false evidence and so subvert court procedures whenever an Irishman is set against an Englishman:

> The Triall hereof have I soe often sene, that I dare Confidentlye avouche the abuse thereof yeat is the lawe of it selfe (as I saide good) and the firste institucion theareof beinge given to all Inglishemen verye rightefull, but now that the Irishe have stepped in to the romes of the Inglishe whoe are now become soe hedefull and provident to kepe them out from hence forthe that they make no scruple of Conscience to passe againste them.[49]

[49] Spenser, *The Works*, IX:66.

Eudoxus replies that he cannot believe that they "make no more Conscience to periure themselves."[50] Irenius reiterates: "so inconscionable are these Comon people, and so little feelinge have they of god, or their owne soules healthe"; they "have no touche of Conscience nor sence of theire evill doinge."[51] The theory of equity argues that when common law does not apply effectively to a particular case, the judge can depart from that law into the authority of conscience. *A View* reports an inversion of this sense of equity. For the inapplicability of common law in Ireland suggests a departure from law, but one that is simultaneously a departure from conscience. In both cases common law is set aside. But because in Ireland the law falters in the absence of conscience, the departure leads not to the personal conscience of the judge, but to the possibility of conscienceless judgment.[52]

In Ireland, therefore, equity and conscience must be put aside out of necessity. Spenser portrays the political difficulty of doing so when Elizabeth is so compassionate. Eudoxus delicately suggests Elizabeth's reaction to Lord Grey's regime:

> If it shall happen that the state of this miserye and lamentable image of things shalbe tolde and felingelye presesented to her sacred maiestye beinge by nature full of mercye and Clemencye whoe is moste inclynable to suche pittifull Complaintes and will not endure to heare suche tragedies made of her people and pore subiectes as some aboute her maie insinuate, then shee perhaps for verye Compassion of suche Calamities will not onelye stopp the streame of such violence and retorne to her wonted mildenes, but allso con them litle thankes which have bene the Authors and Counsellours of such blodye platformes.[53]

Irenius defends Grey as a temperate man, "But that the necessitye of that presente state of things forced him to that violence."[54] The "present state" of things, of Ireland, necessitates rigor and sidelines mercy.[55] The problem is that such a colonial project is hard to defend as justice, particularly to a queen full of mercy. Elizabeth's mistakenly equitable approach is implicitly corrected by Mercilla, who shows true mercy by

[50] *Ibid.*, IX:67.
[51] *Ibid.*, IX:68.
[52] Andrew Hadfield associates *A View* with Jean Bodin's absolutist account of equity, which asserts that when law is overridden, the judge or magistrate is justified in asserting an absolute power. *Edmund Spenser's Irish Experience*, 73–6.
[53] Spenser, *The Works*, IX:159.
[54] *Ibid.*, IX:160.
[55] For a reading of *A View* in terms of necessity, see McCabe, "The Fate of Irena."

not calling off the necessary political violence. The just approach is to steel oneself against all remorse, or pangs of conscience:

> Therefore by all meanes it muste be forsene and assured that after once entringe into this Course of reformacion, theare be afterwardes no remorse or drawinge backe, for the sighte of anie such rufull obiectes as muste theareuppon followe, nor for Compassion of theire Callamityes, seinge that by no other meanes it is possible to recure them, and that these are not of will but of verye urgente necessitye.[56]

This is the course that Artegall and Talus pursue. Gloriana, however, is more like Elizabeth than Mercilla, and calls Artegall back to court before the reformation can be completed:

> But ere he could reforme it thoroughly,
> He through occasion called was away,
> To Faerie Court, that of necessity
> His course of Justice he was forst to stay,
> And *Talus* to revoke from the right way,
> In which he was that Realme for to redresse.
> (27.1–6)

Artegall's return to court is equity checking the rigor of the law – but not therefore improving it. It is not felt as progress in the narrative, as when Britomart calls off Talus, but rather is a misapplication of pity and a corruption of justice. True justice cannot be improved by equity and should not answer to conscience.

So the legend stumbles to a tragic close. Book 5 ends with an equivocal picture of Talus, vainly wishing to chastise Detraction, who is accompanied by Envy and the barking Blatant Beast:

> But *Talus* hearing her so lewdly raile,
> And speake so ill of him, that well deserved,
> Would her have chastiz'd with his yron flaile,
> If her Sir *Artegall* had not preserved,
> And him forbidden, who his heast observed.
> So much the more at him still did she scold,
> And stones did cast, yet he for nought would swerve
> From his right course, but still the way did hold
> To Faery Court, where what him fell shall else be told.
> (xii.43)

---

[56] Spenser, *The Works*, IX:163.

Artegall calls off Talus one last time, an action that any conscientious reader of Book 5 must repeatedly crave. We recall Britomart's equity – but do so only to feel that now such restraint is mistakenly naïve, and politically disastrous. Talus is disturbingly violent, but necessary to the politics of the blatantly real world. The ideological instability of conscience in the Legend of Justice is captured by this final stanza, which offers Talus as an ironic afterimage to the allegory.

In Book 1, Spenser tells an optimistic story about the ability of conscience to exert itself in the private sphere of Holiness. But when conscience moves into the public and political sphere of Justice, it cannot overcome its instability. The House of Holiness can restructure conscience through allegorical personification, but there is no such reorganization in Book 5. Conscience is too diffuse, too parodied, too confusing, too unstable to fit into the public structures of justice. It cannot be cured, and so cannot find a place in the allegory. The final scene of Talus, eager to use his flaile, but mercifully forbidden, but clearly unjustly forbidden, may trigger a sense of conscience. But it is a fleeting sense, without structure and without a strong presence in the political state, at least as Spenser views it.

3

Con-science in Macbeth

It has often intrigued commentators that "conscience" is built out of the Latin word for knowledge, *scientia*, and the prefix *con*, a pairing that goes back to the Greek, *syneidesis*. As C. S. Lewis explains in his discussion of the key word, the prefix *con* can function as an intensifier, so that conscience is to be understood as mere knowledge, a weaker sense that draws close to "conscious." But in what Lewis calls its stronger sense, *con* can be read as a preposition, so that conscience becomes a knowledge with something, or with someone, else.[1] Aquinas takes note of this sense of *con*: "Taking the original meaning of the word, it denotes knowledge ordered towards something, since it means knowledge-along-with-another" (*ST* Ia.79.13, XI:191). Christopher St. German explains: "This worde conscyence which in laten is called conscientia is compowned of this preposicion: cum, that is to say in englysshe: with and with this nowne scientia that is to saye in englysshe knowledge and so conscyence is as moche to say as a knowledge of one thynge with another thynge" (*DS* 87). Lewis calls this stronger sense "consciring," but I will call it "*knowing with.*"

Knowing with can be felt to undergird the more stable conception of personified conscience, in which the allegorized faculty appears as an other person, one capable of dialogue and shared knowledge. But as personification loses its force, as it does in *The Faerie Queene, knowing with* becomes more imperfect, tends to float away from our habitual structures of thought. In this vein, Richard's argument with himself – "Is there a murtherer here? No. Yes, I am./ Then fly. What, from myself? Great reason why" – dramatizes the deep challenge of *knowing with*. Here conscience has no way to name with whom the *knowing with* happens. This becomes a difficult scene of shared knowledge, at once a dialogue

[1] Lewis, *Studies in Words*, 181–213. Also see Pierce, *Conscience in the New Testament*, 18.

and a solipsistically inward experience.[2] This imaginative problem can be seen as a feature of the destructuring Protestant conscience: as the experience of conscience moves toward more inchoate dynamics, the orderly sense of sharing knowledge slides into more incoherent, but more energetic, scenes of *knowing with*.

Accordingly, theorists of conscience are particularly interested in this etymology. In the first chapter of *A Discourse of Conscience*, William Perkins explains:

> And hence comes one reason of the name of conscience. *Scire*, to know, is of one man alone by himselfe: and *conscire* is, when two at the least know some one secret thing; either of them knowing it together with the other. Therefore the name συνείδησις, or *Conscientia* conscience, is that thing that combines two togither, and makes them partners in the knowledge of one and the same secret. Now man and man, or man and Angel can not be combined; because they can not know the secret of any man unlesse it be revealed to them: it remaines therefore that this combination is onely betweene man and God. God knowes perfectly all the doings of man, though they be never so hid and concealed: and man by a gift given him of God knows togither with God, the same things of himselfe: and this gift is named Conscience.
>
> (*DC* 5)

Perkins is alert to the sense that conscience involves actively shared knowledge, between an individual and some other. Reflecting the basic Protestant effort to protect the individual's religious life from other people, such as a confessor, Perkins works his way toward naming this other as God.

But by the end of this passage an alternative to God arises – that conscience is a *knowing with* one's own self. Over the next pages, the inward dynamics of mind and thought seem to capture Perkins's attention far more than the divine. The key passage we have examined already, in which conscience is described as when a man "thinkes with himselfe what he thinks" and as "another person within him" (*DC* 7) – this moment of self-reflection is actually a continuation of his account of the etymology. *Knowing with* becomes the reflexive conscience, something about which Alexander Hume is particularly forthright:

> For the latine word, *Conscientia* (from the quhilk the worde, *Conscience* cummis) is composed of the Preposition *cum*, quhilk signifyis in our language, *with*, & *Scientia*, quhilk signifies *Science*, or Knawledge; as gif

---

[2] See Tilmouth, "Shakespeare's Open Consciences."

wee wald say, the knawledg quhilk man hes inwartly with himselfe, of all his actiounis, wordis, and cogitations.

(*ATC* 13)[3]

The reflexive interpretation of *con-scire* creates a dynamic scene of conscience, one in which the burgeoning of self-consciousness seems to dominate even God's presence. Of course the self-reflection of an individual is no simple thing, so, as with Richard, the emerging energy of subjectivity within conscience becomes quite unsettling. The question "knowing with whom?" does not yield the answer "oneself" with ease. When conscience becomes *knowing with* oneself, the faculty risks slipping into solipsism. And from there, it is vexed by a secularizing answer. Although not Perkins's or Hume's intent, lurking in solipsism is the possibility that no religious conscience at all is functioning, but merely the individual's mistaken mental experience. This is a step toward modernity: the faculty takes on the psychological energies of self-reflection, as conscience in effect blends into consciousness; and simultaneously, conscience disconnects from a divine warrant, potentially secularizing the faculty.

This chapter pursues these two linked tendencies, the emergence of subjectivity in the early modern conscience and the conception of the faculty as merely human. *Knowing with* gives us a set of terms, a scene, in which to observe these otherwise hidden and theoretical dynamics. Such a theoretical turn in this book's argument will necessarily be speculative, as it reaches toward the longer trajectory of early Enlightenment reason, and then beyond that to make contact with some of the key theorists of conscience in modernity, Freud and Judith Butler. But modern theory proves explanatory of Shakespeare's most extended scene of conscience, the play *Macbeth*, which stages a destructuring of *knowing with*, and then investigates the aftermath.

Act 2 Scene 2

Shakespeare finds in Holinshed's *Chronicles* the kernel of his investigation. Kenneth, who furnishes part of the character of Macbeth, murders the king, Malcolm, and is then stricken by conscience. Kenneth,

> could not but still live in continuall feare, least his wicked practise concerning the death of Malcome Duffe should come to light and knowledge of the world. For so commeth it to passe, that such as are pricked in

---

[3] Also see Bourne, *The Anatomie of Conscience*, 6.

conscience for anie secret offense committed, have ever an unquiet mind. And (as the fame goeth) it chanced that a voice was heard as he was in bed in the night time to take his rest, uttering unto him these or the like woords in effect: "Thinke not Kenneth that the wicked slaughter of Malcolme Duffe by thee contrived is kept secret from the knowledge of the eternall God."[4]

Kenneth is afflicted with an unquiet mind, and pricked in conscience. Moreover, conscience has a voice, making what is secret into shared knowledge. Kenneth cannot hope to keep his sin secret, because some other speaker already knows it – and that voice itself makes clear that the knowledge inevitably will be shared with God. Conscience works by undoing secrecy and making sure that knowledge cannot remain private. Such *knowing with* is central to a well-functioning conscience: the next morning Kenneth confesses.

Kenneth's unquiet rest may lie behind Macbeth's lament, "Methought I heard a voice cry, 'Sleep no more!/ Macbeth does murther sleep'" (II.ii.32–3). Like Kenneth, Macbeth hears a voice. But importantly, he is not driven by that voice to confess. Conscience seems to be operating, but without the clarity that Holinshed finds. The voice does not patiently demonstrate *knowing with*, but rather obliquely threatens an end to rest; it does not speak directly to Macbeth, but rather echoes in the night. And the voice of conscience does not connect Macbeth to the divine, but rather remains within the world, as a part of his own mental experience. Conscience seems to be at work, but not coherently or effectively.

In reworking Holinshed, Shakespeare afflicts Macbeth with an experience of *knowing with* which has been fractured and confused. He turns up the volume on Kenneth's unquiet mind and splits the communicating voice into shards. In the aftermath of Duncan's murder both Macbeth and Lady Macbeth undergo a cacophony of sounds and a chaos of sights, their minds reverberating with an overcrowded, overwhelming conscience. If conscience is a *knowing with*, Shakespeare undermines the Macbeths' ability to interpret the object of that preposition – to understand *with what* or *with whom* they know. Immediately after the murder, in the pivotal Act 2 Scene 2, they experience conscience as a chamber of sights and sounds, with each signifier potentially, but incompletely, representing that witness who will communicate their guilt.[5]

---

[4] Holinshed, *The Chronicles of England, Scotlande, and Ireland*, in Bullough, *Narrative and Dramatic Sources*, VII:485. In another possible source, George Buchanan's *Rerum scoticarum historia*, Kenneth is similarly visited by the voice of conscience. *Ibid.*, VII:511.

[5] A. C. Bradley says that Macbeth has the imagination of a poet, through which "he is kept in contact with supernatural impressions and is liable to supernatural fears. And through it, especially,

Macbeth kills his king in the second act, between the first and second scenes, and his entrance in Scene 2 shows him in the first throes of conscience. In his opening words he is startled, and worries that someone is out there: "Who's there? What ho?" (II.ii.8). And then, "I have done the deed. Didst thou not hear a noise?" (II.ii.14). Going from the deed directly to hearing a person or noise, Macbeth is expecting to encounter *knowing with*. In the aftermath of the murder, some voice, some sound, some person must be within a communicable distance, sharing his secret.

In the following lines, Macbeth and Lady Macbeth desperately try to understand what they hear:

MACB.	I have done the deed. Didst thou not hear a noise?
LADY M.	I heard the owl scream and the crickets cry.
	Did not you speak?
MACB.	When?
LADY M.	Now.
MACB.	As I descended?
LADY M.	Ay.
MACB.	Hark! who lies i' th' second chamber?
LADY M.	Donalbain.
MACB.	This is a sorry sight.
LADY M.	A foolish thought to say a sorry sight.

(II.ii.14–19)

To answer Macbeth's confusion, Lady Macbeth first provides an interpretation of the noise which views it as a phenomenon of the natural world. The possibility that it is an owl or crickets would quiet the fear that Macbeth has heard a supernatural voice connected to conscience. But Lady Macbeth immediately undermines her rational explanation by betraying that she too thinks the sound is a person. "Did you not speak?" suggests that the owl and crickets have not set to rest in her own mind the possibility that a voice was what Macbeth heard. They continue inquiring into the sound, but the exchange takes on a dizzying sense of anxiety and doubt: "When?/ Now./ As I descended?/Ay./ Hark!" Here the switching of the stichomythia creates a sense of searching in audience and reader alike, as we ask suddenly, who is speaking? Where on stage or in the line of pentameter is that sound? The question of where Macbeth was when the previous sound echoed remains unresolved, however, as he jumps to another

---

come to him the intimations of conscience and honour . . . . His conscious or reflective mind, that is, moves chiefly among considerations of outward success and failure, while his inner being is convulsed by conscience." *Shakespearean Tragedy*, 352–53.

line of inquiry. "Hark," implies that a new sound is at that very moment audible. Or at least that he thinks it is. And then Macbeth skittishly jumps to a different topic, the tenant of the second chamber. This seems to be motivated by the fear of a real witness to his deed, and so the sense of some other being has developed from the uninterpretable sound, to the possibility of his sin becoming known to the voice of conscience, to the practical fear that the murder was observed by someone in the castle. Each possibility blends together in Macbeth's panic. And Lady Macbeth's one-word answer, that it was the king's son, Donalbain, sinks Macbeth into the feverish state of despair. His response, "This is a sorry sight," may refer to himself: the Riverside, like many editions, adds stage direction implying that Macbeth is looking at his own bloody hands. But these directions are not in the Folio, so Macbeth's words may just as well refer to what has been dominating his despairing mind – possibly the tableau he envisions, in which he has murdered the king in the chamber next to the king's son, or possibly the terrible turn of events in which Donalbain is a material witness. Just like the noise which could be a voice, this is a sight which could be either real or a figure of the imagination. As ambiguity in expression plagues Macbeth, so does ambiguity in sense perception. He seems unable to organize the sounds and sights around him, seems to be focusing now on one, now on the other. But the dominant principle is his feeling that, somewhere within this chamber of echoing sounds and difficult to perceive sights, there is a witness. In the moments after the murder, Macbeth is both wary of and searching for that other who, in the logic of *knowing with*, is privy to his secret and is communicating that shared knowledge.

In these opening moments of their experience with conscience, Lady Macbeth reaches for explanations which would set aside the logic of *knowing with*. First she makes an argument from nature, claiming the sound is an owl or crickets, implying that it is merely an accidental noise from the natural world, and not therefore a voice loaded with moral value. She then turns to an argument from fancy, when she calls his "sorry sight" a "foolish thought." Again, she is denigrating the possibility of conscience *knowing with* by urging that the sight is a product of Macbeth's unreliable mind, rather than some actual other. But Lady Macbeth must work hard to set aside conscience in herself and her husband – as has been seen, she immediately slips out of her feigned innocence of the supernatural with "Did not you speak?" She struggles in the attempt to shove their thoughts away from the portentous world of communicating sights and sounds, but nevertheless continues to reassert her denial of conscience.

Macbeth, however, remains caught in the echo chamber. After "A foolish thought to say a sorry sight," Macbeth says "There's one did laugh in's sleep, and one cried, 'Murther!'" (II.ii.20). Lady Macbeth again tries to push aside the supernatural with a rational, if partial, explanation: "There are two lodg'd together" (II.ii.23), implying that Macbeth had simply overheard a conversation (though this hardly explains why one would refer to murder). But Macbeth carries the voice far into the world of supernatural communication with "Methought I heard a voice cry, 'Sleep no more!/ Macbeth does murther sleep'" (II.ii.32–3). With such exact knowledge, this could only be a supernatural voice, one that, as Holinshed names it, would seem to be conscience. The voice, operating as a *knowing with*, cries out "to all the house" (II.ii.38), sharing in the knowledge of the sin and, as a witness, crying out its tale. Exasperated, Lady Macbeth cuts in: "Who was it that thus cried? Why, worthy thane,/ You do unbend your noble strength, to think/ So brain-sickly of things" (II.ii.41–3). She pushes beyond the chiding "foolish thought" to the outright assertion that Macbeth is sick in the head. Lady Macbeth's second effort to explain away the sounds and sights of conscience lies in the charge of madness.

Macbeth has already thought of this possibility. Before the murder is committed but after the decision to kill is made, as Macbeth readies his intentions, he is haunted by a conscience which is experienced in even more equivocal terms. Conscience here does not communicate with voices and sounds, but as a vision, the "dagger of the mind" which confronts Macbeth in his solitude. Macbeth's preoccupation is whether the dagger he sees is really there, or if it is a product of his mind:

> Is this a dagger which I see before me,
> The handle toward my hand? Come, let me clutch thee:
> I have thee not, and yet I see thee still.
> Art thou not, fatal vision, sensible
> To feeling as to sight? or art thou but
> A dagger of the mind, a false creation,
> Proceeding from the heat-oppressed brain?
>
> (II.i.33–9)

When he cannot touch what he sees, Macbeth assumes that the dagger is "of the mind," and so a false product of a diseased brain. In turning to his own brain as the source, Macbeth cuts off the possibility that the dagger issues from an other – rejecting an interpretation of it as a part of the *knowing with* of conscience. The most common metaphor for conscience's action, that it pricks, is implicit in the image of the dagger.[6]

Macbeth explains away a vision that feels like a warning from his conscience. But in the same soliloquy conscience sneaks back into his thoughts in an indirect manner, by means of the figure of Tarquin. Contemplating his own intentions, Macbeth imagines a night full of witchcraft, and in this landscape personifies "withered murder" who "with his stealthy pace,/ With Tarquin's ravishing strides, towards his design/ Moves like a ghost" (II.i.54–6). In Shakespeare's earlier rendering of the scene in "The Rape of Lucrece," the rapist Tarquin takes his ravishing strides – he "stalks" toward Lucrece (354) – only after a dispute of conscience:

> Thus graceless hold he disputation
> 'Tween frozen conscience and hot burning will,
> And with good thoughts makes dispensation,
> Urging the worser sense for vantage still;
> Which in a moment doth confound and kill
>   All pure effects, and doth so far proceed
>   That what is vile shows like a virtuous deed.
>   (246–52)

Macbeth imagines murder on the other side of Tarquin's encounter with conscience – that is, his language reveals how his own murderous action will proceed only in the wake of failed conscience. If Macbeth has begun to undermine conscience, as Lady Macbeth will do extensively in the play, his mind shows itself to be, on some level, very aware of what he is doing. The complexity of the allusion to Tarquin, however, registers just how ambivalent Macbeth's experience of conscience is at this moment. Unlike the unanimous chorus of voices judging Richard III a villain, Macbeth's conscience flickers with the impossibility of deciding whether the dagger is real or not, and hints at its knowledge through the trails of literary allusion. Macbeth's conclusion concerning the dagger appears as perfectly contradictory: "There's no such thing:/ It is the bloody business which informs/ Thus to mine eyes" (II.i.47–9). He decides that the dagger is unreal, and at the same time names it as a piece of information issuing from the bloody business – as a signifier of conscience.

The play itself, mischievously supporting Lady Macbeth, further attenuates Macbeth's conscience by suggesting that the dagger is a real

---

[6] As it is in Hamlet's resolution "to speak daggers to her but use none" (III.ii.396) before the closet scene with Gertrude.

weapon. For much of Act 2 Scene 2 Macbeth thoughtlessly clutches a pair of real daggers whose bloody materiality is all too obvious. The entire chamber of Act 2 Scene 2 ends, moreover, with a similar materializing of the sound of knocking. When Lady Macbeth leaves and Macbeth again finds himself alone, he hears a knock within and declares, "Whence is that knocking?/ How is't with me, when every noise appalls me?/ What hands are here?" (II.ii.54–6). Once again in the realm of overheard sounds, everything feels portentous and barely understood. For all we know the knocking hands are hands of the mind. But then Lady Macbeth returns to insist that the knocking is an ordinary sound, coming from the south entry (II.ii.63). And in the Porter Scene which follows, the knocking is parodied in its mundane materiality, both as sounds now clearly emanating from a door, and in the Porter's drunken mimicking of the repeated noise: "Knock, knock, knock!" (III.i.3). Just as Lady Macbeth insists, the sounds and sights that present themselves as Macbeth's conscience seem to be merely the physical phenomena of the everyday world. We emerge from Act 2 Scene 2 enmeshed in a conscience that is loud and portentous and threatening, but also potentially meaningless in its naturalism.

Despair and Disenchantment

When Macbeth and Lady Macbeth struggle with a conscience that is ambivalently divine and disenchanted, they confront conditions that, in the Protestant understanding, are commonly called despair. *Macbeth's* shrieking owls, plotting witches, and visiting ghosts make for a landscape like that of Despayre's cave, where Redcrosse sees "the ghastly Owle,/ Shrieking his balefull note," and "all about it wandring ghostes did wayle and howle" (I.ix.33.6–9). A guilty conscience feels much the same for Redcrosse and Macbeth, and, as discussed in Chapter 2, it felt this way to many in the period. William Perkins's "perturbations," or what Richard Greenham called "hurly burlyes," name how the experience of a guilty conscience could include a frightening, often disorienting, experience of visions and dreams. As Hume describes it: "Yea it wil appeare to himselfe, that al the creatures of God are animate, as it were, and conspired against him" (*ATC* 42–3).

For one caught in a despairing conscience, a main concern is to distinguish between experiences that are legitimately of the wounded conscience, and those which can be explained as merely natural. This is the problem of knowing the difference between conscience and melancholy. Conscience and melancholy both can lead to distempered mental experiences, and so can be easily confused; conscience is the more real and important one. As Timothy Bright explains, "Whatsoever molestation riseth directly as a proper object of the mind, that in that respect is not melancholicke, but hath a farther ground then fancie, and riseth from conscience."[7] Or as Perkins says, the afflictions of conscience have "a true and certain cause," while melancholy suffers when "the imagination conceiveth a thing to be so, which is not so."[8] The important border between conscience and melancholy is the border between what belongs to the greater theological realm of sin and salvation, and what belongs to the body.

This is the interpretive problem of Act 2 Scene 2, as Macbeth and Lady Macbeth struggle to comprehend its crickets and owls and daggers. On the one hand, they are surrounded by an enchanted world, supernaturally signifying their guilt in the greater theological economy. On the other hand, Lady Macbeth, explains away the echo chamber either as merely natural or as a product of brain sickness or melancholy. Lady Macbeth's skepticism is a concerted effort to disenchant conscience. The same interpretive problem extends beyond Lady Macbeth's arguments into the greater events of the play. In Macbeth's vision of Banquo's ghost, no one else can see what Macbeth sees, and so Lady Macbeth implores him: "This is the very painting of your fear. This is the air-drawn dagger which, you said,/ Led you to Duncan" (III.iv.62–4). Similarly, the play cultivates an ambiguity over whether or not the witches have supernatural power, challenging the audience to determine whether to interpret them naturally or supernaturally.[9] *Macbeth* repeatedly brings us to the border between natural and supernatural, biological and theological, as Stephen Greenblatt argues: "Shakespeare achieves the remarkable effect of a nebulous infection, a bleeding of the demonic into the secular and the secular into the demonic."[10]

---

[7] Bright, *A Treatise of Melancholy*, 193.

[8] Perkins, *The Whole Treatise*, 195.

[9] Bradley, *Shakespearean Tragedy*, 341–46. Significantly, one of Shakespeare's sources, Reginald Scot's *The Discoverie of Witchcraft*, is also a key source for Keith Thomas, who describes the text as "the standard sceptical position." *Religion and the Decline of Magic*, 572. Scot's skepticism extends to ghosts, omens, witchcraft, and dreams, among other supernatural elements pertinent to *Macbeth*. Scot is also careful to keep conscience away from the supernatural: "But that witches or magicians have power by words, herbs, or imprecations to thrust into the mind or conscience of man, what it shall please them, by vertue of their charmes, herbs, stones, or familiares, etc: according to the opinion of Hemingius, I denie." *The Discoverie of Witchcraft*, 181. On Scot's influence, see Strier, "Shakespeare and the Skeptics."

[10] Greenblatt, "Shakespeare Bewitched," 124. Also see Garber, *Dreams in Shakespeare*, 88–138.

The skeptical calculus resulting from this ambiguity matters, for our purposes, because it has the potential to block conscience. Lady Macbeth's arguments for natural sounds and brain-sickly visions are an effort to contain an overwhelming scene of *knowing with*. If it is merely natural, it is not, as Hume puts it, as if "al the creatures of God are animate, as it were, and conspired against him." As Lady Macbeth well knows, skepticism toward ghosts, or the portentous sights and sounds of Act 2 Scene 2, can banish the functioning of *knowing with* from the mind, thus controlling conscience. When it is understood to function through *knowing with*, conscience tends toward the enchanted forms of personification and animism. But it also proves susceptible to disenchantment.

So the Protestant conscience intersects with the larger, familiar narrative of modern secularization, with the expansion of skepticism and disenchantment. Robert Scribner describes how disenchantment in the Reformation destabilized what he calls the "moralized universe," a world in which supernatural intervention, in the form of portents and signs, marks how human sin is legible in the world. Scribner argues that "The Protestant elaboration of the moralized universe had the effect of increasing anxiety among those it affected. Deprived of the protective means inherent in the Catholic sacramental system, Protestants found themselves prey to anxiety that was hardly allayed by invoking the Protestant doctrine of providence."[11] *Macbeth* calls forth such a moralized universe and simultaneously discredits it, casting *knowing with* into an unstable position, as conscience bends to disenchantment.

A disenchanted conscience clearly takes part in the larger historical trajectory of rational religion. The scene of conscience, so intimately captured by theorists and poets, is stripped down and sometimes entirely evacuated by seventeenth-century skepticism. Robert Burton, for example, disconnects conscience from the divine by suggesting that the natural condition of melancholy can itself explain conscience: "much melancholy is without affliction of conscience, as Bright and Perkins illustrate by four reasons; and yet melancholy alone again may be sometimes a sufficient cause of this terror of conscience."[12] The Cambridge Platonists can be viewed as championing a religion of conscience, particularly in

---

[11] Scribner, "The Reformation, Popular Magic, and the 'Disenchantment of the World,'" 486. Max Weber first uses the phrase "the disenchantment of the world" in "Science as Vocation," 155.

[12] Burton, *The Anatomy of Melancholy*, III:iv.2.3. Among examples of genuinely wounded consciences, Burton cites Richard III and Kenneth.

their emphasis on morality and reason.[13] But they do not theorize the workings of conscience, and generally move away from discussing the faculty directly. Nathaniel Culverwell's "candle of the Lord" binds "*in foro Conscientiae*," but seems to replace conscience more than amplify it.[14] This key Cambridge Platonist metaphor functions very much like conscience, enlightening and providing divine guidance to the individual; in shedding enchanted associations, conscience seems to melt into light and Right Reason.[15]

In the wake of these latitude men, John Locke's *An Essay Concerning Human Understanding* is usually credited with taking the decisive step toward a secular conscience, when he asserts that conscience can be formed within us not by divine creation, but rather through "Education, Company, and Customs of their Country," and that it "is nothing else but our own Opinion of Judgment of the Moral Rectitude or Pravity of our own Actions."[16] Locke's remarkable assertion of a secular and human origin is accompanied by an overall neglect of the faculty in the *Essay*, as consciousness takes its place. This secularizing is furthered in Shaftesbury's account, which replaces a "religious conscience" with a "moral or natural conscience" that is explicitly disenchanted: "No one is esteemed the more conscientious for the fear of evil spirits, conjurations, enchantments." The scene of conscience operates not through *knowing with*, but through reason and its inherent harmonizing: "there must in every rational creature be yet further conscience, namely, from sense of deformity in what is thus ill-deserving and unnatural."[17]

Closer to Shakespeare's moment, and an early landmark in this rationalizing trajectory, is Edward, Lord Herbert of Cherbury's *De Veritate* (1624). Best known as the central expression of Cherbury's proto-deist philosophy, *De Veritate* is also fundamentally a work about

[13] G. A. J. Rogers says Henry More's *An Explanation of the Grand Mytery of Godliness* (1660), makes "as strong a case for the primacy of conscience as perhaps did anybody in the seventeenth century." "The Other-Worldly Philosophers," 13.

[14] Culverwell, *An Elegant and Learned Discourse*, 58. Also see Greville, *The Nature of Truth*.

[15] Robert A. Greene argues for the "candle of the Lord" as *synderesis* metamorphosed. "Synderesis, the Spark of Conscience," 213–14.

[16] "I doubt not, but without being written on their Hearts, many Men may, by the same way that they come to the Knowledge of other things, come to assent to several Moral Rules, and be convinced of their Obligation. Others also may come to be of the same Mind, from their Education, Company, and Customs of their Country; which *Persuasion however got, will serve to set Conscience on work*, which is nothing else but our own Opinion of Judgment of the Moral Rectitude or Pravity of our own Actions." Locke, *An Essay*, I.iii.8, 70.

[17] Cooper, Third Earl of Shaftesbury, *Characteristics*, 209. On the secularization of conscience in the Enlightenment, see Andrew, *Conscience and its Critics*, 79–113; Strohm, *Conscience*, 37–58.

conscience.[18] As part of its transformative religious skepticism, *De Veritate* turns away from nearly all forms of organized worship and divine revelation, creating a religion based entirely on innate ideas. This shift to the inward experience of knowledge makes Cherbury's a religion of conscience. But it is a conscience entirely removed from supernatural revelation, or what Scribner calls the moralized universe. *De Veritate* does not pursue a full secularizing of conscience – Cherbury's deism is not atheism – but it does strip down the scene of conscience, enacting a disenchanting of *knowing with*.

Cherbury celebrates conscience as "the most important principle of all," declaring that, "It is so essential to us that there is no hope of inner peace except when it is brought into due conformity. In it, above all, the great contract of salvation is expressed and eternal blessedness assured, and it is to it that all the common notions are referred."[19] Much of Cherbury's handling of conscience is standard Protestantism, as it assures salvation, judges right and wrong, and links humans to the divine. But his insistence on "conformity" is unique, reflecting Cherbury's location of conscience at the center of his particular philosophical system.

De Veritate develops a complex system of knowing truth based upon innate ideas, "Common Notions" that are in every person. These common notions inform four classes of faculties, Natural Instinct, Internal Apprehension, External Apprehension, Discursive Thought.[20] We are able to discern truth about an object or concept through what he calls "analogy," when one of these faculties "conforms" with the object or concept: "All truth according to this doctrine consists of conformity."[21] The second class of faculties, Internal Apprehension, which mediates between the higher and lower faculties, is essentially identical with conscience.[22] Conscience is "the bond between all other apprehensions" within Internal Apprehension, and, more expansively, it holds together all four faculties: "For conscience finds its only satisfaction in the right conformity of all the faculties."[23] Conscience, for Cherbury, is particularly necessary to the

---

[18] Cherbury promises in *De Veritate* that he will publish an "entire treatise on Conscience," which may refer to the incomplete *De Causis Errorum*. That text, however, has little that is directly on conscience. Herbert, *De Veritate*, 186.

[19] *Ibid.*, 184.

[20] *Ibid.*, 115.

[21] *Ibid.*, 88.

[22] *Ibid.*, 147.

[23] *Ibid.*, 185.

central goal of establishing the analogy between faculty and object, and its workings are understood as conforming or not conforming.

But what conformity actually is, Cherbury admits, is elusive. He attempts to distinguish conformity from perception, but unsuccessfully:

> it is neither the faculty nor the object which perceives; the act of perception is achieved by our mind when these principles react upon each other and conformity results, as it were from the conflict, that is when we sense ourselves in the act of perceiving – precise terms are lacking. So what we sense or apprehend in the depths of our mind is the pure act of conformity.[24]

Conformity is hard to describe because it is specifically not a process that involves sense perception or material bodies or other familiar ways of organizing relationships. It is a purer mental event: "In this investigation I wish the coarse physical structure of the faculties stripped off and broken away in order that the divine intellectual types may appear in all their purity."[25] It is this pure mental experience, "stripped" of all "physical structures" that characterizes the functioning of conscience. It seems to work by a kind of congruence, or what Cherbury often calls harmony. So it creates an experience that is based on geometry or proportion rather than on the personifications and sensory stimuli that make up the scene of voices and visions in *knowing with*. Cherbury strips away *knowing with* from conscience, anticipating Shaftesbury in his rational and geometric faculty.

This skeptical dismantling of the scene of *knowing with* is most famously enacted in Hobbes's *Leviathan*. Led by his materialism, Hobbes draws near to Cherbury's incipient deism, evincing a deeply skeptical attitude toward revealed religion, or "daemonology." Without the possibility of enchanted communication, Hobbes downgrades *knowing with* to mere metaphor:

> When two, or more men, know of one and the same fact, they are said to be Conscious of it one to another; which is as much as to know it together. And because such are fittest witnesses of the facts of one another, or of a third; it was, and ever will be reputed a very Evill act, for any man to speak against his *Conscience*; or to corrupt, or force another so to do: Insomuch that the plea of Conscience has been always hearkened unto very diligently in all times. Afterwards, men made use of the same word metaphorically, for the knowledge of their own secret facts, and secret thoughts; and therefore it is Rhetorically said, that the Conscience is a thousand witnesses. And last of all, men, vehemently in love with their

---

[24] *Ibid.*, 159.
[25] *Ibid.*, 159.

own new opinions (though never so absurd,) and obstinately bent to maintain them, gave those their opinions also that reverenced name of Conscience, as if they would have it seem unlawfull, to change or speak against them; and so pretend to know they are true, when they know at most, but that they think so.

(*Lev.* I:7, 48)

Many familiar details from the discourse of conscience can be found here. Hobbes describes conscience as shading into consciousness, as a witness, and as *knowing with*. But in this important moment, Hobbes insists that *knowing with* is not real. It is only a metaphor, a bit of rhetoric that covers up its entirely natural origin in the mundane act of sharing knowledge with another person. As in Cherbury's *De Veritate*, the scene of *knowing with* is disenchanted and silenced.

As a result, conscience for Hobbes is fundamentally solipsistic, no more than personal opinion. Calling *knowing with* a metaphor is, in Hobbes's system, to imply that conscience itself is an abuse.[26] It is not just deceptive, but an indication of the abusiveness of the notion of conscience itself. For Hobbes offers this account of conscience as an illustration in a larger discussion of the human tendency to elevate personal opinion to the exalted level of truth, even divine law. His skepticism toward the faculty is intended to deny private conscience any authority beyond the individual. This makes sense as part of Hobbes's larger argument that the social contract transfers all authority and judgment to the sovereign. Suspicious of it as a political threat, Hobbes undermines private conscience in order to set up the faculty elsewhere as operating strictly in the public sphere, so that "the Law is the publique Conscience" (*Lev.* II:29, 223). Here we begin to glimpse how the disenchanted conscience contributes to the formation of a political subject. As will be discussed in Chapter 5, the abstraction of conscience in *Leviathan* is central to the formation of the possessive individualism that enables liberal contract and sovereign political authority.

Lady Macbeth never attains the disenchanted conscience of Cherbury, much less the political authority theorized by Hobbes. Forging her way through the sounds and sights of the echo chamber, she reaches for political power as she reaches for a conscience that functions in the increasing quiet of rational thought, dwindling so that it perhaps may not bother

---

[26] Metaphor names discourse which is false: it is one of the "abuses of speech" when people "use words metaphorically; that is, in other sense than that they are ordained for; and thereby deceive others." *Lev.* I:4, 26.

her at all. But as it moves toward its tragic conclusion, Shakespeare's play refuses to let conscience fade. Instead it stages a return of a spectacularly functioning faculty: Lady Macbeth, who would deny conscience as superstition, experiences it in Act 5 as an overwhelming and significant force. It is a force that responds to disenchantment by shifting the scene of *knowing with* into the unconscious mind, thereby turning Lady Macbeth toward the horizon of modern subjectivity.

The Uncanny Conscience and Subjectivity

In her skeptical argument in Act 2 Scene 2, Lady Macbeth insists that the blood on Macbeth's hands is merely physical blood, and not a supernatural signifier of the divine. "Go get some water,/ And wash this filthy witness from your hand," she says. Macbeth nevertheless cries out, "Will all great Neptune's ocean wash this blood/Clean from my hand?" So Lady Macbeth persists: "A little water clears us of this deed;/ How easy is it then!" (II.ii.43–65). Merely material, the blood should easily wash off, and that is that. But of course the blood remains visible to her, and in Act 5 becomes the emblem of her great struggle with conscience: "Out, damn'd spot! out, I say!"; "What, will these hands ne'er be clean?"; "Here's the smell of the blood still. All the perfumes of Arabia will not sweeten this little hand" (V.i.35–52). The sight of blood, and now even its scent, return to Lady Macbeth's mental experience. Alongside shifting bits of remembered events, her perception of the portentous spot marks the return of the flashing sights and echoing sounds of Act 2 Scene 2.

Following Lady Macbeth's own lead, her "slumbery agitation" might be explained away like the daggers of Macbeth's mind. The bloody spot might be taken as "a false creation,/ Proceeding from the heat-oppressed brain." But Shakespeare puts a doctor in the scene to dispel this possibility. "This disease is beyond my practise" he observes, and then:

> Unnatural deeds
> Do breed unnatural troubles; infected minds
> To their deaf pillows will discharge their secrets.
> More needs she the divine than the physician.
> God, God forgive us all!
>
> (V.i.71–5)

Lady Macbeth has an infected mind, but it is not of a biological origin, and so she needs a divine, not a doctor. The most the Doctor can do is pray. Just as Perkins, Hume, and Bright carefully distinguish conscience from melancholy, so Act 5 begins with a clear diagnosis. Lady Macbeth has insistently used her skepticism and materialism to argue away conscience, but in Act 5 it returns. Fittingly, *knowing with* also returns. The Doctor admonishes the Gentlewoman for being an inappropriate witness: "Go to, go to; you have known what you should not" (V.i.46). But the Gentlewoman insists that the *knowing with* is not between humans, but is between Lady Macbeth and God: "She has spoke what she should not, I am sure of that: heaven knows what she has known" (lines 48–9).

When Macbeth in turn becomes witness to this scene of conscience, he seeks refuge in the same familiar skepticism. Fully committed to his own unconscientious path, and well schooled in Lady Macbeth's argument for material accounts of the experience of conscience, he presses the Doctor for a cure:

> Canst thou not minister to a mind diseas'd,
> Pluck from the memory a rooted sorrow,
> Raze out the written troubles of the brain,
> And with some sweet oblivious antidote
> Cleanse the stuff'd bosom of that perilous stuff
> Which weighs upon the heart?
>
> (V.iii.40–5)

Vainly, Macbeth wishes the disease were something a physician could heal. But his clumsy repetition of the vague and untheological "stuff" marks his distance from any understanding of the workings of conscience. It is obvious that the remedies of the physician are utterly beside the point; the natural explanation is thoroughly parodied. In Act 5, then, conscience reappears, returning to effectiveness after it has been seemingly surmounted. In Act 2, Lady Macbeth wanted Macbeth to "wash this filthy witness" from his hand, but now the blood, not simply material blood, is perceptible on *her* hands. She is thrust back into the sights and sounds and smells that witness her guilt, and this time she does not explain them away, but rather experiences them as a fulsome conscience.

If conscience returns, it is important that it returns in a dream. Dreams are themselves an important site of early modern disenchantment, as interpreters disagreed, as with conscience, whether they were forms of supernatural revelation, or merely the physiological effects of the humours and the brain.[27] Richard's conscience is manifest first in

---

[27] Holland, "'The Interpretation of Dreams' in the Renaissance," 30–1. Also see Scot, *Discoverie of Witchcraft*, 178.

his dream, as the accusing ghosts of his victims. Similarly, in Holinshed, Kenneth's unambiguous voice of conscience comes to him in a dream. Act 2 Scene 2 can be seen as an exercise in bringing Kenneth's dream into the waking world, mapping the *knowing with* of conscience onto the real. There it falters: in the light of day, skepticism can too easily undo conscience. But conscience then regains its purchase, establishing the scene of witnessing by returning to the darker passages of dreams. The move from Kenneth's dream to Lady Macbeth's, however, makes a significant difference. While Kenneth's hears the voice of conscience clearly, Lady Macbeth hears no speeches and sees no ghosts. Instead she experiences a disjunctive replay of past events, calling out "why then 'tis time to do't" (V.i.35); "who would have thought the old man to have had so much blood in him?" (39–40); "I tell you yet again Banquo's buried" (63–4); "To bed, to bed; there's knocking at the gate" (66–7). And of course most inescapably, she sees and smells Duncan's blood on her hands. Lady Macbeth's dream is a disruptive and non-linear experience, capturing what in the modern world Freud calls dream-work.

The spots of blood reactivate conscience, but in the mode of a return of the repressed. What returns is the sense of an enchanted scene of *knowing with*, a scene that had been repressed by Lady Macbeth's skepticism. This amounts to a step along the trajectory of disenchantment, but also to a reversal and step backward, toward enchantment. Conscience again functions as a *knowing with*, but this experience is now psychologically complicated. It is marked by skepticism as well as ambivalence about that skepticism – it unfolds in a mind that has doubted, and then doubted that doubt. This complex conscience, with its participation in disenchantment and its proximity to the unconscious, might best be described as uncanny.

According to Freud, the uncanny particularly names the reappearance of something "familiar and old-established in the mind, and which has become alienated from it only through the process of repression."[28] The uncanny occurs in two kinds of reappearances, either repressed infantile complexes, or "when primitive beliefs which have been surmounted seem once more to be confirmed."[29] It is the latter, the return of surmounted primitive beliefs, which resembles conscience in Act 5. The primitive belief, what Freud calls the "omnipotence of thoughts," is "the old animistic conception of the universe" in which spirits populate the

---

[28] "The Uncanny" in *The Standard Edition*, 17:241.
[29] *Ibid.*, 17:249.

world and magic works upon us.[30] This understanding of the world is a thing of the past: the modern mindset disbelieves in the omnipotence of thoughts, and carries around the memory of it only in the unconscious. From within a present skepticism, the uncanny is felt as a return of repressed animism and belief in magic. The supernatural breaks through our conscious, skeptical position:

> We – our primitive forefathers – once believed that these possibilities were realities, and were convinced that they actually happened. Nowadays we no longer believe in them, we have *surmounted* these modes of thought; but we do not feel quite sure of our new beliefs, and the old ones still exist within us ready to seize upon any confirmation. As soon as something *actually happens* in our lives which seems to confirm the old, discarded beliefs we get a feeling of the uncanny.[31]

The uncanny, then, arises when we are skeptical of the supernatural, but are momentarily challenged to reconsider that skepticism. It names the condition felt by an unbeliever when he or she suddenly doubts that unbelief. This is not the same as a return to belief – rather it is an arrival at an ambivalent kind of belief, one that is hesitant or perhaps embarrassed, and which contains within it the suspicion of its own baselessness.

This return from skepticism not only captures the experience of Lady Macbeth, but the play itself is uncanny in that, in Freud's words, "the distinction between imagination and reality is effaced."[32] It regularly asks the audience to think through the very issue that Macbeth and Lady Macbeth worry when they consider the dagger, the owls, or Banquo's ghost. This is the conscience that *Macbeth* stages, not simply a faculty that is experienced in the enchanted terms of *knowing with*, but one that is felt as an uncanny return of *knowing with* after such superstition has been surmounted.

Such a conscience anticipates the disenchantment of *knowing with* by such figures as Cherbury and Hobbes. And it is also a familiar modern experience, in particular forming one of Freud's main examples of the uncanny. Discussing the idea of the double, Freud cites conscience as a central form of the uncanny in the modern world:

> The idea of the "double" does not necessarily disappear with the passing of primary narcissism, for it can receive fresh meaning from the later stages of

---

[30] *Ibid.*, 17:240.
[31] *Ibid.*, 17:247–8.
[32] *Ibid.*, 17:244.

the ego's development. A special agency is slowly formed there, which is able to stand over against the rest of the ego, which has the function of observing and criticizing the self and of exercising censorship within the mind, and which we become aware of as our 'conscience.'[33]

The process of gazing critically back upon oneself so closely resembles the supernatural dynamics of the double that conscience becomes a place in which surmounted animism commonly returns. Conscience thrusts the modern mind back into the older superstitious forms. The double, which is the scene of *knowing with*, returns despite disenchantment. And so it returns tinged with the sense of the uncanny.

The essay on the uncanny is written four years before *The Ego and the Id* (1923), in which Freud begins to develop his most complete understanding of the conscience as a key part of the ego ideal or super-ego.[34] Freud's detailed structure of ego, id, and super-ego allows him to theorize a discrete faculty that is capable of turning back on itself in order to observe and judge: "As a child grows up, the role of father is carried on by teachers and others in authority; their injunctions and prohibitions remain powerful in the ego ideal and continue, in the form of conscience, to exercise the moral censorship."[35] The formation of conscience is explained as an internalization of external prohibitions, a process that takes place through the ego identifying with abandoned cathexes of the id, particularly the renunciation of Oedipal desires – a far more rationalized and structured story than the uncanny appearance of a double. But when Freud says these early ego identifications "always behave as a special agency in the ego and stand apart from the ego in the form of a super ego," it becomes clear that his thinking is continuous with the essay on the uncanny, in which he says "A special agency is slowly formed there, which is able to stand over against the rest of the ego."[36] Conscience is eventually submitted to a full rationalization in *The Ego and the Id* and *Civilization and its Discontents*, but in "The Uncanny" Freud is still pondering the strangeness of a faculty that seems to function in the old,

[33] *Ibid.*, 17:235.

[34] The role of the super-ego in explaining guilt and conscience is then most fully developed in *Civilization and Its Discontents*, chapters 7 and 8. *Ibid.*, 21:123–45.

[35] *Ibid.*, 19:37. Similarly, in *Civilization and its Discontents*: "A great change takes place only when the authority is internalized through the establishment of a super-ego. The phenomena of conscience then reach a higher stage. Actually, it is not until now that we should speak of conscience or a sense of guilt." *Ibid.*, 21:125.

[36] *Ibid.*, 19:48.

surmounted terms of animism.[37] The uncanny marks the strange, reluctant sense that superstition may still be explanatory. Some more rational explanation is surely out there, but for the moment the older way of thinking prevails.

The same striving for explanation that we see in Freud's modern theorization of conscience, and a similar sense of the uncanny, is legible in the passage that is at the center of this book's larger argument, the self-reflective conscience of Perkins:

> For there must be two actions of the understanding, the one is simple, which barely conceiveth or thinketh this or that: the other is a reflecting or doubling of the former, whereby a man conceives and thinkes with himselfe what he thinks. And this action properly pertaines to the conscience. The minde thinks a thought, now conscience goes beyond the minde, and knowes what the minde thinks: so as if a man would go about to hide his sinnefull thoughts from God, his conscience as an other person within him, shall discover all. By meanes of this second action conscience may beare witnes even of thoughts, and from hence also it seemes to borrow his name, because conscience is a science or knowledge ioyned with an other knowledge: for by it I conceive and know what I know.
>
> (*DC*, 6–7)[38]

In this expansion of *knowing with*, God hovers behind the faculty as the real witness who shares knowledge. But at the same time, conscience is a "doubling" of thought within the self, and becomes "as an other person within him." The double does not supplant God, since the force of "as" is to cast the "other person" as a figure of speech or possibly a dramatic role. In other words, Perkins acknowledges his ambivalence about this way of conceiving of the faculty. But even if it is simultaneously marked as a surmounted idea, Perkins's double acts with palpable energy and effectiveness. It does the key work of bearing witness, and it

---

[37] Freud observes, "The fact that an agency of this kind exists, which is able to treat the rest of the ego like an object – the fact, that is, that man is capable of self-observation – renders it possible to invest the old idea of a 'double' with a new meaning and to ascribe a number of things to it – above all, those things which seem to self-criticism to belong to the old surmounted narcissism of earliest times." *Ibid.*, 17:235.

[38] Thomas Merrill's edition of Perkins records a textual variant on the key word "doubling," providing "doubting" in its place. Perkins, *William Perkins 1558–1602*, 7. But "doubling" fits the sense of the passage better, and has a more authoritative provenance. The only edition of *Discourse of Conscience* published in Perkins's lifetime has "doubling," *DC*, 7. "Doubling" also appears in the first editions of the *Works*: (1603), 620; (1605), 620. "Doubting" enters into the next *Works* (1609), 511, and appears in collections thereafter.

embodies the etymology of *knowing with*, creating a scene of conscience as a dynamic space of shared knowledge.

As early modern England attempts to capture the scene of conscience, to describe what the experience is like, there is often a strain of embarrassment at the effort. The scene of *knowing with* feels superstitious or not really descriptive, and it creates an ambivalence which is difficult to locate in the topography of the early modern mind. Freud would call this ambivalence the uncanny, and would locate its origin in the unconscious.[39] Arguably, the uncanny can also be discerned in most of the literary scenes of conscience so far examined. It can be found as Launcelot Gobbo debates with a comically archaic personification of conscience. It is palpable as Richard investigates his own relationship to conscience: "What do I fear? Myself? There's none else by./ Richard loves Richard, that is, I am I." It is in the surprising emergence of conscience in the robot, Talus, as if he were a creation of E. T. A. Hoffman, and in the fevered imagination that often lies between melancholy and the despairing conscience. As the Protestant conscience is disengaged from scholastic structures, rationalism simultaneously beckons, with its enlightened and skeptical world view. As a result, theorists and poets capture an experience that both acknowledges the persuasiveness of modernity and feels the uncanny return to older structures.

An uncanny conscience implies the modern topography of the unconscious mind in Shakespeare and early modern thought, which may seem anachronistic. But the concept of the uncanny is useful to this study not because it supplies us with precise psychological structures – relative to Freud's later work on conscience, the uncanny hardly offers precision – but because it begins to capture a certain kind of inwardness that is central to the early modern conscience. The uncanny shows how the energies of early modern disenchantment are congruent with the energies that circulate in the topography of the unconscious mind, with conscience negotiating between earlier enchanted structures and modern psychological structures. That these energies characterize the early modern conscience makes sense if we recall that conscience in the period is simultaneously consciousness, and that it is bound up with emerging subjectivity.

Indeed, Judith Butler has argued in *The Psychic Life of Power* that subjectivity and the topography of the unconscious are themselves formed in alignment with the self-reflective conscience. Meditating on power and

---

[39] A key impetus to Freud's theorization of the super-ego in *The Ego and the Id* is the observation that conscience seems to work partly in the unconscious mind. *The Standard Edition*, 19:26–7.

subjectivity in Hegel, Nietzsche, Freud, and Althusser, Butler identifies a reflexive turn in the form of self-consciousness, self-reproach, and bad conscience. This turn functions as a "tropological inauguration of the subject," so that subjectivity, and the unconscious with it, emerge within the self-reflective conscience.[40] Butler's argument builds on Nietzsche's, that bad conscience is an internalization of external prohibitions, an understanding also central to Freud, as well as Foucault.[41] To this story, Butler adds the observation that this very internalization is what creates the subject, so that the reflexive subject is "understood paradoxically not merely as the subordination of a subject to a norm, but as the constitution of a subject through precisely such a subordination."[42] The internalization of prohibition is not simply the subject turning on itself, because before that internalization there was no subject to make a turn. Conscience, according to Butler, is simultaneously subjection to external power and the creation of an autonomous subject. This is accompanied by a repression of the state of subjection, so that the autonomous subject is also now the modern possessor of an unconscious: "If the effect of autonomy is conditioned by subordination and that founding subordination or dependency is rigorously repressed, the subject emerges in tandem with the unconscious."[43]

In a discussion of Althusser, Butler shows how the subject, hailed by a policeman, internalizing guilt as he or she turns, is actually brought into being as a subject. This process is conscience:

> Conscience cannot be conceptualized as a self-restriction, if that relation is construed as a pregiven reflexivity, a turning back upon itself performed by a ready-made subject. Instead, it designates a kind of turning back – a reflexivity which constitutes the condition of possibility for the subject to form. Reflexivity is constituted through this moment of conscience, this turning back upon oneself, which is simultaneous with a turning toward the law. This self-restriction does not internalize an external law: the model of internalization takes for granted that an "internal" and "external" have already been formed. Instead, this self-restriction is prior to the subject. It constitutes the inaugurating reflexive turn of the subject.[44]

---

[40] Butler, *The Psychic Life of Power*, 3.

[41] See Nietzsche, *On the Genealogy of Morals*, 84–91. The conscience as an inward colonization of power is at the center of Foucault's description of the state as a new form of pastoral power: "this form of power cannot be exercised without knowing the insides of people's mind, without exploring their souls, without making them reveal their innermost secrets. It implies a knowledge of the conscience and an ability to direct it." "The Subject and Power," 214.

[42] Butler, *The Psychic Life of Power*, 66.

[43] *Ibid.*, 7.

[44] *Ibid.*, 114–5.

Butler's chapter on Althusser is titled "Conscience Doth Make Subjects of Us All." Although she does not discuss *Hamlet*, and her book does not extend its argument prior to Hegel, Butler insightfully calls out this key passage of early modern conscience. Hamlet's third soliloquy, steeped in self-consciousness, conscience, and emerging subjectivity, could well be advanced to support her argument. Even more clearly, Perkins's reflexive conscience matches with Butler's focus on the productive self-reflection of the conscience. For Butler, "Conscience is the means by which a subject becomes an object for itself, reflecting on itself, establish itself as reflective and reflexive."[45] For Perkins, conscience is "a reflecting or doubling of the former, whereby a man conceives and thinkes with himselfe what he thinks." In Butler's argument, the self-reflective turn, in which the ego is perceived as an object in the world, is precisely what creates the topography of the modern subject, with its space of inwardness and with the unconscious.[46] A similar construction of spatiality can be discerned in Perkins, when "The minde thinks a thought, now conscience goes beyond the minde, and knowes what the minde thinks." Going beyond in order to turn back on itself, Perkins's conscience creates a topography of inwardness in the very way that Butler describes in modernity.

The destructured Protestant conscience clearly anticipates the dynamics that Butler locates in modern theorists. Perkins's self-reflective conscience emerges in the absence of the *synderesis* and its structural functioning. Similarly, the theorists of conscience seek to capture the workings of the faculty in order to further the authority of the private conscience over the authority of confessors. Following Butler's analysis, we may speculate that the early modern conscience internalizes these external forms of power – *synderesis*, confessor – making them part of itself, and therefore becoming self-reflective. But in performing this turn, it also sublimates the external power, and so produces the unconscious and subjectivity. My argument has been that *knowing with* is an early modern location for this turn. Usefully, it is a scene closer to the intellectual and theological world of early modernity than Althusser's scene of hailing. Rather than the police and law, power takes the form of the

---

[45] *Ibid.*, 22.

[46] "The 'turn' that marks the melancholic response to loss appears to initiate the redoubling of the ego as an object; only by turning back on itself does the ego acquire the status of a perceptual object . . . . The ego itself is produced as a *psychic object*; in fact, the very articulation of this psychic space, sometimes figured as 'internal' depends on this melancholic turn." *Ibid.*, 168.

divine, and of the enchanted moral universe authorized by divinity, as the reflexive conscience produces a modern subject.[47]

By staging the experience of conscience as *knowing with*, Act 2 Scene 2 maps an animist world saturated with external powers. The moralized universe promises that each human action, and each object or sight or sound, communicates with a greater divine justice, casting the Macbeths into a world of powerful external prohibitions. Then Act 5 relocates that power within Lady Macbeth, as the energetic functioning of her conscience. This is not a mere internalization of prohibition, as Nietzsche describes – Lady Macbeth does not become a saint or an ascetic. Rather, she becomes a subject in Butler's sense, and so becomes capable of experiencing conscience within the unconscious dynamics of dream-work. As she sees and smells blood on her own hands, Lady Macbeth's iconic moment of conscience is crackling with the power and energy that circulated in the external prohibitions of Act 2 Scene 2. This dynamic network of power has been internalized as a reflexive and energetic individual conscience.

Gunpowder

It is the political energy of such a conscience that I would emphasize in concluding this chapter. When *Macbeth* is read as a play about conscience, it is usually for its connection to one of the greatest challenges to political authority in the period, the Gunpowder Plot.[48] Among the plotters was the Jesuit Henry Garnett, who was tried and executed in the same year as *Macbeth* was probably staged. The sensational trial revealed Garnett's authorship of *A Treatise of Equivocation*, which uses the casuistic tradition of equivocation, or amphibology, to justify rebellion.[49] It is Garnett whom the Porter seems to call out as the "equivocator, that could swear in both the scales against either scale, who committed treason enough for God's sake, yet could not equivocate to heaven" (II.iii.8–11).

---

[47] Anthony Cascardi argues that subjectivity and self-consciousness develop within disenchantment, as products of the struggle between reason and enchantment: "Although the subject may be seen as empowered to gain distance from and to master a natural world rendered correspondingly 'disenchanted' or 'desouled,' the goal of reason must consist in the avoidance of a 'fall' out of consciousness back into enchantment." *The Subject of Modernity*, 55.

[48] Huntley, "Macbeth and the Background of Jesuitical Equivocation"; Wills, *Witches and Jesuits*, 93–105; Mullaney, *The Place of the Stage*, 116–34. Also see Frank Kermode's introduction to *Macbeth* in *The Riverside Shakespeare*, 1356–7, and Stephen Greenblatt's introduction in *The Norton Shakespeare*, 2569–70.

[49] See Sommerville, "'The New Art of Lying'"; Zagorin, *Ways of Lying*, 153–220.

From within the excessively inward experience of conscience in Act 2 Scene 2, the knocking suddenly reveals a public perspective, acting as a reminder that private conscience can also exert a profound influence on the public spheres of justice and politics.

Garnett's techniques provide a way of controlling conscience, so as to enable individuals to avoid the power of the state. The title page of his treatise promises to make a false oath conscientious:

> Whether a Catholicke or any other person before a magistrate beyng demaunded uppon his oath whether a Prieste were in such a place, may (notwithstanding his perfect knowledge to the contrary) without Periury and securely in conscience answere, No, with this secreat meaning reserved in his mynde, That he was not there so that any man is bounde to detect it.[50]

Just as conscience connects the individual's knowledge to God, so an oath shares this knowledge outwardly, with the court or the magistrate – through the oath, the scene of *knowing with* expands to include the public sphere of law and politics.[51] But scandalously, Garnet disconnects this public circuit of knowledge. One technique, mental reservation, involves intentionally not vocalizing key details to the interrogator. This creates two very distinct meanings, and segregates them between public utterance and the internal voice of the conscience. For example, "whan beyng demaunded whether John at Style be in such a place, I knowinge that he is there in deede, do say neverthelesse 'I know not,' – reserving or understanding within myselfe these other wordes (to th'end for to tell you)."[52] God shares an inward knowledge, but this truth is not for the court or magistrate. Similarly, the technique of equivocation depends upon a linguistic situation in which not everyone shares in the meaning. So if I am asked whether a stranger is lodging in my house, according to Garnett I could answer: "'he lyeth not in my howse,' meaning that he doth not tell a lye there, althoughe he lodge there."[53] A pun splits the sentence into two different assertions, making the truth accessible only in the inward scene of *knowing with* between speaker and God. But this is enough: as priests hiding from the law by mental reservation or equivocation, "we hope we may declare the innocency of our conscience."[54]

---

[50] Garnett, *A Treatise of Equivocation*, title page. The treatise itself went unpublished until the nineteenth century, but is referred to and summarized in the trial. Anon., *A True and Perfect Relation*, H4v-I3r. Also see Parsons, *A Treatise Tending to Mitigation*.

[51] See *New Catholic Encyclopedia*, s.v. "Oaths," X:496; Gray, *Oaths and the English Reformation*.

[52] Garnett, *A Treatise of Equivocation*, 9.

[53] *Ibid.*, 49.

[54] *Ibid.*, 83.

What Garnett's casuistry offers is a technology for manipulating the scene of *knowing with*. At the trial, Attorney General Edward Coke repeatedly expresses outrage that Jesuit priests absolved the conspirators: equivocation and mental reservation undermine the state and its machinery as surely as does gunpowder.[55] So the Porter insists on the folly of such a technology. The equivocator "could swear in both the scales against either scale . . . yet could not equivocate to heaven." That is, he could attempt to finesse his oath so that it says two things at once, weighing on both scales of justice – but still God knows the truth. As *Macbeth* makes clear, Garnett's kind of control is inimical to the Protestant conscience, and doomed to fail. Increasingly destructured, the reformed faculty resists human efforts to master it. When the Porter breaks in on the echo chamber of Act 2 Scene 2, the dynamism of the Protestant conscience, even as it tilts toward the troubled imaginary of despair and melancholy, or the unstable self-reflection of consciousness, has the virtue of resisting any efforts to control it. It will out.

A destructured conscience that breaks into the public sphere offers a defense against political machinations, protecting the Jacobean state from its perceived Jesuit enemies. But we can observe that the destructured conscience, by breaking into the public sphere, also creates a politics infused with conscience. What happens in the private conscience may also happen in public politics. The faculty becomes the now-visible point of contact between the individual's inward experience and the public sphere.

In this light, as conscience shapes the early modern subject, it is also shaping a political subject. Judith Butler describes a relay of power that leads to the formation of subjectivity: "The power that initiates the subject fails to remain continuous with the power that is the subject's agency. A significant and potentially enabling reversal occurs when power shifts from its status as a condition of agency to the subject's 'own' agency."[56] Similarly, in the uncanny space of a disenchanting conscience, the energies of *knowing with* undergo an enabling reversal. Skepticism breaks off the power of the moralized universe and establishes the solipsism of *knowing with* oneself. Self-reflection, meanwhile, creates a space in which power can be contained within the subject. The power which was previously part of the moralized universe now becomes the possession of this conscientious subject. What results is a conscientious subject with the features of possessive individualism, owning its own power to act.

A self-possessed subject is capable of the basic liberal voluntarist position, giving consent to contract and political obligation.[57] It also has the potential for ideological agency. After all, Althusser's basic argument is that subjectivity is bound to ideology, the one calling forth the other, so that subjectivity is the condition of ideological being. As conscience binds with subjectivity, it also therefore binds with the possibility of personal ideology, making it the means by which individual judgments enter into the public sphere. Conscience creates a subject that is set up for an active and ideological politics. This is something like what Michael Walzer describes as the achievement of the saints who first "constructed a theoretical justification for independent political action," heralding "a new integration of private men . . . into the political order, an integration based on a novel view of politics as a kind of conscientious and continuous labor."[58] The individual becomes a conscientious actor in the public sphere; in its most revolutionary expressions, conscience gives sovereignty to the individual.

This political subject, conscientious and ideologically energetic, is the focus of the second half of this book, as the argument turns from the inward scene of conscience to the public sphere, and to the lead role that conscience plays in the politics of mid-century England. This can be persuasively told as a progressive story of the emerging liberal subject, autonomous and rational. As *Macbeth* warns us, however, the conscientious subject appears with an unconscious. It carries with it the uncanny remains of its formation, an inward scene of *knowing with* that is not fully surmounted. The conscientious subject cannot simply be the thin subject of liberal contract, but also must be thick with the complexities of *knowing with* and self-reflection, as well as salvation and despair. It forms a possessive individual, but one who is also still possessed by pre-secular origins. This ambivalence becomes legible in the seventeenth century's public discourses of conscience. As the destructured and uncanny conscience becomes public, as the next chapter shows, it flows into two very opposite discursive streams, a casuistry that frames the faculty as rational and communicable, and an antinomianism that conceives of conscience as inspiration. Recognizing both streams will allow us to register the complexity and energy of conscience's entrance into the public sphere of politics.

[57] Macpherson, *The Political Theory of Possessive Individualism*, 3.
[58] Walzer, *The Revolution of the Saints*, 2.

4

Casuistry and Antinomianism

Herbert's "Conscience"

As the first half of this book has studied the inward experience of conscience, a key question has been how that scene translates to action –
how it has looked for individuals such as Hamlet or Talus or Macbeth
to act in the external world. Here a continuing line of inquiry will map
these dynamics onto the more collective space of discourse: how do the
inward conceptions of private conscience become the external conceptions of public conscience? This discursive inquiry is elicited by the way
that, moving into the Caroline decades, the reflexive and private conscience spills out into the public sphere, mattering more than ever as a
way to think through political and ideological claims. The destructured
conscience remains a determinate force in the middle seventeenth century, but it is translated into the discourses of public expression.

Such a translation, from Protestant inwardness to the external Caroline
world, happens to be one of the legacies of George Herbert's poetry.
From the moment *The Temple* offered Herbert's "private ejaculations" in
publication, this most intimate of early modern verse has called forth
a concerted effort to associate it with public discourses. Isaak Walton
influentially portrayed Herbert in High Anglican terms.[1] But Royalists
and several kinds of Puritans could also claim him.[2] Modern criticism
has hunted for Herbert's public affiliations, and has located him in nearly
every part of the theological-political spectrum.[3] It is no doubt a product
of Herbert's limber and experimental thinking that he can be aligned
with such a variety of ideologies. But it also reflects an imperative of

---

[1] "It was hardly to Walton's purpose to remind his readers that George Herbert's oldest brother,
Edward, Lord Herbert of Cherbury, although 'a man of great learning and reason,' was also notori-
ously unorthodox." Summers, *George Herbert*, 28.
[2] Hutchinson, *The Works of George Herbert*, xliii–xliv.
[3] Veith, "The Religious Wars in George Herbert Criticism."

the historical moment: there is a need to think through how the strong dynamics of Protestant inwardness play out in the increasingly turbulent and consequential public realm. Herbert is a useful touchstone for such an inquiry, a place in which to ask how the reflexive conscience translates to public discourse.

A number of Herbert's best-known poems feel their way from private experience to a more communal scene of shared communication. Often, for instance, the poet's inward ruminations are interrupted by another voice, a "friend" or, as is often thought, God or Jesus, turning the poem into dialogue, e.g. "The Collar," "Redemption," "Jordan (II)," and "The Pilgrimage." In each of these the turn to dialogue feels welcome, tending to solve the poet's difficulties. But something very different happens when Herbert explicitly portrays conscience. In "Conscience," the poet's whole goal is to silence his interlocutor, whom he derides as a "Pratler." This poem captures the familiar Protestant experience of a wounded conscience, and like *Macbeth* it struggles with an uncanny scene of *knowing with*.

Herbert's Conscience has a voice and is nearly a personification. But it is puerile and annoying:

> Peace pratler, do not lowre:
> Not a fair look, but thou dost call it foul:
> Not a sweet dish, but thou dost call it sowre:
> Musick to thee doth howl.
> By listning to thy chatting fears
> I have both lost mine eyes and eares.
>
> (ll 1–6)[4]

Hardly soothing, the voice of conscience makes things foul and sour. Its prattling and chatting fill the poet's mental experience with uncontrolled racket. So he begs for an end to this echoing chamber:

> Pratler, no more, I say:
> My thoughts must work, but like a noiselesse sphere;
> Harmonious peace must rock them all the day:
> No room for pratlers there.
>
> (ll 7–10)

The remarkable image of the mind working "like a noiselesse sphere" gives shape to a private place outside of *knowing with*. Conscience is imagined as a mental experience that cannot be captured by sound or language. The

---

[4] All quotations are from Helen Wilcox's edition, *The English Poems*.

same thing happens in "Windows," where Herbert suggests that a properly functioning conscience has little to do with the momentary extension of the spoken word: "but speech alone/ Doth vanish like a flaring thing,/ And in the eare, not conscience ring" (ll 13–15). Here conscience not only escapes prattling, but resists organization by the senses, pushing into abstraction. What will "ring" in the conscience is something that occurs in the glass of a window; how the conscience will "work" is like the perfectly abstract geometry of a sphere. This kind of abstraction looks very like the disenchanted conscience theorized by the poet's brother, Edward, Lord Herbert of Cherbury, who strips away the scene of *knowing with* by theorizing a conscience that works by "conformity" and "analogy" rather than voices or visions.[5] The abstract and geometric image of the "noiselesse sphere" is for Helen Vendler "the quintessence of Herbert at his best."[6]

But in "Conscience" this quintessence is only glimpsed, never attained. Instead, the poem returns in the final stanzas to the noise and bluster of *knowing with*. The poet strives to attain the noiseless sphere by controlling and silencing the voice of conscience. To that end he tastes his savior's blood "at his board," i.e. Communion, and at first the "physick" seems successful, leaving Conscience "not a word;/ No, not a tooth or nail to scratch,/ And at my actions carp, or catch" (16–18). But then it turns out that the sacrament does not work, so that the poem ends with the poet still trying to quiet prattling conscience:

> Yet if thou talkest still,
> Besides my physick, know there's some for thee:
> Some wood and nails to make a staffe or bill
> For those that trouble me:
> The bloudie crosse of my deare Lord
> Is both my physick and my sword.
> (ll 19–24)

---

[5] Herbert and his elder brother differ on many religious fundamentals, so critics have generally read them in opposition. But it is hard to imagine that Cherbury's notorious and challenging views had no influence on his brother. Religious skepticism often infiltrates the poetry of *The Temple* – as a thought experiment it works quite well to imagine the free-thinking speaker of "The Collar" as Cherbury. Intriguingly, *The Temple* and *De Veritate* each were almost dedicated to the other's author: an early manuscript of *De Veritate* is dedicated to George Herbert, while a draft of Nicholas Ferrar's preface to *The Temple* seems to have included a dedication to Cherbury. Hutchesen, "Critical Discussion" in Herbert, *Lord Herbert of Cherbury's De Religione Laici*, 20; Doerksen, "Nicholas Ferrar," 24–6. On the brothers' relationship, see Held, "Brother Poets"; John Drury has recently argued for similarities in several matters of temperament and theology, including an emphasis on introspection and natural revelation. *Music at Midnight*, 103–9.

[6] Vendler, *The Poetry of George Herbert*, 236.

The voice of conscience continues its childish prattling, and the poet chastises too much and without effect, sounding like a frustrated parent. At the poem's end the prattler is not successfully disciplined, but is rather joined by the poet in bluster and noise: even as he says he wants quiet, the poet impatiently threatens ("there's some for thee"), and tries to cow the prattler with an excess of wood, nails, staffe, bill, blood, cross, and sword. *Knowing with* is not an impressive experience, but, as with Launcelot Gobbo's personification, begins to feel parodied. The rational image of the "noiselesse sphere" has surmounted the primitive or childish conscience, but uncannily *knowing with* returns, fitting in with Herbert's habit of combining intense belief with an archly skeptical demeanor, what T. S. Eliot has described as simultaneous sincerity and insincerity.[7]

How to place this challenging inward scene of conscience in the broader public discourses of Herbert's period? Camille Wells Slights makes an influential argument for reading the whole of *The Temple* as engaged in the habits and techniques of seventeenth-century casuistry. She shows the poems stressing practical cases, demonstrating problem solving through logic and reason, and entertaining doubts but ultimately securing obedience.[8] And she reads "Conscience" as exemplary of Herbert's casuistry in that it "diagnoses" an over-scrupulous conscience, and turns to the sacrament and the mysteries of faith in order to contain the unruly voice of conscience.[9] In this reading the poet's voice becomes infused with the calm reason of a spiritual advisor guiding the consciences of his flock. This matches Herbert's tendency in *The Temple* toward an intimate pastoralism, as well as his overt commitment to casuistry in *The Priest to the Temple*, where he asserts that the country parson "greatly esteemes also of cases of conscience, wherein he is much versed. And indeed, herein is the greatest ability of a Parson to lead his people exactly in the wayes of Truth."[10]

However, this casuistic reading of "Conscience" may seem overly sanguine about the poet's ability to "recover health" and quiet the prattling faculty. After all, the sacrament does not enact a cure, and the poet himself descends into the noisy childishness of the Pratler. The imperfect

[7] Eliot sees this ambivalence as a hallmark of Herbert's poetry: "The greater the elevation, the finer becomes the difference between sincerity and insincerity, between the reality and the unattained aspiration. And in this George Herbert seems to me to be as secure, as habitually sure, as any poet who has written in English." Eliot, "George Herbert," 334.
[8] Slights, *The Casuistical Tradition*, 183–246.
[9] *Ibid.*, 197–8.
[10] Herbert, *The Complete English Works*, 202.

ending, and its disconcerting violence, suggest that the poem does not conform to what Slights calls "the casuistical paradigm of transforming confusion to clarity through understanding."[11] It is less about calm reason and obedience than it is about the insistent and harsh assertions of a conscience that resists the technologies of control.

Paying more attention to this tone, Sidney Gottlieb reads "Conscience" in a quite opposite context, as an engagement with radical Puritanism. The prattler, he argues, represents a Puritan preacher, a "nonconforming, radical Protestant, a danger not only to one's peace of mind but also to one's church and society."[12] The poet is still trying to contain a too-loud conscience, only instead of the public discourse of casuistry, the inward scene of *knowing with* is mapped onto the discourse of the Puritan pulpit. Gottlieb does not specify which Puritans Herbert is satirizing, but Daniel Doerksen has argued for a larger affinity with Richard Sibbes, and Nigel Smith has spotted the poem "Conscience" used in later antinomian polemic.[13] These readings reflect an important development: in the 1630s and 1640s, conscience is increasingly discussed by Puritans in the public discourses of pulpit and print shop. Particularly among the Calvinist and Puritan preachers whom William Haller has called the "fraternity of spiritual preachers," conscience is frequently invoked, and made central to the elect's claims for inspiration, and for a political ideology full of what Gottlieb describes as "urgency, anger and militancy."[14]

That "Conscience" can be read as engaged with casuistry or as engaged with radical Puritanism sheds important light on the way that the faculty was entering into the public sphere. In the decades leading up to the civil war, as conscience becomes an increasingly important political force, the inwardness of its theological functioning shifts toward the external events and discourses of politics. The shift happens in two quite divergent streams: through the rational and practical divinity of casuistry, and through the inspired, often antinomian, claims of the radical Puritans. Just as both discourses can be persuasively read onto Herbert's "Conscience," so both are common terms in which conscience was understood as it entered into seventeenth-century politics. These two streams, antinomianism and casuistry, will be the subjects of this chapter.

---

[11] Slights, *The Casuistical Tradition*, 238.

[12] Gottlieb, "Herbert's Case of 'Conscience,'" 113–14.

[13] Doerksen, "Show and Tell"; Smith, "George Herbert in Defence of Antinomianism." Elizabeth Clarke discusses Herbert's nearness to, but suspicion of, antinomianism, *Theory and Theology*, 179–223.

[14] Haller, *The Rise of Puritanism*, 64. On the entire Puritan circle, see 49–82. Gottlieb, "Herbert's Case of 'Conscience,'" 114.

Casuistry

Critical accounts of the early modern conscience have tended to focus on casuistry. This has been an important project, which has recaptured the intellectual complexity of casuistry in the face of its dismissal by figures such as Pascal and Alexander Pope. The scholarship has come from many fields, including studies in ethics, such as Jonsen and Toulmin's, historical collections such as Braun and Vallance's, philosophical approaches such as that of Leites, and an array of theological investigations, such as those of Keenan and Shannon, Wood, and McAdoo.[15] Literary criticism has seen a number of books on conscience as casuistry, such as those by Slights, John Wilks, Lowell Gallagher, Meg Lota Brown, and Ceri Sullivan.[16]

The dominance of a casuistical conscience in our critical understanding is not surprising, given the numerous works that early modern England produced, by Jeremy Taylor, Robert Sanderson, Henry Hammond, William Ames, and William Perkins, among others.[17] Moreover, the English casuists make a show of their efforts, drawing attention to the project of a Protestant casuistry, as when Taylor begins *Ductor Dubitantium* by lamenting that in the Reformed churches "though in all things else the Goodness of God hath made us to abound, and our Cup to run over; yet our labours have been hitherto unimploied in the description of the Rules of Conscience and Casuistical Theology."[18] The anxiety for a Protestant casuistry reflects competition with Rome, with its extensive casuistic tradition. But it also issues from the challenge of reinventing the practice in order to meet the needs of reformed religion. Having abandoned private confession, and suspicious of works, Protestant casuistry focuses less on the fine details of sacraments and penance than is found in the Catholic tradition.[19] There is also resistance to the Catholic reliance on Church authorities to solve cases, which often takes the form of rejecting

---

[15] Jonsen and Toulmin, *The Abuse of Casuistry*. Braun and Vallance, eds., *Contexts of Conscience*. Leites, ed., *Conscience and Casuistry*. Keenan and Shannon, eds., *The Context of Casuistry*. Wood, *English Casuistical Divinity*. McAdoo, *The Structure of Caroline Moral Theology*.

[16] Slights, *The Casuistical Tradition*. Wilks, *The Idea of Conscience*. Gallagher, *Medusa's Gaze*. Brown, *Donne and the Politics of Conscience*. Sullivan, *The Rhetoric of the Conscience*.

[17] Taylor, *Ductor Dubitantium*. Sanderson, *De Obligatione Conscientiae*. Sanderson was translated by Robert Codrington in *Several Cases of Conscience*. Hammond, *Of Conscience*. Ames, *CPC*. Perkins, *The Whole Treatise*.

[18] Taylor, *Ductor Dubitantium*, "Epistle Dedicatory." For similar pronouncements see *CPC* "To the Reader," and Thomas Pickering's letter to the reader in Perkins, *Whole Treatise*.

[19] "The more typical works of seventeenth-century casuistical divinity are elaborate discussions of general principles, with particular cases introduced mainly by way of illustration and not as of first importance." Wood, *English Casuistical Divinity*, 49.

Probabilism, and thrusts scripturalism and reason forward as better means of resolution.[20] These are basic Protestant principles, which make the very deliberate project of improving upon Catholic casuistry appear as an essential movement in seventeenth-century England.

But we should not make the mistake of thinking that the discourse of conscience is identical to the discourse of casuistry. By insisting on two streams of conscience, casuistic and antinomian, this chapter takes issue with a valorization of casuistry that has read conscience too narrowly. The problem is, when our picture is dominated by casuistry we run the risk of missing the early modern conscience's more theoretical manifestations. Casuistry's purpose is to locate conscience in the practical world, bending it toward the practical conclusions of cases. In so doing, it tends to organize and contain the increasingly private and inchoate energies that we have seen emerging from the theorists of conscience. If this study has so far highlighted a dynamic of destructuring within Protestant theorists, then the subsequent Protestant casuistry can be seen as a turn back toward structure. Under the demand for practical applications, destructuring becomes restructuring. This restructuring has the important effect of allowing the faculty to be communicated. The Protestant conscience that would slip into an inchoate privacy is made communicable from one person to another, so that it can participate in the public discourse of practical casuistry.

Camille Wells Slights describes casuistry as a process in which "the self-conscious turning back of the mind on itself is united with a focus on specific, practical action."[21] The inchoate and inward dynamics of the self-reflective conscience are submitted to a set of real-world demands, with the imperative that they yield clear solutions and actions. The conscience that serves such a casuistic process must be conceived of in relatively organized terms, containing the destructuring that was a product of Luther's renovations. So William Ames, in a chapter titled "Of Conscience examining and reviewing actions" makes relatively little room for the scenes of inwardness that are typical of the theorists of conscience. While explaining the act of "reviewing" actions, Ames

---

[20] Taylor laments that Catholic casuistry relies on "canons and the Epistles of Popes for authentick warranties," and asserts that they must "rely only upon Scriptures and right Reason." *Ductor Dubitantium*, iv. On the matter of authority, see McAdoo, *The Structure of Caroline Moral Theology*, 79; Wood, *English Casuistical Divinity*, xviii. On probabilism, see Stone, "Scrupulosity and Conscience." Brown compares Catholic and Protestant casuistry, *Donne and the Politics of Conscience*, 24–34, 50–61.
[21] Slights, *The Casuistical Tradition*, xiv.

draws as near as he ever does to the kind of self-reflection that emerges in Perkins. But compared to Perkins, Ames is terse and minimally introspective: "This reviewing is a reflect act of the understanding, whereby a man understandeth, and with judgment, weigheth his own actions with their circumstances" (*CPC* I:17). There is no thinking about thought, or any sense of the complexity of mind. The experience of self-reflection is never developed, here or anywhere else in Ames's extensive work on conscience.

The reflexive and destructured conscience is contained in Ames by the very structure that the theorists had dismantled – by the bipartite structure of *conscientia* and *synderesis*. While Luther, Calvin, Woolton, Perkins, Hume, and others move the Protestant conscience away from *synderesis*, Ames very explicitly returns to it. Although Ames emphasizes his debt to Perkins, he immediately disagrees with his assertion that conscience is a power or faculty, insisting instead that it is an act (*CPC* I:2–3). This return to the scholastic categories marks a significant shift in the structure of conscience. As discussed in Chapter 1, when Perkins makes conscience a power rather than an act, he is elevating its importance as part of his rejection of *synderesis*. So when Ames defines conscience as an act, he is paving the way for a more fundamental departure from Perkins: in the next chapter, and as the entire subject of the chapter, Ames reinstates the scholastic concept of *synderesis*. The first chapter, "The definition of conscience" is followed by, "Of the synteresis or Principles and rules by which Conscience judgeth" (*CPC* I:2–6). Ames offers a typical definition of *synderesis* as the knowledge of what we should do or shun "still conserved in mans mind even after his fal." He then goes on to show how it offers the proposition for the syllogism that structures the judgments of conscience (*CPC* I:4). Once again conscience is submitted to the authority of *synderesis*, and to the rational and logical structure of syllogism.

The return to *synderesis* and syllogism is characteristic of nearly all Protestant casuistry. Robert Sanderson argues against those who would take conscience and *synderesis* as identical, and supplies a standard definition as "the habit of the first principles, about Good and Evill, from whence conclusions are deduced, out of which proceedeth Conscience."[22] In his description of conscience, Jeremy Taylor turns to Aquinas and *synderesis*, "or the general repository of moral principles or measures of good." And he then lays out a series of syllogisms, led by *synderesis*, which he calls "the Rule of conscience, or the first act of

[22] Sanderson, *Several Cases*, 15. Also see 30, 133.

conscience as it is a Rule and a Guide."²³ Robert A. Greene describes the disappearance of the term *synderesis*, tracing it as it descends into a satirized position as an "inkhorn" term, before disappearing entirely. But he is mistaken when he says that the last "serious and sustained subscription to the theory of synderesis" in English is in Christopher St. German's *Doctor and Student* – working against this clear path toward extinction, the Protestant casuists make one last, very serious, effort to attach *synderesis* to conscience.²⁴

Casuistry's turn to *synderesis* and syllogism surrounds the Protestant conscience with a rational structure. The casuistic stream of conscience, much more than the antinomian, accentuates reason and its role in forming judgments. Sanderson, for example, defines conscience as "a faculty, or a habit of the practical understanding, by which the mind of Man doth by the discourse of reason apply that light with which he is indued to his particular moral Actions."²⁵ The discursive and rational structures of *synderesis* and syllogism form a kind of exoskeleton of support around the Protestant conscience. So in Ames, the "reflect act of the understanding" is explicitly submitted to external rules and laws. Reflection becomes part of a "reviewing" of actions in which "The *actions* and the *rule* must be compared together," and "The rule of this triall or judgement, must not be our *naturall reason*, the *custome of others* or the like; but the *Law*, or *revealed* will of God" (*CPC* I:17–18).²⁶ Conscience is linked systematically to rule and law through the *synderesis*:

> This conclusion therefore dependeth partly on that generall Law, which is pronounced by the *Synteresis*, in the *major* Proposition; and partly, on that *Reviewing* of the action or condition which is contained in the *minor* Proposition. So that it gathereth together the strength of the former acts of Conscience, and maketh the judgement thereof perfect.
>
> (*CPC* I:19)

²³ Taylor, *Ductor Dubitantium*, I:9–11. Also see Fenner, *A Treatise of Conscience*, 44. Ames's brother-in-law, Phineas Fletcher, creates a personification "Synteresis" in *The Purple Island*, VI. 61–2, *Poetical Works*, II:82.

²⁴ Greene, "Synderesis, the Spark of Conscience," 208.

²⁵ Sanderson, *Several Cases*, 3. Regarding Jeremy Taylor, Robert Hoopes says that "pure reason and practical reason are reconciled in right conscience, which is to define right conscience as right reason in conduct," *Right Reason*, 167. Also see Wood, *English Casuistical Divinity*, 67; McAdoo, *The Structure of Caroline Moral Theology*, 66–9; Slights, *The Casuistical Tradition*, 56–9.

²⁶ L. John Van Til argues that the most important feature of Ames's conscience is that it is dialectical and bound up in logic, making it "not so much an internal function of the self as it was an external process regulated by a rational dialectic method." *Liberty of Conscience*, 57.

Supported by rules and the forward march of logic, Ames's conscience arrives at "perfect" judgments, which is to say complete and reliable conclusions to the particular case of conscience. The casuistic project of solving cases reshapes the Protestant conscience, embedding it in a discursive and orderly context of laws and rules.

A theorist of conscience such as Perkins, foregrounding Protestant faith, pictures the faculty bound up in matters of election, assurance, and despair. These cannot yield clear or finished solutions, but rather call forth a conscience that is necessarily incomplete and in process – that is more unfolding experience and inward reflection than a structured system with a fixed endpoint. But the casuist's attention to practical problems brings conscience into a process that can and should yield answers, or "perfect" judgments. Rather than the inchoate energies of thought about thought, Ames pictures an orderly review of rules. Rather than the recursive turnings of self-reflection, Ames's conscience unfolds in the bipartite structure of conscience and *synderesis*. And this conception of conscience allows Ames the casuist to deliver a long list of conclusions, covering an array of practical actions, from drunkenness, to whether confession is necessary, to manslaughter, to the duties of marriage (*CPC* III:78, IV:34, V:183, V:205).

Casuistry's turn to laws and rules is even more obvious in Jeremy Taylor. *Ductor Dubitantium* has as its subtitle "Or The Rule of Conscience," and each chapter is organized around a series of rules. Rule 1, of course, defines conscience as a faculty that operates by the dictates of rules and measures: "Conscience is the minde of a Man governed by a rule, and measured by the proportions of good and evil."[27] This sense of proportion and the ideal of governance by rule suggest how the casuistic conscience extends order and structure from the workings of the private conscience into the public sphere. Taylor is particularly wary of the way that conscience falls away from the rational adherence to rules, creating an unstable politics in the public arena:

> Nothing is more usual, then to pretend Conscience to all the actions of men which are publick, and whose nature cannot be concealed . . . Ask a Schismatick why he refuses to joyn in the Communion of the Church? He tels you, it is against his Conscience: And the disobedient refuse to submit to Laws; and they also in many cases pretend Conscience . . . And so Suspicion, and Jealousie, and Disobedience, and Rebellion are become conscience.[28]

---

[27] Taylor, *Ductor Dubitantium*, I:1.
[28] *Ibid.*, I:26–7.

When Taylor turns to human laws, his first Rule codifies the faculty's necessary political obedience: "The Conscience is properly and directly, actively and passively, under pains of sin and punishment, obliged to obey the Laws of men."[29]

Here casuistry discusses how the private conscience translates to public, political discourse. Just as importantly, casuistry serves as the very means by which conscience becomes public discourse. In the mode of casuistry, Taylor enumerates eight arguments against the subjection of conscience to human law. He then responds carefully to each, rejecting the claim central to the antinomian stream, that "To submit the conscience to any law or power of man, is to betray our Christian liberty."[30] Human laws bind the conscience, Taylor asserts, "not by vertue or formal energy of the civil power, but the authority and power of God."[31] Over the course of 430 pages, Taylor articulates multiple cases that arise around this issue, such as whether human law obliges conscience in public as well as secret, or whether laws oblige outside of the superior power's dominion. Taylor's case studies do not always arrive at absolute obligation. But even when the answers are multiple and ambiguous, the effect is to surround the individual conscience with a web of discursive and logical connections. Each case becomes a place in which the individual is tied to law and enmeshed in public discourse, so that casuistry itself becomes the occasion for the creation of political obligations.

As Slights shows when discussing the Engagement Controversy, casuistic analysis of the problem of allegiance to the Commonwealth often did not yield precise political positions, so much as it worked "to imitate the process by which man can reach right decisions, that is, to embody the mode of thinking it recommends."[32] This is to recognize a casuistic mode that extends beyond the manuals, to shape, as many critics have argued,

---

[29] *Ibid.*, III:3. Similarly, Sanderson asserts that "you cannot keep your Conscience upright, and safe, unlesse you be subjected; Therefore humane Laws do oblige the Conscience." *Several Cases*, 179. Hammond says there is a single rule for conscience, and "*law* is this only rule." *Of Conscience*, 8.

[30] Taylor, *Ductor Dubitantium*, III:4.

[31] *Ibid.*, III:16. The most common support for this position is Romans 13:5. *Ibid.*, III:7. William Fenner asserts a "secondary and relative" bond of conscience to the magistrate, which allows him to interpret Romans 13:5 as saying "The Apostle there speaketh of Magistrates; and he telleth us that their laws bind our consciences in relation to Gods, and therefore we must be subject unto them for conscience sake." *A Treatise of Conscience*, 267–9. Ames argues that only God can properly and immediately bind the conscience, "Yet nevertheless humane Lawes are to bee observed out of conscience towards God, Rom 13." *CPC*, II:167.

[32] Slights, *The Casuistical Tradition*, 52. Slights discusses Robert Sanderson's "The Case of the Engagement," which can be found in *Nine Cases of Conscience*. Also see Wallace, *Destiny His Choice*, 9–68.

how early modern England discussed and solved major issues of political authority. Lowell Gallagher, for example, describes "the dissemination of casuistry in the central legal and political documents of the Tudor government, and, finally, in the Anglican establishment."[33] Casuistry, moreover, asserted itself not just through arguments and ways of thinking, but through the practical act of swearing oaths. Justin Champion argues that "Political casuistry was one of the main ways central government was authorized: oaths of allegiance, oaths *ex officio*, and oaths of association, were tendered to the adult male population at moments of crisis and as commonplace reaffirmations of obligation."[34]

With its focus on reason and rule and law and obligation, casuistry tilts conservative. H. R. McAdoo points out that "Practically all the leading English moralists and casuists were bishops."[35] Indeed, Robert Sanderson was Bishop of Lincoln, Jeremy Taylor was Bishop of Down and Connor in the Irish church, and Joseph Hall of Norwich. Plus, many had close ties to the crown: Sanderson and Hammond both served as chaplains to Charles I; Taylor was a member of Charles's court in Oxford, and dedicates *Ductor Dubitantium* to Charles II. The key exception is William Ames, who was a leading Puritan voice and nonconformist. Ames, though, was in many ways a conservative Puritan, for example in his strong opposition to Arminius.

I would not want to lose the insight that casuistry is in some basic ways a conservative force – but a better description of this quality would be that Protestant casuistry tends toward communicability. The destructured conscience, with its reflexivity, remains private, in the sense that it cannot be told to others. It is not readily understood or analyzed as a complete faculty, as if from the outside. It is not easily described or located in language. And it asserts a closed kind of sovereignty over external powers and laws, resisting becoming enmeshed in political obligations and entering only uneasily into political discourse. In casuistry, on the other hand, conscience does not elude structure, but rather reasserts it. Supported by *synderesis*, the casuistic conscience becomes part of a larger discourse of logic and rules. It is therefore not understood as a self-enclosed, sovereign power, but is rather a power that functions within the practical and public worlds of case divinity and political obligation. Casuistry constructs a conscience that can be described and discussed

---

[33] Gallagher, *Medusa's Gaze*, 6.
[34] Champion, "Willing to Suffer," 18.
[35] McAdoo, *The Structure of Caroline Moral Theology*, 65.

between people, that can be part of the larger discursive network of laws and obligations, and so that can be communicated in the public world.

Accordingly, Slights's focus on casuistry leads her to relatively sanguine conclusions about how conscience makes itself felt in public. In her reading, Herbert "uses strategies of reasoned argument and self-analysis to resolve problems of moral doubt," and Hamlet is "a man of acute moral reason who resolves perplexing moral problems with rigor and discrimination," arriving at a perfect conscience; her assertion that "the casuistical paradigm pervades almost everything that Milton wrote" reveals Samson as a "hero of conscience" who in a redemptive ending experiences "rousing motions" that are a product both of "careful analysis" and Grace.[36] Ceri Sullivan, on the other hand, reads the period's lyric poetry quite differently, in that she sees Donne, Herbert, and Vaughn as departing from the communicability of casuistry. While Sullivan describes casuistry as syllogistic and legalistic, she sees in the poets a turn to "extreme tropes of failed communication."[37] Different from the logic and order of casuistry, conscience in lyric is an experience of incomprehension, enigma, and broken-off speech. Herbert's "Conscience" exemplifies the poets feeling "God nagging them to listen, rather than feeling him perform mighty speech acts upon them."[38] Sullivan arrives at a very different poetics, but begins with the same assumptions about casuistry, that it constructs for conscience an orderly entrance into the public world.[39]

The restructuring that makes conscience communicable, that inscribes it in public discourse, amounts to a containment of the inchoate Protestant conscience. Ames and Taylor and others wage an intentional campaign to build a Protestant casuistry, which often reads as a deliberate effort at restructuring a conscience that, in its descent from Luther and Calvin, had become too wild. This can particularly be felt in the reception of William Perkins as a casuist – a reception that is not wrong, but is also not the whole story. In this study Perkins has been the key representative of the theorists of conscience, and, the reader may have noticed, was not part of the above discussion of casuistry. Yet he is commonly cited as a father of English casuistry, who, according to Thomas

---

[36] Slights, *The Casuistical Tradition*, 182, 105, 247, 284.
[37] Sullivan, *Rhetoric of the Conscience*, 11. On casuistry see 11–38.
[38] *Ibid.*, 224.
[39] Wilks and Brown generally view conscience through a casuistic lens like that of Slights and Sullivan. Gallagher differs in seeing casuistry as constructing a less stable discourse for conscience, closer to a Bakhtinian sense of discourse.

Merrill, "set a pattern for all later work in Protestant moral divinity."[40] Receiving Perkins exclusively as a casuist, however, elides his influence on the antinomian stream of seventeenth-century conscience, covering over the more radical implications of his theology.

Perkins's early work clearly places him as a theorist of conscience. His first book on conscience, *A Case of Conscience: The Greatest There Ever Was* claims in its title to be doing casuistry. But in a purely Calvinist vein, its whole focus is on the question of election – so that the text pushes aside the multiple cases typical of casuistry, asserting a single, essential case. As in Luther and Calvin, conscience is oriented toward salvation and faith, rather than works, and so it becomes a theoretical more than a practical faculty. *A Discourse on Conscience* covers the experience of conscience more expansively, but retains a theoretical focus on the whole person. It is here that the reflexive and destructured private conscience receives its full articulation. *A Discourse*, furthermore, has none of the trappings of the manuals of casuistry – no index of topics or divisions into subjects, no effort to resolve multiple problems arising from worship or the practical world.

Perkins's third major work on conscience does look more like casuistry, from its title, *The Whole Treatise of the Cases of Conscience*, to its willingness to engage in a set of practical cases on such matters as sacraments and oaths. But this text was published posthumously, and it appears that the editor, Thomas Pickering, exerted considerable influence on its final shape. Pickering's Epistle is a manifesto for Protestant casuistry, listing the extensive failings of Catholic casuistry, and arguing that in Protestant churches casuistry "should be more taught, and further inlarged, then it is."[41] In the address to the reader, Pickering then claims that in presenting this book of casuistry he has dealt faithfully with Perkins's writings, without material additions. But he adds that "it was thought to be convenient to distinguish it into Bookes according to the severall distinct parts, the Bookes into Chapters, the Chapters that were most capable of division into sections."[42] What Pickering adds is the organizational superstructure that allows the text to be used as a practical reference. This practical apparatus, designed for quick reference by topic, is one of the most recognizable

[40] Perkins, *William Perkins 1558–1602*, xx. Also see Wright, "William Perkins: Elizabethan Apostle of 'Practical Divinity'"; Wood, *English Casuistical Divinity*, 68. Slights uses Perkins as paradigmatic of casuistic thinking throughout *The Casuistic Tradition*, relying primarily on the *Whole Treatise*.
[41] Perkins, *Whole Treatise*, "Epistle Dedicatory."
[42] *Ibid.*, "To the Reader."

features in the genre of casuistry; Pickering's editing brings Perkins into conformity with the deliberate project of a Protestant casuistry. But from the outset there is an evident tension between apparatus and text. The "Preface" to Book 1 is said in its heading to declare the "Ground and Order of the Treatise." But the paragraphs that follow read instead like a short sermon, beginning with a verse from Isaiah and unfolding with little effort at a systematic declaration of what is to follow.[43] *The Whole Treatise* is most likely a series of only loosely related sermons left among Perkins's papers, stitched together into the format of a casuistry manual. In fact, James Keenan argues that it is less a book of casuistry than a devotional manual, in the tradition of Ignatius.[44]

The point here is not to separate Perkins from casuistry, as he no doubt exerted significant influence on the tradition. Rather, it is to recognize that Perkins was more theorist of conscience than practitioner of case divinity. Pickering stresses a part of Perkins's approach to conscience, initiating a legacy in casuistry that continues to influence critics today. But this legacy turns our gaze away from Perkins's theoretical leanings. In this way it takes part in the containment of the destructured Protestant conscience, and it elides Perkins's more radical legacy, among Puritan preachers and within the antinomian stream of conscience.

Antinomianism

For the theorists of conscience, a focus on election pulls the faculty away from the practical, toward the more theoretical domain of the whole person. A conscience that is too scrupulously attuned to practical questions, such as those raised by vows and works and the Law, is liable to suffer the pricks of despair. A healthy conscience instead is oriented toward faith, and is instrumental in Christian liberty. Following this trajectory, as conscience begins to enter more fully into the public discourse of the seventeenth century, it is increasingly imagined as the site in which an individual's Christian liberty becomes a form of political expression. As the faculty within which, and through which, the saints received assurance of election, conscience leaves behind reason, and obedience to law, and begins to take on qualities of inspiration and antinomianism.

At the core of this development are radical Puritan preachers, who think conscience functions in a close relationship with the Holy Spirit.

---

[43] *Ibid.*, 1.
[44] Keenan, "Was William Perkins' *Whole Treatise of Cases of Conscience* Casuistry?"

Richard Sibbes, in *The Saint's Priviledge* (1638), does not see conscience as unfolding in a rational or orderly way, but rather as working together with the inspiration of the Holy Ghost:

> Againe, the sending of the Holy Ghost is necessary for this conviction, because hee alone must set downe the soul and make the conscience quiet, who is greater then the conscience. Conscience will clamour thou art a sinner, the Holy Ghost convinces, in Christ thou are righteous.[45]

Thomas Goodwin asserts in *A Childe of Light Walking in Darknesse* (1636) that the Spirit operates together with conscience, and that their conjunction makes the difference between a regenerate and a despairing conscience:

> And hence it is that when Gods Spirit forbeareth to witnesse with conscience, the goodness of our estates, and ceaseth to embolden and encourage conscience by his presence, and the sprinkling of Christs blood upon it against the remaining defilement; that then our consciences are as apt to fall into feares and doubts and self-condemnings.[46]

This language echoes Herbert's "Conscience" and other familiar scenes of *knowing with*. But the scene has a new actor in it: the Spirit is now also present, witnessing with conscience. As this section will show, in the Caroline years conscience becomes intertwined with the Spirit, taking on many of the qualities of inspiration, and, in its more extreme expressions, pushing into the totalizing inspiration of antinomianism. Such an inspired conscience is the very opposite of the casuistic stream, where the faculty is taken to function in a rational and structured manner, aligned conservatively with law and political power.

In a certain sense, the blending of conscience and Spirit is not a radical innovation, but simply fulfills the Protestant assertion that conscience is freed from the Law by the intervention of Grace. In his 1535 commentary on Galatians, Luther credits the Spirit with regenerating conscience that has been ensnared by the Law: "The true use of the Law, on the other hand, cannot be measured by any price, namely when the conscience that has been confined under the Law does not despair, but becomes wise through the Holy Spirit" (*LW* 26:345). However, this claim that conscience works jointly with the Spirit is a rare occurrence in a commentary that is one of Luther's main assertions of faith over works.

---

[45] Sibbes, *The Saints Priviledge*, 500.
[46] Goodwin, *A Childe of Light*, 42.

Although conscience is discussed extensively, it is everywhere else aligned only with despair and terror, with the strictures of the Law or the tyranny of the Pope – and so kept separate from the Spirit or Grace.[47] Similarly, Calvin regularly aligns conscience with suffering under the Law, and Spirit with the freedom of election – but never brings the two together.[48] For Luther and Calvin, conscience comes up almost exclusively when discussing works and the Law, as a site of suffering. They do not theorize the experience of the regenerate conscience in detail, and so rarely articulate it in terms of the Spirit.

It appears to be in the work of William Perkins that Spirit and conscience come together. The latter half of *A Discourse of Conscience* gives significant attention to the individual's experience of conscience as a site of freedom and certainty. Having been broken down by works, the conscience recovers from despair into Christian liberty, and in Perkins's description the Spirit plays a decisive role:

> Thus I have in some part made manifest that an unfallible certenty of pardon of sinne and life everlasting is the property of every renued conscience. Now therefore I will proceede further to consider how this certenty is caused and imprinted in the conscience. The principall agent and beginner thereof is the Holy ghost, inlightning the minde and conscience with spirituall and divine light.
>
> (*DC* 138–9)[49]

In blending Spirit and conscience Perkins is following the authority of Scripture. Romans 9:1 explicitly brings Spirit and conscience together: "I lie not, my conscience bearing me witnesse in the Holy Ghost."[50] Perkins cites this verse in an account of the certain persuasion that can come to the elect through conscience (*DC* 141). He also turns in several places to Romans 8:15–16, which is a commonly cited proof text for the idea of election: "but ye have received the Spirit of adoption, whereby we crie Abba, father. The same Spirite beareth witnesse with our spirit, that we are the children of God." Although these verses do not mention conscience, Perkins discerns the common activity of the faculty, witnessing.

---

[47] E.g. "The two devils who plague us are sin and conscience, the power of the Law and the sting of sin (1Cor1.56). But Christ has conquered these two monsters." *LW* 26:26.

[48] See *Inst.* II:v.5, 121, where the Holy Ghost visits the elect with liberty, but the reprobate are "pressed with witnesse of conscience." The same separation holds true throughout *Inst.* III:xx, "Of Christian Liberty."

[49] Also see *ATC* 66, 71, 109; Greenham, *Paramythion*, 77; Huit, *The Anatomy of Conscience*, 109, 321–2.

[50] This and the next quotation are from the 1560 Geneva Bible.

So he cites Romans 8 and adds the gloss: "Now the spirit of man here mentioned is the mind or conscience renued and sanctified" (*DC* 143).[51] Conscience is not identical with the Spirit, but is rather identified with the "spirit of man." But under the aegis of Romans 8 conscience has acquired a description as a spirit, which was not present before. And it has acquired a way of functioning with the Holy Spirit, so, Perkins says, "That which gods spirit doth testify to the conscience, the conscience can again testifie to us. But Gods spirit doth testify to the conscience of a man regenerate that he is the child of God" (*DC* 143–4). Enlightened by the Spirit and witnessing with it, conscience takes on a significantly inspirational dimension.[52]

In the following decades, the inspired conscience regularly appears among the many Puritans who were influenced by Perkins. Perkins shaped the seventeenth-century conscience not only through his extensive writings, but also through preaching in the Puritan ferment at Cambridge in the 1580s and 1590s. Along with Richard Greenham, Perkins exerted enormous influence over a Cambridge scene that has been described as a "Puritan Academe, with a touch of Little Gidding."[53] Perkins's protégé William Ames begins *Conscience With the Power and Cases Thereof* by recalling Perkins's influence over his Cambridge students, and how "left he many behind him affected with that study" of conscience (*CPC* A2v).[54] Among these was John Downame of Christ's College, who in his popular treatise, *The Christian Warfare* (1604), repeatedly argues for the assurance of election resulting from the joint functioning of Spirit and conscience: "whatsoever the spirit of God doth testifie in the heart and conscience of a man, and doth fully assure him thereof, that he is to beleeve, and of that he ought undoubtedly to be assured."[55] Also among these was Thomas Taylor, who edited Perkins's sermons on Jude, calling himself one of Perkins's "ordinary hearers in Cambridge."[56] Taylor, in *The Progresse of Saints to Full Holinesse* (1631),

---

[51] Also see *DC* 109: "Now that the spirit of God doth give this testimony to the conscience of man, the scripture is more then plaine. Rom 8:16."

[52] Conscience is also aligned with Spirit in the Hebrew Bible, where *ruach* is often interpreted as a Hebrew word for the faculty.

[53] Porter, *Reformation and Reaction*, 217.

[54] Ames also credited Perkins's Cambridge preaching with initiating his conversion experience. Sprunger, *The Learned Doctor William Ames*, 11.

[55] Downame, *The Christian Warfare*, 211. Also see 217, 463, 519.

[56] Porter, *Reformation and Reaction*, 264. Taylor also calls him "judicious Mr. Perkins, from whose gracious mouth and Ministery I received in my youth often the same holy truth, as now in his fruitfull writings appeareth every where." *Regula Vitae*, 208.

frequently brings Spirit and conscience together, saying that God speaks to the elect "Inwardly, by the still voice of his Spirit to the conscience."[57] And among these were Richard Sibbes and Thomas Goodwin, quoted above as examples of the inspired conscience.[58] All of these were part of the "brotherhood of preachers," as William Haller describes them, who "looked mainly to Cambridge as their seminary."[59]

As in Perkins, the conjunction of conscience and Spirit emerges in Calvinist discussions of election, and often finds authority in the same verses from Romans. Richard Sibbes, in *A Fountain Sealed* (1638), describes the process by which a saint is assured of election in terms of a dual witnessing, relying on Romans 8:15–16: "one witnesse is the Spirit of man which knowes the things that are in man; the other witnesse is the Spirit of God, witnessing to our spirits that we are the children of God." He then cites Romans 9:1 to support the assertion, exactly following Perkins, that the Spirit of man in Romans 8 is the conscience:

> Here is light added to light, witnesse added to witnesse, the greater witnesse of the Spirit to the lesse of our Spirits: the Apostle joynes them both together, My conscience bears me witnesse through the holy Ghost.[60]

Samuel Petto, who cites Sibbes's *A Fountain Sealed*, uses Romans 8:16 as his text for the entire sermon, *The Voice of Spirit*. He also argues that "our spirit" from that verse means conscience: "the Spirit is said to witnes with our Spirit. Its testimony, irresistibly overcometh our Spirit, i.e. our Conscience, it causeth them to conclude the same thing: and so there is a joynt-testimony."[61]

In such joint testimony, the functioning of conscience becomes intimately bound up in the functioning of the Spirit. Yet the relationship between Spirit and conscience is often unclear. Thomas Goodwin calls the Spirit "the superior part of the understanding conscience," but sometimes treats conscience and Spirit as synonyms.[62] Sibbes often uses

---

[57] Taylor, *The Progresse of Saints*, 371. Also see 24,194–7, 239, 371

[58] Goodwin describes arriving at Cambridge after Perkins's death, but finding that "the town was then filled with the discourse of the power of Mr Perkins' ministry, still fresh in most men's memories." Quoted by Ian Breward in Perkins, *The Work of William Perkins*, 9.

[59] Haller, *Liberty and Reformation*, 11. Other major Puritan voices coming out of Cambridge include William Gouge, John Dod, Samuel Ward, John Cotton, and Roger Williams. See Haller, *Rise of Puritanism*, 49–82; Porter, *Reformation and Reaction*, 217–67; Webster, *Godly Clergy*, 15–35.

[60] Sibbes, *A Fountaine Sealed*, 206–7. Sibbes frequently places conscience at the center of the Spirit's assurance, 40, 42, 57, 58–9, 206, 224–6.

[61] Petto, *The Voice of the Spirit*, 11. For similar uses of Romans, also see Downame, *Christian Warfare*, 519; Taylor, *The Progresse of the Saints*, 194, 238–9; Symonds, *The Case and Cure*, 429–31.

[62] Goodwin, *A Childe of Light*, 83, 21–2.

conscience and Spirit interchangeably, and declares that "when the spirit joynes with conscience, then God speaks indeed, then there is light upon light."[63] But Sibbes also asserts that the Spirit is "above conscience" and works upon it, so that it "purifieth the conscience."[64] Thomas Taylor places conscience under Spirit, but then says that conscience, "being renewed is called also by the name of Spirit." Cause and effect are hard to disentangle. For Taylor, sometimes a quiet conscience is the cause of a sanctified Spirit, sometimes it is the product of the Spirit.[65] It becomes difficult to describe exactly how conscience and Spirit work – but this fits into the often impressionistic qualities of inspiration. The insertion of the Spirit into the scene of *knowing with* tends to push the conscience into a space of ecstatic inspiration, which is difficult to describe or communicate with precision.

So there emerges an increasingly vatic understanding of the experience of the faculty. Conscience is often described as a scene of washing in the justifying blood of Christ, so that the faculty is regenerated through a fluid and highly metaphorical process. Sibbes says that "The bloud of Christ being sprinckled on the heart by the Spirit, doth pacifie the conscience in assuring it that God is pacified by bloud."[66] Similarly, Walter Craddock says that God "washeth that mans conscience, by the bloud of his Son; that is, his Spirit applies the vertue of the bloud of his Sonne to our Soules, and Consciences, to make them pure and peaceable."[67] Taylor, like Sibbes, describes the regenerate conscience as enlightened by light: it rejoices "that it hath gotten a sweete glimpse of light and favour from God: it rejoyceth in that it hath got a sight of Jesus Christ."[68] Blood, water, and light: these are the powerful but imprecise images often deployed in the increasingly antinomian discourse of the saints. In the same way, Herbert's "Conscience" is ambivalent about a faculty that functions within the violent and ecstatic scene of Christ's blood. But, as Nigel Smith has shown, such metaphors are central to the many sincere

[63] Sibbes, *A Fountaine Sealed*, 42–3.

[64] *Ibid.*, 74, 226, 57.

[65] Taylor, *The Progresse of the Saints*, 194, 217, 239.

[66] Sibbes, *A Fountaine Sealed*, 161.

[67] Craddock, *Gospel-Holinesse*, 51. Also see Goodwin, *A Childe of Light*, 42: "And hence it is that when Gods Spirit forbeareth to witnesse with conscience, the goodness of our estates, and ceaseth to embolden and encourage conscience by his presence, and the sprinkling of Christs blood upon it against the remaining defilement; that then our consciences are as apt to fall into feares and doubts and self-condemnings."

[68] Taylor, *The Progresse of the Saints*, 184. Also see 44.

claims for perfection in England.[69] While most of the Puritan preachers following Perkins stop short of extreme claims for the inspired conscience, the joining of conscience and Spirit can also be found among the most radical expressions of antinomianism.[70]

John Eaton, one of the most outspoken antinomian voices, conceives of conscience as entirely purified by inspiration. In *The Honeycombe of Free Justification* (1642) he argues for a Christian liberty in which conscience is entirely sinless:

> if the peace of conscience casting out the accusations, terrors and condemnings of conscience, doe reigne in your heart, then it shewes plainly, that in truth you yeeld to Christ the glory of his blood and righteousnesse in making both you and your consciences of unjust just, that is *perfectly holy and righteous from all spot of sinne in the sight of God freely.*[71]

Free justification asserts that the elect are not just made righteous by Christ, which is the standard Protestant notion, but are made perfectly so, without any sin. The elect partake of the divine, and by implication are above the authority of any other law – a powerful and controversial antinomian claim.[72] Eaton, making the faculty instrumental to free justification, asserts that it can become entirely spotless. Similarly, Henry Denne, antinomian preacher and Leveller, argues that while the body is sinful, the conscience is a site of total perfection:

> The called of God (even the most upright of them) have sin in the flesh, they have sin in the conversation. But they have no sin, neither can they have any sin in the conscience: for the true faith of Gods elect, and sin in the conscience, can no more stand together then light and darknesse.[73]

For Luther and Calvin and many of their followers, conscience is trapped in a despairing relationship to works, its tendency to move away from structure leading to instability and suffering. In *Hamlet*, a perfect conscience seems suspicious. But here the inspired conscience pulls away from despair, and in its most antinomian expression promises the very opposite – what was inchoate becomes perfect.

[69] Smith, *Perfection Proclaimed*, 229–339.

[70] Sibbes and Thomas Taylor both wrote against antinomians, but should be seen as inhabiting a less extreme position in an ongoing dialectic. As David Como argues, "mainstream Puritanism gave birth to antinomianism not once, nor even twice – but multiple times." *Blown By the Spirit*, 131.

[71] Eaton, *The Honeycombe of Free Justification*, 90.

[72] See Como, *Blown by the Spirit*, 176–218; Haller, *The Rise of Puritanism*, 208–17.

[73] Denne, *The Man of Sin*, 12. Also see Wilkerson, *The Saints Travel*, 86–7; Craddock, *Gospel-Holinesse*, 51.

In another typically antinomian position, certain members of Denne's congregations at Fenstanton and Warboys held such an exalted understanding of the conscience that it was viewed as even more authoritative than Scripture. According to church records,

> They answered, the light in their consciences made it manifest. We told them we had not so learned Christ, as to be guided by their fancy, and therefore we desired them to prove what they said by the scriptures. They replied that the light in their consciences was the rule they desired to walk by. We granted that an enlightened conscience was a guide; but we demanded by what the conscience should be enlightened? They answered, "not by the scriptures, for the conscience was above the scriptures; and the scriptures ought to be tried by it, and not that by the scriptures."[74]

As Geoffrey Nuttall has argued, the most radical question raised by antinomian theology is "whether the Word is to be tried by the Spirit, or the Spirit by the Word."[75] Here the perfection of the individual conscience not only promises freedom from human law and custom, and from ecclesiastical authority, but even from the Bible.

For these congregants conscience becomes more authoritative than Scripture, so that they claim to be ruled by "the light in their consciences." This phrase becomes a familiar Quaker tag, as their enthusiastic emphasis on a theology of "light" extends into the workings of conscience. The phrase echoes throughout George Fox's journal, as when he writes to a group at Ulverston, "To the light in all your consciences I speak, with which Christ Jesus enlightens you."[76] Fox gives this light many of the functions usually associated with conscience, such as witnessing and condemning. Or, for another example among many, in a letter to Cromwell, Fox concludes by appealing to Cromwell "as a witness against all wicked inventions of men and murderous plots, which answered shall be with the light in all your consciences, which makes no covenant with death, to which light in you all I speak, and am clear."[77] Emerging as central to individual inspiration, conscience has become a critical piece of Quaker antinomianism. Perkins's merging of conscience and Spirit has many gradations, and "the light in their

---

[74] *Records of the Churches*, 115–16. Quoted in Nuttall, *The Holy Spirit*, 37.

[75] Nuttall, *The Holy Spirit*, 28. The Spirit was initially understood in Protestant theology as illuminating Scripture and authorizing the individual's interpretation of the sacred text. But antinomians and Quakers came to find the Spirit entirely within themselves, separate from the text of the Bible and with greater authority than the Bible. *Ibid.*, 20–33.

[76] Fox, *Journal*, 143.

[77] *Ibid.*, 198. See Moore, *The Light in their Consciences*.

consciences" can be seen as its extreme expression. So Nuttall observes that "from one angle the evolution of Puritanism may be seen as an increasing preoccupation with conscience, til the strain proved too great, and Antinomianism set in."[78]

Two Streams

While the antinomian conscience functions in "joynt-testimony" with the Spirit, casuists have little to say about conscience and the Spirit. Rather, Jeremy Taylor warns against the dangers of enthusiasts, who "obtrude their fancies upon the world, and yet not being able to prove what they say, pretend the Spirit of God to be the author of all their theoremes."[79] When the saints set about describing the functioning of the antinomian conscience, they turn to the familiar metaphors of inspiration: liquid and light and breath and the blood of Christ. The plasticity and imprecision of this language contrast starkly with the descriptions of casuistry's bipartite conscience, which moves from the rule of *synderesis*, through the logical language of syllogism, to a practical conclusion. The antinomian conscience explicitly rejects the Old Testament Law, and in its extreme forms places the faculty above the Protestant common ground of Scripture. But the casuistic conscience is nomian, so to speak – it is guided by *synderesis*, informed by the authority of Scripture, and fully enmeshed in the rules and obligations of practical cases. Gathering together these differences, we could say that the casuistic conscience is communicable from one person to another, and so enters easily into the public discourses of law and politics, while the antinomian conscience constructs a private authority that resists communicability, and so it enters public discourse in a less malleable, less communal way.

Jeremy Taylor elsewhere articulates incommunicability as a key problem with inspiration, when he argues against the Spirit as authorizing interpretation of Scripture:

> For put case the Spirit is given to some men enabling them to expound infallibly, yet because this is but a private assistance, and cannot be proved

---

[78] Nuttall, *The Holy Spirit*, 36. Leo Solt says that "Antinomians turned the antennae of their consciences to fresh but fragmentary manifestations of truth revealed by the Holy Spirit." *Saints in Arms*, 99.

[79] Taylor, *Ductor Dubitantium*, 45. Taylor briefly admits that the Spirit can influence the conscience through direct revelation, but never adopts the enthusiastic language of Sibbes and the others. *Ibid.*, 12, 43. Ames glances at inspiration in a discussion of Vocation, citing Romans 8:16 and Romans 9:1–2, but making no claims about the Spirit. *CPC*, II:9–10.

to others, this infallible assistance may determine my own assent, but shall not inable me to prescribe to others, because it were unreasonable I should, unless I could prove to him that I have the Spirit.[80]

An individual may be persuaded, but he or she cannot then persuade others. Inspiration cannot be proved, which is to say it cannot enter into discourse and be submitted to reason, or to the negotiations and adjustments of the practical world. A conscience bound up with the Spirit is strong, but it must remain private. When such a conscience enters into public discourse, it remains fundamentally inaccessible, removed from others in the public by its position outside of discourse.

In its isolation from adjustment and compromise, the inspired conscience may seem all the more powerful, as it maintains an ideologically pristine and unchallengeable quality. In this way it begins to take on the energy and conviction of revolution. Richard Sibbes, describing how the Holy Ghost reveals righteousness to the consciences of the elect, declares:

> Where the soule is convinced of the righteousnesse of Christ, there the conscience demands boldly: It is God that justifies, who shal condemne? It is Christ that is dead and risen againe and sits at the right hand of God; who shall lay anything to the charge of Gods chosen. So that a convinced conscience dares all creatures in Heaven and Earth, it works strongly and boldly.[81]

Not only among Puritan preachers, but among Quakers, the antinomian preachers of the New Model Army, and among the Levellers, the inspired conscience enters public discourse as a revolutionary force. It exerts an energetic kind of sovereignty, resisting the adjustments of communication, and elevating the individual as a potentially comprehensive exception to all other forms of power.

But as the antinomian stream gives rise to an energetically sovereign conscience, it flows alongside the more orderly and conservative stream of casuistry. These two very opposite discourses, both present, show what a wide set of possibilities there are for the conscience – with each individual and in every discourse, the faculty is capable of both casuistic obligations and antinomian revolutions. Such ambivalence in early modern public discourse can be understood as a product of the ambivalence this study has described in the private discourse of the destructured conscience. The example of George Herbert's "Conscience" suggests that

---

[80] Taylor, *Discourse of the Liberty of Prophesying*, 163–4.
[81] Sibbes, *The Saints Priviledge*, 507.

uncanny scenes of *knowing with* may in fact make possible the period's broad and ambivalent political uses of conscience. Just as a reader of "Conscience" can turn toward either casuistry or antinomianism, so an early modern subject can turn either way, or both ways, when translating the private experience of conscience into public action or ideology.

So the destructured conscience can be read in opposite directions, both as rational casuistry and as inspired antinomianism. It can plausibly lead toward a public context in which the faculty is susceptible to description and therefore part of the debates and adjustments of communication. This casuistic stream makes conscience into a commonwealth-building force, conservative in its emphasis on law, and communal in its facilitation of reason and discourse in the public sphere. Alternatively, private conscience can plausibly lead toward a context in which the faculty resists articulation and therefore stands outside persuasion and other forms of discursivity. This antinomian stream makes the faculty into an atomizing force, a sovereign conscience that gives shape to the possessive individual, and pushes toward revolution. During the Civil War, the scene of conscience becomes more important than ever to public discourse, though no less inchoate, as it shapes the political subject and its relation to the public sphere.

5

Public Discourses: Toleration, Revolution, Sovereignty

The two streams mean that conscience enters public discourse ambivalently, with both antinomian and casuistic understandings sheltering in the single word "conscience." Such complexity does not paralyze, but rather, this chapter suggests, proves to be productive. In the antinomian stream can be felt a strong forward current, toward a conception of the private conscience that is increasingly sovereign. It has a liberating and expanding logic, leading to absolute conceptions of the rights of the individual, and toward revolutionary conceptions of conscientious action. But running against this stream is the casuistic understanding, which reinserts the individual conscience into law and public communication. It limits what would be revolutionary, and it organizes and makes communicable what would be inchoate. As conscience enters into public discourse, the antinomian and casuistic streams pull it in differing directions, building an energy that makes the faculty central to the politics of the Civil War.

The casuistic and antinomian streams are meant to capture key qualities in the discourse, and are not meant to be comprehensive. A full account of conscience in seventeenth-century public discourse would have more to say, for example, about natural law, Arminianism, and republicanism. These two, admittedly stylized, categories, however, help describe an interrelated set of issues at the center of the political landscape, including reason and inspiration, the sovereign conscience and its place in the public sphere, and the obligations of the political subject. To pursue these, this chapter offers three cases from the politics of mid-century England: the toleration crisis of the 1640s, the emergence of Leveller democracy and revolution, and Hobbes's reaction.

Liberty of Conscience

Conscience takes a central place in public discourse in the 1640s, when "liberty of conscience" becomes a watchword for all who struggle for religious toleration. "Give me the liberty to know, to utter, and to argue freely according to conscience, above all liberties," Milton declares in *Areopagitica* (*CPW* II:560). In the same year, 1644, William Walwyn titles the first chapter of *The Compassionate Samaritan* "Liberty of Conscience Asserted"; Henry Robinson pleads for toleration in *Liberty of Conscience*; and Roger Williams publishes the most radical statement of toleration of the period, *The Bloudy Tenent of Persecution, for Cause of Conscience*.[1] Williams argues that, "It is the will and command of God, that since the coming of his Sonne the Lord Jesus a permission of the most Paganish, Jewish, Turkish or Antichristian consciences and worships, be granted to all men in all Nations and Countries." Even Jews and Turks should be tolerated, because "it is no prejudice to the commonwealth if liberty of conscience were suffered to such as do fear God."[2] Spurred by Independent protest against the Presbyterians of the Westminster Assembly, conscience publicly authorizes freedom of worship and resistance to ecclesiastical authority. And so it becomes the name for individual religious sovereignty in the public sphere.

Liberty of conscience has multiple roots in the Reformation. Luther's conclusion at the Diet of Worms, "I cannot and I will not retract anything, since it is neither safe nor right to go against conscience. I cannot do otherwise, here I stand, may God help me, Amen," lays the foundation (*LW* 32:112–13). Sebastian Castellio, D. V. Coornhert, and Michel Montaigne all raise their voices on the continent for liberty of conscience.[3] In sixteenth-century England, it was championed by Thomas More, as well as by the resistance to the Marian state, as described in Foxe's *Acts and Monuments*, especially the account of James Hale. And in Jacobean England it was critical to the Baptists and nonconformists returning from Dutch exile, such as Leonard Busher, who publishes *Religions Peace* from Amsterdam in 1614, criticizing English bishops because they "force and constrayne men and womens consciences."[4]

---

[1] Pointing to these classic texts, John Coffey calls 1644 a "fundamental turning point" in which a national consensus for the admissibility of persecution falls apart. *Persecution and Toleration*, 47. For a concise account see Coffey, "The Toleration Controversy."

[2] Williams, *The Bloudy Tenent*, a2v.

[3] Castellio, *Concerning Heretics*; Coornhert, *Synod on the Freedom of Conscience*; Montaigne, "Of Freedom of Conscience." Also see Skinner and van Gelderen, *Freedom and the Construction of Europe*.

[4] Busher, *Religions Peace*, 10. Busher's text is republished in 1646 with an expanded title, *Religions Peace or a Plea for Liberty of Conscience*. Also see Helwys, *A Short Declaration* and *Obiections Answered*. On the Baptists and Nonconformists of the early seventeenth century, see Jordan, *The Development of Religious Toleration*, 1:261–321; Tolmie, *The Triumph of the Saints*, 69–84.

These antecedents are all expressions of Protestant sectarianism, which positions conscience as the primary site of liberty in the 1640s.[5] In the toleration crisis, the faculty takes on a politically active quality, especially as a form of resistance to the collective impingements of law and temporal authority. This emerging sense of conscience as a site of individual resistance is in significant ways an expression of the antinomian stream that the last chapter described. When conscience works in conjunction with the Spirit, it tends to ignore human law, and, in its more enthusiastic expressions, to set up beyond all discursiveness and communicability. Shedding these restraints, a kind of autonomy takes hold in which the individual alone can understand the workings of conscience. Tucked into the individual, beyond the reach of law or description or political power, the liberated conscience accrues a strongly private power. So throughout the debate are phrases that frame the faculty as under siege – laments against those that impose on "tender consciences" or that would "assault" consciences, or, in the phrase Milton often uses, that would be "forcers of conscience."[6]

Essential to most arguments for liberty of conscience, accordingly, is an effort to insulate the faculty from law and magistrate. Joshua Sprigge's *The Ancient Bounds or Liberty of Conscience* (1645) for example, admits duties for magistrates and for synods such as the Westminster Assembly, but insists that these "cannot reach the mind, and judgement, and conscience."[7] As Henry Vane summarizes, conscience operates purely within the individual, unsusceptible to interference from external power, and entirely outside the domain of law:

> In matters of Religion, the Magistrate is but a fellow-Servant with us, and we must all stand or fall to one Master. But in matters concerning our neighbour, he is appointed a Judge and Ruler between us, and we must stand or fall to his Judgement. We may, and ought to give up our outward estates to the determination of another for Peace sake, but our Consciences in Religion are none of ours to dispose of.[8]

---

[5] Of course England continues to struggle with toleration in the interregnum and Restoration. On the interregnum see Worden, "Toleration and the Cromwellian Protectorate." On the Restoration, see Grell et al., *From Persecution to Toleration*.

[6] Goodwin et al., *An Apologeticall Narration*, 26. Robinson, *Liberty of Conscience*, 40. Milton, "On the New Forcers of Conscience Under the Long Parliament"; *Eikonoklastes*, *CPW* III:488; *Of Civil Power*, *CPW* VII:242.

[7] Sprigge, *The Ancient Bounds*, 22–3.

[8] Vane, *Zeal Examined*, 11. Roger Williams characteristically adopts the most absolute principle, asserting a total separation of the civil power of the magistrate from spiritual matters. *The Bloudy Tenent*, "To the Right Honorable."

Such sovereignty of individual conscience has its theological foundation in Luther's notion of the two kingdoms, which posits two separate
governments and kinds of law, one under God and one under temporal
authority. Luther warns that "when the temporal authority presumes to
prescribe laws for the soul, it encroaches upon God's government and
only misleads souls and destroys them." The protected space of God's
kingdom he aligns with conscience: of the individual Christian, he says,
"How he believes or disbelieves is a matter for the conscience of each
individual."[9] And yet Luther argued for extensive obedience to temporal
authority, and countenanced significant influence over spiritual matters
by Church leaders.[10] Similarly, Calvin asserts a version of the two kingdoms, but, as his Christian commonwealth and the burning of Michael
Servetus indicate, he allows the magistrate considerable authority over
conscience. So in the discussion of Christian Liberty in the *Institutes*,
when Calvin describes the importance of separating the spiritual and
temporal kingdoms, his first concern is not the protection of individual
liberty, but the risk that conscience may overly embolden the individual.
He argues primarily against this possibility: "that which the Gospell tea-
cheth of the spirituall libertie, we shall not wrongefully drawe to the civil
order, as though Christians were according to the outward government
lesse subject to the lawes of men, because their consciences are at libertie
before God" (*Inst.*, III.xix.15, 348).[11] Calvin separates conscience from
the magistrate, but simultaneously argues back to obedience.

William Perkins, however, does not shy away from the challenge the
Protestant conscience presents to political authority. In *A Discourse of
Conscience*, after theorizing the inward experience, Perkins develops an
extended discussion of how human law is an "improper binder" of conscience (*DC* 38). Perkins carefully preserves the separation of conscience
from the temporal kingdom:

> As for the laws of men, they want power to commaund conscience. In deede
> if it were possible for our governours by law to commaund mens thoughts
> and affections, then also might they command conscience; but the first is
> not possible, for their lawes can reach no further then to the outward man,

[9] *Temporal Authority: To What Extent It Should Be Obeyed*, LW 45:105, 108. See Althaus, *The Ethics of Martin Luther*, 43–82; Thomason, *The Political Thought of Martin Luther*, 36–61.
[10] See Ozment, "Martin Luther on Religious Liberty."
[11] Also see IV:xx, "Of Civile Governement." On Calvin's evolving positions on toleration, see Witte, "Moderate Religious Liberty in the Theology of John Calvin." On the ambivalence of Calvin and Calvinism toward liberty of conscience, see Coffey, "The Language of Liberty in Calvinist Political Thought."

that is, to bodie and goods, with the speaches and deedes thereof; and the ende of them all is not to maintaine spirituall peace of conscience, which is betweene man and God, but only that externall and civill peace which is betweene man and man. And it were not meete that men should commaund conscience, which cannot see conscience and judge of all her actions, which appeare not outwardly and whereof there be no witnesses, but God and the conscience of the doer. Lastly men are no fitte commanders of conscience because they are no lords of it, but God himselfe alone.

(*DC* 57–8)

Perkins was a political moderate who remained within the Church his whole life. So any deliberate program of resistance is unlikely. His clear willingness to allow conscience to oppose law, however, can be seen as a natural product of his theorizations of the faculty. His destructured conscience emphasizes individual experience at the expense of more collective discourses such as law. It is inward and inchoate, and so tends to slip out of order and rule. It is reflexive, and so does not offer points of contact with external authorities, but rather turns back on itself, creating a solipsistic faculty that isolates it from outside entanglements and sources of power, such as the magistrate. And as was argued in the last chapter, Perkins's conscience resists the kind of practical discourse that shapes casuistry, as it includes the Spirit in its workings, giving sway to the faculty's antinomian center.

Meanwhile, there are numerous affiliations between those expressing an antinomian conscience and those arguing for liberty of conscience. Thomas Goodwin, one of the Puritan preachers who saw conscience functioning in conjunction with the Spirit, was also an author of *An Apologeticall Narration* (1643), the first important text in the toleration debates. In order to separate themselves from Presbyterian uniformity, Goodwin, Philip Nye, and the other authors recount their experiences during their Dutch exile, making the claim that they had attained a liberated relationship with conscience, one that was authoritative precisely because it operated through the Spirit. They describe their exile as

leaving us as freely to be guided by that light and touch Gods Spirit should by the Word vouchsafe our consciences, as the Needle toucht with the Load-stone is in the Compasse: And we had (of all men) the greatest reason to be true to our own consciences in what we should embrace, seeing it was for our consciences that we were deprived at once of what ever was dear to us.[12]

---

[12] Goodwin et al., *An Apologeticall Narration*, 3.

With the responsiveness of a compass, conscience indicates the Spirit in an entirely unmediated way. It functions in isolation from human law or the technologies of casuistic reasoning, just as the exiled authors were isolated from England and its church. Over the course of the tract, the experience of exile serves as the main argument for liberty of conscience, so that the isolated and private conscience authorizes their independence from the authority of the Westminster Assembly.

Conscience is free from the encroachments of temporal power precisely because it is so closely bound up in the antinomian functioning of the Spirit. Henry Robinson argues that even a "misled conscience" cannot be corrected by human intervention because that would violate the close relationship between conscience and God:

> tis a folly of all follies the most ridiculous, for a man to put out his owne eyes, renounce his owne reason, infatuate his owne understanding, and proscribe the Holy Ghost himselfe (for the Spirit of God cannot long beare witnesse together with our spirits, Rom 8.16. save according to our owne eyes, reason and understanding) that he may be beholding to others to let him see and understand by proxie.[13]

Citing the key text from Romans for the antinomian conscience, Robinson carves out a faculty that must be protected from forcing, lest the Holy Ghost be proscribed. The antinomian John Saltmarsh begins his argument for liberty of conscience with the sovereign authority of the Spirit, asserting that "[t]he consciences of men are under a Spiritual and immediate interpreter of the Word, even as the Spirit of the Lord, in all things of Spirited cognizance, as every Scripture-truth or Truth, in the Word is." Any persecution or control by the magistrate therefore has the result "that our consciences are not under the Lord Jesus, and his Spirit immediately in the things of God, but under the interpretations of men."[14]

Not only is the antinomian conscience resistant to persuasion or coercion by others, but it operates as an irresistible force even within the individual. William Walwyn's first reason for liberty of conscience is that "what judgement soever a man is, he cannot chuse but bee of that judgement."[15] Such an absolute conscience is supported by Walwyn's belief in free justification. Reflecting on the toleration crisis, he later describes how he "had long before been established in that part of doctrine (called then, Antinomian) of free justification by Christ alone;

---

[13] Robinson, *John the Baptist*, 30.
[14] Saltmarsh, *The Smoke in the Temple*, 24–5.
[15] Walwyn, *The Compassionate Samaritan*, 6–7.

and so my heart was at much more ease and freedom, then others, who were entangled with those yokes of bondage, unto which Sermons and Doctrines mixt of Law and Gospel, do subject distressed consciences."[16] Free justification elevates individual faith above sermons and even above Scripture, so that there is no modifying, or subjecting, the conscience once it has been shaped by the Spirit.

As the individual conscience acquires such a bedrock quality, it becomes a necessary precondition of truth. Here liberty of conscience moves beyond a negative liberty.[17] Several toleration texts, such as Robinson's *Liberty of Conscience* and Milton's *Areopagitica*, not only defend conscience from external forcers, but make the case for a progressive revelation.[18] Truth can be pursued only if conscience is free to experiment with new ideas, so that Joshua Sprigge sees liberty of conscience as "a necessary advantage to the truth," because it is only through such freedom that truth will be revealed.[19] In the careful search for truth, the possibility of heretics must be tolerated because, as Henry Vane declares, even a seeming heresy could be a "forerunner of some true spiritual liberty."[20] With truth progressively discovered through a positive liberty of conscience, the faculty begins to take on a pattern of ideological expansion. If one idea should be tolerated, then arguably the next one should be as well; when a perfect understanding of truth depends on a perfect liberty, then any limit to conscience becomes a threat to true religion. In this way liberty of conscience during the 1640s tends to expand outward, pushing toward increasing liberty, and toward its most pure expression, an absolute toleration.

It would be a simplification, however, not to notice that in the 1640s liberty of conscience was still far from the principle of absolute toleration. With the exception of Roger Williams, tolerationists were likely to exclude many parties. Atheists were almost universally denied toleration, and arguments for the suppression of heresy limited any number of Protestant sects. Calls for liberty of conscience often seemed little more than a bid for freedom for the author's own creed, a "double standard," which, John Coffey points out, was a far cry from the "principled

[16] Walwyn, *Walwyn's Just Defence*, 8.
[17] "Not freedom from but freedom to," as Isaiah Berlin puts it. "Two Concepts of Liberty," 131.
[18] Robinson, *Liberty of Conscience*, 49. See Milton's famous image of Truth, hewn like Osiris into a thousand pieces, requiring a careful search, *CPW* II:549.
[19] Sprigge, *The Ancient Bounds*, A4v.
[20] Vane, *Zeal Examined*, 33.

rejection of all religious persecution."[21] Joshua Sprigge, for example, demands liberty from the interference of the magistrate, but is careful to except cases of "manifest scandall and danger to mens soules and consciences, as Arrianisme, Socinianisme, Familisme."[22] William Walwyn demands "Liberty of conscience be allowed for every man . . . and no man be punished or discountenanced by authority for his opinion, unlesse it be dangerous to the State," which is the common formula for denying toleration to Catholics, whose presumed allegiance to the Pope was felt to be a threat to the state.[23]

Conscience does not simply release England into the modern liberal notion of toleration. In fact, the faculty was regularly claimed by opponents of toleration.[24] Adam Steuart (who is the "A.S" named by Milton as a forcer of conscience) begins his response to *An Apologeticall Narration* by declaring: "I am perswaded in my conscience, that your opinion of Independency, &c. if it were admitted . . . could not but prove the root of all sort of Schisms, and Heresie, and consequently the utter overthrow of Christs Universall Militant Church here upon Earth."[25] This is a clever gambit, for if conscience is to be authoritative, then Steuart's conscience should carry as much weight as those of the dissenters. Responding to the authors' claim in *An Apologeticall Narration*, quoted above, that the Spirit directed their conscience "as the Needle toucht with the Load-stone," so that they had "the greatest reason to be true to our own consciences," Steuart responds with the example of Presbyterians who had been exiled for religion: "Had they not (I say) as great reason to be true to their consciences, as ye can have?"[26]

Samuel Rutherford, another of Milton's forcers, produces one of the most comprehensive rebuttals to liberty of conscience, arguing against John Goodwin, Henry Robinson, Roger Williams, Joshua Sprigge, and John Saltmarsh, among others, in *A Free Disputation Against*

---

[21] Coffey, *Persecution and Toleration*, 54. A. A. Seaton remarks, "those who raise the cry for liberty usually mean liberty for themselves." *The Theory of Toleration*, 46.

[22] Sprigge, *The Ancient Bounds*, 4.

[23] Walwyn, *The Compassionate Samaritan*, 5. On the exclusion of Catholics see Norah Carlin, "Toleration for Catholics."

[24] Justin Champion points out, "Conscience then was not a concept simply monopolized by the dissidents but lay at the very heart of the operations and understandings of state power. Conscience was an instrument of order and government." "Willing to Suffer," 15.

[25] Steuart, *Some Observations*, "To the Divines." Or see the Anonymous, *Anti-Toleration*, 9: "That he whose conscience tells him Toleration is unlawful, cannot but oppose Toleration in his place, else he playes the hypocrite, and sins against his conscience."

[26] Steuart, *Some Observations*, 10.

Pretended Liberty of Conscience (1649). He explicitly places conscience under the authority of synods, and argues extensively against the sovereignty of the antinomian conscience: "Conscience is a servant, and a under-Judge onely, not a Lord, nor an Absolute and Independent Soveraigne, whose voice is a Law, therefore an Idolatrous and exorbitant rule of Conscience is here also to be condemned."[27] Rutherford begins his argument by re-defining conscience in the structured terms of the casuists. Citing William Ames among several earlier casuists, he discusses the scholastic categories of power, habit, and act, makes room in conscience for the bipartite structure of *synderesis*, and describes its functioning in terms of a syllogism.[28] Concerning the destructured and sovereign faculty of the tolerationists, "No rule can be falser, and more crooked then the conscience."[29]

But even as the casuistic stream often contains the liberating current of antinomianism, the overall debate creates a productive and exploratory scene of conscience. Rutherford warns that if toleration has place, "Conscience is hereby made every mans Rule, Umpire, Judge, Bible, and his God, which if he follow he is but at the worst, a godly pious, holy Hereticke, who feareth his conscience more than his Creator."[30] Ironically, despite being enrolled in Milton's sonnet, Rutherford anticipates *Paradise Lost* and Milton's "umpire conscience," articulating a vividly sovereign version of the faculty. Similarly, in the push and pull of the toleration debate, the outline of absolute toleration is frequently discernible. As the expansive logic of liberty of conscience pushes toward increasing purity, disputants on both sides regularly call out their opponents for inconsistency and hypocrisy, and so give voice to more expansive toleration. Henry Robinson wonders at "such who both persecute others and are yet persecuted themselves; but is it not strange that any man should be so plunged in ignorance, and passionately transported, as to make a conscience of doing that which himselfe confesses to be evill in others?"[31] Robinson means the Presbyterians, and makes his case by pointing out how contradictory it is for figures such as William Prynne, who suffered persecution at the hands of the bishops, to turn around and support it against Independents. But antitolerationists are also eager to point out

---

[27] Rutherford, *A Free Disputation*, 10.
[28] *Ibid.*, 2–7.
[29] *Ibid.*, 116.
[30] *Ibid.*, "To the Reader."
[31] Robinson, *John the Baptist*, 53. Walwyn worries that the Presbyterians are particularly intolerant "as slaves usually are when they becomes masters." *The Compassionate Samaritan*, 18.

inconsistency in the Independents. Steuart points to the intolerance of John Cotton and expects that the five authors of *An Apologeticall Narration* would deny Presbyterians their doctrinal preferences: "If any man incited the State not to allow you a peacable practice of your new Religion, they did according to their conscience, as your New-England men do with those of our Religion, as some say, that some of you five would do with us."[32] The charge of hypocrisy makes commonplace the possibility of unfettered toleration, even when the ideal is opposed.

Supporting both sides of the toleration debate, conscience becomes a kind of machine of political exploration, a means by which the public discourse of the 1640s feels its way around the sovereignty of the individual and the principle of toleration. This exploration is so effective because it is itself a continuing scene of conscience. It may be easy for the modern reader to focus on the glaring contradictions, as when Independents will not tolerate Catholics. But the important point is that even in these contradictions, we can see the drawing and redrawing of conscience – the shape it is given by its liberties, as well as by the rules that restrict it. Toleration is explored within this scene, on the stage provided by conscience, where *knowing with* can take place, where inwardness can be described and understood, where individual judgment and its relationship to the public sphere can be tested. In the dynamic public discourse of the toleration debate, the private conscience is experienced as the central player. What emerges is an increased familiarity with the idea of a sovereign conscience that, when it enters into public discourse, can exceed all other obligations. The sovereign conscience attains an ideological coherence, and an undeniable political energy.

These are on clearest display in *Areopagitica*. Paralleling the ambivalence of the larger toleration crisis, the text is intolerant toward Catholics, and not absolutely opposed to censorship. It also, as will be discussed in Chapter 6, displays a complex blend of reason and inspiration. But in its comprehensive engagement with the boundaries between private conscience and public discourse, *Areopagitica* operates as a kind of machine of exploration, expanding well into the reaches of liberty and modern liberalism. Milton names conscience as the highest liberty, and in the oration's most eloquent moments, evokes a political subject of revolutionary energy, one that labors in the deep mines of knowledge, that sallies forth to race after truth, not without dust and heat, and that is capable, in

---

[32] Steuart, *Some Observations*, 61. Also see Rutherford, *A Free Disputation*, 50.

Milton's vision of a political future, of becoming a member of a Nation of Prophets (*CPW* II:562, 515, 556). Roger Williams articulates an absolute toleration, but does so in a relatively inert political philosophy; Milton, in comparison, imagines a conscientious politics that has not ceased to resonate in our liberal era.

Levellers

Radical assertions of liberty of conscience in 1644 made little practical headway with the Westminster Assembly. Chapter 20 of the 1646 Westminster Confession, "Of Christian liberty, and liberty of conscience," blocks Christian liberty entirely from the political sphere by describing conscience as lacking any power in ecclesiastical or civil matters. An individual cannot, under the pretense of Christian liberty, practice or publish freely, but "may lawfully be called to account, and proceeded against by the Censures of the Church, and by the power of the Civil Magistrate."[33]

But if the more antinomian expressions of conscience are rejected by the Assembly, they find sympathy within the radical politics that take aim at the monarchy. All three of the main Leveller authors cut their teeth on the toleration debates: William Walwyn most notably, with *The Compassionate Samaritan*, but also Richard Overton, with *The Araignement of Mr. Persecution* (1645), and John Lilburne, with *A Copy of a Letter* (1644), a response to William Prynne.[34] Paralleling the toleration debates, Levellers fought most bitterly with Presbyterians: the first major Leveller petition, Overton and Walwyn's *A Remonstrance of Many Thousand Citizens* (1646), is addressed to the Presbyterian-controlled Parliament. In addition to calling for Lilburne's freedom and the natural political rights of the people, *A Remonstrance* argues that "neither you nor none else, can have any power at all to conclude the People in matters that concerne the Worship of God, for therein every one of us ought to be fully assured in our owne mindes, and to be sure to Worship him according to our Consciences."[35] The argument for toleration blends easily with the democratic vocabulary of the Levellers.

---

[33] Anon., *The Humble Advice*, 35–6.

[34] Andrew Sharp includes Walwyn's other major statement for religious toleration, *Tolleration Justified and Persecution Condemned* (1646) as one of the earliest entries in the anthology *The English Levellers*, 9–30.

[35] Overton and Walwyn, *A Remonstrance*, 12. Also see Overton, *An Arrow against All Tyrants*, in Sharp, *The English Levellers*, 64.

The Levellers are often linked with the discourses of natural law, but their revolutionary energy largely derives from the theological foundations of liberty of conscience.[36] This conforms to the genealogy discerned by William Haller, A. S. P. Woodhouse, and others, that Puritan theology gives birth to fundamental principles of political liberalism.[37] Blair Worden has described the frequent articulation of "civil and religious liberty" in the 1640s, arguing that the merging of political and religious spheres becomes foundational to liberal discourse.[38] Their clearest point of contiguity is in the emergence of the sovereign conscience in public discourse, and, along with it, a political subject that possesses a revolutionary degree of sovereignty.

This is a political subject not just worthy of protection from forcers, but one that has a wide franchise and individual rights. These are asserted in the ongoing Leveller manifesto *An Agreement of the People*, which David Wooton calls "the first proposal in history for a written constitution based on inalienable natural rights."[39] After setting up the terms of the franchise, *An Agreement* sets out a list of reservations, which the people's Representatives cannot infringe. First among these constitutional rights is that no magistrate will have the power "to restrain any person from the professing his faith, or exercise of religion according to his conscience in any house or place."[40] Liberty of conscience is the Leveller First Ammendment.[41] The second denies the Representatives the ability to

---

[36] Brian Manning argues that, "Central to the Leveller programme was the demand for religious liberty – for each individual to be free to hold what opinions in religion his reason told him to be true and to worship God in the way his conscience told him to be right, without interference from the state or state-church. This involved carving out for the individual an area of autonomy beyond the reach of any human power." "The Levellers and Religion," 78. On the emergence of Leveller organization out of the toleration crisis, see Tolmie, *The Triumph of the Saints*, 144–72.

[37] Haller, *Liberty and Reformation*. Woodhouse, *Puritanism and Liberty*, Introduction, 65–9. Scholarly debate has seen a contest between such Whiggish readings and revisionist readings. For an account of the positions, and an argument for a "post-revisionist approach," see Coffey, *Persecution and Toleration*, 1–7. Also see Patterson, *Early Modern Liberalism*.

[38] "Until the civil wars the pressures on conventional thinking to merge the higher and lower concepts both of Christian liberty and of liberty of conscience were more or less withstood. During them the distinctions broke down. The fragmentation of the Puritan movement, and the debates over ecclesiology and religious compulsion, brought a new urgency to the practical dimensions of the liberty of the spirit and conscience. To many minds the liberty of Christians in Christ, and the liberty they might enjoy in their ecclesiastical arrangements, became even harder to distinguish," *God's Instruments*, 324.

[39] Wooten, "Leveller Democracy," 412.

[40] Lilburne, *Foundations of Freedom*, 11.

[41] This met immediate opposition, however, even within the New Model Army. This exact article in *The Agreement* was the occasion for the Whitehall Debates of 1648, in which the full extent of the right of liberty of conscience was contested. As a further indication of the mingling of religious and political conscience, in addition to Levellers, several present at Whitehall were important

impress soldiers, "every mans conscience being to be satisfied in the just-nesse of that cause wherein he hazards his life."[42] Conscience is first pro-tected against forcing, and then becomes the foundation for the assertion of what is just in the public sphere, by each soldier. Conscience becomes the place in which the subject assumes a role in ideological politics.

The soldiers of the New Model Army fight for such a conscien-tious politics. Early in the Army's confrontation with the Presbyterian Parliament, the issues are quite practical: Parliament sought to disband the army; the army sought back-pay and to avoid enlistment in Ireland. The army's first major statement, *A Solemn Engagement of the Army* (June 5, 1647), focuses on disbandment and the soldiers' grievances, making no ideological claims of political judgment. In fact at the end it disa-vows any action against magistrate or Parliament, and disavows liberty of conscience.[43] But *A Solemn Engagement* also initiated the General Council in the army, which gave seats to the Agitators who were to push the Leveller agenda. Reflecting this influence, the next important docu-ment, *A Representation of the Army* (June 14), strikes a more democratic posture. In its subtitle it declares that it addresses "the Just and funda-mental Rights and Liberties of themselves and the Kingdom." And after rehearsing earlier practical grievances, *A Representation* takes on the more principled language of the Levellers, asserting repeatedly that their inten-tion is the "securing of our owne and the Kingdoms rights, liberties, and safety."[44] In shifting from practical grievances to this more principled reg-ister, the petition specifically invokes conscience as an indication of the soldiers' authority to plead for such matters:

> especially considering that we were not a meer mercenary Army, hired to serve any Arbitrary power of a State, but called forth and conjured by the severall Declarations of Parliament, to the defence of our owne and the peoples just Rights and Liberties; and so we took up Armes in judge-ment and conscience to those ends.[45]

Precisely because they acted according to conscience and their own judg-ments, the soldiers have the authority to act upon the democratic ideals

---

voices for toleration, including Philip Nye and Joshua Sprigge. The debates read like a spirited replay of the toleration crisis. See Woodhouse, *Puritanism and Liberty*, 125–78. Also see Gentles, *The New Model Army*, 207–8.

[42] Lilburne, *Foundations of Freedom*, 11.

[43] England and Wales Army, *A Solemn Engagement*, 26.

[44] England and Wales Army, *A Representation*, 43.

[45] *Ibid.*, 39. Ian Gentles calls *A Representation* "a full-dress political programme." *The New Model Army*, 178–9.

of "the peoples just Rights." Conscience becomes the occasion and source of political assertiveness, a positive guarantor of rights and an origin for political action. The Leveller goal of securing possession of their rights and liberties is supported by the fact that they have secured possession of their own selves – rather than selling their actions as mercenaries, they are soldiers of conscience.

The rarefied space of "judgement and conscience" heralds a new kind of politics, as the phrase proves to be a touchstone in subsequent Leveller arguments. In *The Case of the Armie Truly Stated*, published four months later, the Agitators and Fairfax complain that the issues expressed in *A Representation* had not been addressed. Moving beyond practical matters, they return to the document where "pag.6. it is declared that the Army took up Armes, in judgement and conscience, for the peoples just rights and liberties." They lament that since then Parliament has tried "to perswade the Soldiers and Agitators, that they stand as Soldiers only to serve the State, and may not as free Commons claime their right and freedome."[46] Parliament would have the soldiers of the New Model Army be merely servants of the state. What the Levellers fight for is the idea that, having taken up arms in conscience, they are subjects in possession of rights and freedoms, and are actors in a world of ideological possibilities.

The following month, an early version of *An Agreement of the People* (November 3) includes a call to New Model officers and soldiers to sign the petition for democratic reforms. The expectation for continued commitment to the Leveller ideals is based on the army's previous conscientious actions: "because we are confident, that in judgment and Conscience, ye hazarded your lives for the settlement of such a just and equall Government, that you and your posterities, and all the free borne people of this Nation might enjoy justice and freedome."[47] The phrase sticks in the mind of Henry Ireton, so that in preparation for the reading of *An Agreement* at the Putney debates, Ireton anticipates the key words:

> we have carried the name of God (and I hope not in show, but in reality), professing to act, and to work, as we have thought, in our judgments and consciences, God to lead us; professing to act to those ends that we have thought to be answerable and suitable to the mind of God, so far as it hath been known to us.[48]

---

[46] Fairfax, *The Case of the Armie*, 4–5. Also in Woodhouse, *Puritanism and Liberty*, 431.
[47] Bear, *An Agreement*, 12. Also in Woodhouse, *Puritanism and Liberty*, 448.
[48] Woodhouse, *Puritanism and Liberty*, 49.

Ireton invokes "judgments and consciences," however, in a speech against the Agitators, as the faculty also serves the side of the Grandees. Ireton argues for limits to the sovereignty of conscience, as part of Putney's long consideration of whether the army can break past engagements. On the one side, the Leveller Colonel Thomas Rainborough asserts that conscience is a legitimate authority for breaking an engagement: "I am wholly confident that every honest man is bound in duty to God and his conscience, let him be engaged in what he will, to decline it when he sees it to be evil."[49] Conscience is so sovereign that it can override any past engagement. Ireton, in contrast, is horrified at how judgment and conscience threaten engagements, for in doing so they seem to threaten the very principle of political obligation: "And therefore when I hear men speak of laying aside all engagements to consider only that wild or vast notion of what in every man's conception is just or unjust, I am afraid and do tremble at the boundless and endless consequences of it."[50] The Grandees rejected most Leveller positions, and soon after the mutiny at Ware was put down, John Wildman, Leveller writer and Agitator at Putney, publishes a bitter denunciation of Ireton and Cromwell. He twice reminds them that in *A Representation* the army had "declared that they took up Armes in judgement and conscience." This proves Ireton and Cromwell's "palpable Hypocrisie in their Declarations or else their grosse Apostacie from their first principles."[51] Wildman concludes by calling Ireton and Cromwell mercenaries, which in Leveller parlance is the very opposite of a conscientious actor.[52]

Throughout the Putney debates, Ireton and Cromwell resist Leveller agitation by attempting to undo the coherence and bedrock force of the sovereign conscience. Their resistance is essentially an effort to direct conscience out of the flow of the antinomian stream, and toward the casuistic. Cromwell challenges the sovereign conscience at its core, by attempting to reign in antinomian claims for divine inspiration: "we should all take heed of mentioning our own thoughts and conceptions with that which is of God."[53] In a fascinating anticipation of *Samson Agonistes*, Cromwell frequently brings up the problem of judging whether

---

[49] *Ibid.*, 13–14. Also see John Everard, described in the Putney manuscript as "Buff-Coat," 34.

[50] *Ibid.*, 27.

[51] Wildman, *Putney Projects*, 3, 11. Also see Woodhouse, *Puritanism and Liberty*, 475.

[52] Wildman, *Putney Projects*, 46. Also see Woodhouse, *Puritanism and Liberty*, 69.

[53] Woodhouse, *Puritanism and Liberty*, 103.

an apprehension is "of God" or not, identifying this hermeneutic as the particular office of conscience:

> If in those things we do speak, and pretend to speak from God, there be mistakes of fact, if there be a mistake in the thing or in the reason of the thing, truly I think it is free for me to show both the one and the other, if I can. Nay, I think it is my duty to do it; for no man receives anything in the name of the Lord further than to the light of his conscience appears.[54]

As with the antinomian preachers, conscience is intertwined with inspiration, even to the point of invoking "the light of conscience." But Cromwell also considers it a duty to cast a skeptical gaze on inspiration, as a way to contain its excesses and errors.

Cromwell also challenges the sovereign conscience by attempting to foil its privacy, connecting it to the more communal discourses of the casuistic stream. Responding to Leveller claims that conscience can justify breaking past engagements, Cromwell insists that "Our engagements are public engagements. They are to the kingdom, and to every one in the kingdom that could look upon what we did publicly declare."[55] Through the lens of public obligation, conscientious action will not assert the sovereignty of the individual, but rather will subordinate the individual's perspective to that of the public:

> Those who do apprehend obligations lying upon them . . . that they would clearly come to this resolution, that if they found in their judgments and consciences that those engagements led to anything which really cannot consist with the liberty and safety and public interest of this nation, they would account the general duty paramount to the other, so far as not to oppose any other that would do better for the nation than they will do.[56]

Cromwell invokes the ideological position of "judgments and consciences," which the Levellers align with the sovereign conscience. But now conscience is subject to public interest, as political obligation to the nation is stronger than the private, antinomian faculty. Cromwell makes conscience less sovereign by attaching it securely to the public realm.

Cromwell at Putney is often more casuistic than we might expect, asserting a conscience that has more to do with practical facts and reason and communicability, and less to do with private inspiration. Under the

---

[54] *Ibid.*, 101.
[55] *Ibid.*, 16. Ireton, hoping to quell resistance to engagements, warns that they should "take heed, that we may consider first engagements so far as they are engagementes publicly of the Army. I do not speak of particular engagements; I would not have them considered, if there be any." *Ibid.*, 50.
[56] *Ibid.*, 107.

pressure of Leveller radicalism, Cromwell is pulled away from his anti-nomian instincts.[57] So in the scene of conscience that unfolds at Putney, the faculty continues to support all sides. It can look like the sovereign conscience of Leveller democracy, and like the more orderly and communicable conscience of Grandee politics. In the debates, what emerges is a scene in which the private conscience meets the public sphere, and in the back and forth of the scene, a political subject takes shape.

C. B. Macpherson calls this early modern formation a first example of possessive individualism. Macpherson discerns a "proprietorial quality" in Leveller individualism, so that the individual has "a property in his own person and capacities," and based on this property, "Levellers grounded all their claims for specific rights, civil, religious, economic, and political."[58] This was, according to Macpherson, "a leap in political theory as radical as Galileo's formulation of the law of uniform motion" – a leap into the political subject of modern liberalism.[59]

The basic innovation of possessive individualism lies in "deducing political obligation from the supposed or observed facts of man's nature," which is to say that political obligation has its origin in the individual, rather than God.[60] Here is formed a deontological subject that exists prior to rights and obligations. It, rather than an external law, is the fundamental source of political justification, making it the liberal subject that Michael Sandel calls an "Archimedean point" of origin.[61] This Archimedean point, justifying rights and obligations, is in many ways identical to the sovereign conscience. Both the possessive individual and the sovereign conscience provide the origin and authority for individual political actions. Both coincide with the assertion of rights and the formation of obligations. Both make possible emerging liberalism.

The fit is not exact with Macpherson, as in his argument possessive individualism is a secular phenomenon, a product of seventeenth-century market forces. As long as conscience is the little god within, the faculty cannot be Macpherson's anthropocentric origin to political obligation.[62] However, the early modern conscience is pre-secular in

---

[57] On Cromwell's more antinomian conscience, see Lobo, "Early Quaker Writing."

[58] Macpherson, *The Political Theory of Possessive Individualism*, 142.

[59] *Ibid.*, 77.

[60] *Ibid.*, 15.

[61] Sandel, *Liberalism and the Limits of Justice*, 20–2.

[62] Macpherson briefly characterizes Leveller claims for religious freedom as "property in one's own mental and spiritual person," but otherwise does not address religious sources of the liberal subject. *The Political Theory of Possessive Individualism*, 142.

varying degrees: when conscience functions through the Holy Spirit, it is more directly linked to a divine origin, and when it is disentangled from antinomianism and made casuistic, it becomes more anthropocentric. In the uncanny shuttling between these modes, conscience can take on the qualities of possessive individualism, appearing as an Archimedean point; it can also be powerfully and energetically theological, crossing the border between a pre-secular understanding of the individual, and the deontological subject of modern liberalism. In the complex scene of the early modern conscience, the faculty can serve all sides, and in doing so gives rough shape to the liberal subject. It is no surprise, then, to find it also serving the philosophy most explicitly ranged against the Levellers, a philosophy that is also commonly associated with the emergence of the liberal subject, that of *Leviathan*.

Conscience in *Leviathan*

As discussed in Chapter 3, Hobbes undermines the inward scene of *knowing with*, and with it the authority of private conscience. He argues that "conscience" signifies a more communicable and shared way of knowing: "When two, or more men, know of one and the same fact, they are said to be Conscious of it one to another; which is as much as to know it together." As a private faculty, the word is only used "metaphorically, for the knowledge of their own secret facts, and secret thoughts." The individual conscience is merely a metaphor, and so is an abuse. For in Hobbes's view, private conscience is politically destructive, lending an overwhelming authority to what would otherwise just be personal opinion, and thereby giving power to those who are "vehemently in love with their own new opinions (though never so absurd)" (*Lev.* I:7, 48).[63] *Leviathan* is clearly responding to the Civil War, and it is likely that Hobbes's vehement men and new opinions are such radical voices as the Levellers and the Puritan preachers who invoke conscience so often in the 1640s.[64] Indeed this etymology does the same thing as Cromwell's response to the Agitators at Putney, separating conscience from the private sphere, in order to establish it as a public faculty.

This recasting of conscience as public is essential to Hobbes's commonwealth. In order to preserve the authority of the sovereign, Hobbes

[63] Similarly, inspiration is a mere metaphor. *Lev.* III:34, 278.
[64] David Wooton argues for *Leviathan* as a response to the Levellers. *Divine Right and Democracy*, 56–8.

particularly fears the private determination of morality: it is one of the diseases of a commonwealth "That every private man is Judge of Good and Evil Actions" (*Lev.* I:29, 223).[65] Closely related is another doctrine said to weaken the commonwealth, that individual conscience is so authoritative that "whatsoever a man does against his Conscience, is sinne." In response, Hobbes takes aim at the absolute sovereignty of the faculty, the idea that one is obligated to obey even an erring conscience. Hobbes concedes that in the state of nature this is so, since the individual has no other rule. But when there is civil law, private conscience is not sovereign:

> yet it is not so with him that lives in a Common-wealth; because the Law is the publique Conscience, by which he hath already undertaken to be guided. Otherwise in such diversity, as there is of private consciences, which are but private opinions, the Common-wealth must needs be distracted, and no man dare to obey the Soveraign Power, farther than it shall seem good in his own eyes.
>
> (*Lev.* II:29, 223)

In the politics of the 1640s, conscience has become too private and too isolated from the legal filiations of the commonwealth. Its radical consequences are contained by theorizing a "publique Conscience."

This is to return conscience to the casuistic stream, where it is understood as a communicable faculty, governed by law. And yet the assertion that "the Law is the publique Conscience" creates a strange new form for the faculty. Casuistry surrounds the familiar private conscience with the practical exigencies of cases. Hobbes instead translates it entirely into a public and legal structure. In light of its theological foundations, there is something nonsensical about a public conscience. How can we understand the scholastic categories of power, habit, and act, or the bipartite structure of *synderesis* and *conscientia*, mapped onto the idea of law? How does the Protestant emphasis on salvation, or Calvinist despair, pertain to a conscience that is collective? The inescapably inward and psychological dynamics of conscience would seem to apply to the idea of a public faculty – to reverse Hobbes – only metaphorically.[66]

---

[65] In *De Cive* "the private knowledge of Good and Evil . . . cannot be granted without the ruine of all Governments." Hobbes, *De Cive*, XII.6, 150.

[66] There is some precedence for a public conscience. The Chancery was often known as the court of the King's conscience, which expands the faculty beyond the borders of the individual, locating it in law. But this tradition has more to do with the mystical idea of the king's two bodies than Hobbes is likely to admit into his materialist system. See Hanson, *From Kingdom to*

But if a public conscience is hard to imagine in its functioning, it does fit well with the mechanism of contract that makes *Leviathan's* artificial sovereign. Hobbes asserts that private conscience is essential to natural law, as "The Lawes of Nature oblige in Conscience always," but adds an important qualification: "but in Effect then onely where there is Security." Alongside this note, he explains, "The Lawes of Nature oblige *in foro interno*; that is to say, they bind to a desire they should take place; *but in foro externo*; that is, to the putting them in act, not alwayes." He reasons that in a state of nature, anyone who did follow conscience, acting modestly and fulfilling all promises, would be the only one doing so, and would "make himselfe a prey to others, and procure his own certain ruine" (*Lev.* I:15, 110).⁶⁷ Conscience cannot be acted upon because it would contradict the right to survival. Only after the social contract has created a commonwealth can conscience take effect – but now transformed into a public conscience. Just as contract transfers sovereignty from the individual to the sovereign, so conscience is translated from the private individual to the public and artificial domain of law.

In Hobbes's commonwealth, conscience cannot be private. Private conscience threatens the sovereign precisely because it has itself become sovereign – raising the possibility of a nation of sovereigns, each an exception to the law. So Hobbes degrades conscience into metaphor and reconstitutes it in strictly public terms. And yet, even as it is carried across into a public faculty, private conscience does not actually go away. Rather, in Hobbes's *Leviathan* the private and sovereign conscience repeatedly returns into view, in surprising but crucial places. Hobbes does not, and cannot, banish private conscience from his system because it is too productive of political obligation to be fully elided.

First, private conscience serves a crucial purpose as a conduit for natural law, the gateway through which the laws of nature become obligations in the commonwealth. As Perez Zagorin points out, natural law is the foundation of Hobbes's theory of contract: the second law is to form contracts in the pursuit of peace (*Lev.* I:14, 92), and the third is that contracts must be kept (*Lev.* I:15, 100).⁶⁸ As natural laws, these spurs to contract are felt through conscience – "The Lawes of Nature oblige in Conscience always" – so that the formation and keeping of

---

Commonwealth, 253–80. On the idea of a public person, see Hill, "Covenant Theology and the Concept of the Public Person."

⁶⁷ Also see Hobbes, *De Cive*, III.27, 72.
⁶⁸ Zagorin, *Hobbes and the Law of Nature*, 30–65.

contracts rely on the functioning of conscience. When conscience facili-
tates natural law it is part of Hobbes's argument showing, according to
Zagorin, "the way of egress from the state of nature" into the commonwealth.[69] So even if conscience is only felt in the commonwealth as
public, it arrives at that contractual status because of its (possibly imper-
ceptible) private functioning in the state of nature.

The private conscience not only is a conduit from nature to contract,
but it continues to exert itself within the commonwealth through the
sovereign, who has a conscience and maintains full use of it. Unlike
the relationships within a commonwealth, the relationship between one
sovereign and another remains in the state of nature, in which each sovereign has the right to procure his own safety, as well as that of his people.
So the "Law of Nations," Hobbes asserts, is the "Law of Nature," as the
relationship between sovereigns is to be understood in terms of natural
law. And here private conscience remains in effect, as the "court" of
natural law:

> And the same Law, that dictateth to men that have no Civil Government,
> what they ought to do, and what to avoyd in regard of one another, dicta-
> teth the same to Common-wealths, that is, to the Consciences of
> Soveraign Princes, and Soveraign Assemblies; there being no Court
> of Naturall Justice, but in the Conscience onely.
>
> (*Lev.* II:30, 244)

Furthermore, the sovereign's conscience extends beyond foreign relations, exerting significant authority over the spiritual lives of domestic
subjects. In the commonwealth, the sovereign can appoint a pope or any
form of ecclesiastical government, "as they please, so they doe it out of a
sincere conscience of which God onely is the Judge" (*Lev.* III:42, 378).
The king's conscience, in private communication with God, directs the
entire ecclesiastical apparatus, from appointments to teaching, preaching,
and sacraments (*Lev.* III:42, 373–5). It is worth noticing how Hobbes's
Erastianism in some ways takes the form of liberty of conscience. True,
it belongs only to the sovereign – but just as tolerationists have been
demanding, conscience, rather than custom or Church authorities, serves
to determine how to worship.

Beyond these temporal arrangements, Hobbes reserves for the sovereign the power to interpret Scripture, which amounts to an authority

---

[69] *Ibid.*, 44. On the intertwining of conscience and natural law in the seventeenth century, see Kahn,
Wayward Contracts, 29–56.

over individual salvation. Even the ten commandments are merely good counsel in themselves, and only become laws when a sovereign is able to enforce them (*Lev.* III:42, 356–60).[70] In *De Cive*, Hobbes places the sovereign's conscience directly over his subject's salvation when he asks whether sovereigns sin against the law of nature "if they cause not such a doctrine, and worship, to be taught and practised (or permit a contrary to be taught and practised) as they beleeve necessarily conduceth to the eternal salvation of their subjects?" He answers, "It is manifest they act against their conscience."[71] For Hobbes, conscience is understood in its basic Protestant task of determining salvation, and the fact of the sovereign's representation of the subject through contract means that the king's own private conscience, with all of its beliefs and persuasions, guides religion in the commonwealth. In this way the Protestant conscience is turned into law and made public, and in this way Christian sovereigns do the work of *knowing with*, being "the onely Persons, whom Christians now hear speak from God" (*Lev.* III:43, 405).[72]

And still the private conscience in *Leviathan* is not wholly accounted for: beyond the sovereign, it continues its presence even within the commonwealth's subjects. After all, if private conscience is part of the state of nature, and if its efficacy is evident in so much of the sovereign's power, it cannot be easily denied a place in each individual. For Hobbes all people are equal, so what is natural in the king's person is also natural in each individual. In the chapter on vain philosophies, Hobbes gives surprising authority to the individual conscience in his argument against inquisition:

> There is another Errour in their Civill Philosophy (which they never learned of Aristotle, nor Cicero, nor any other of the Heathen,) to extend the power of the Law, which is the Rule of Actions onely, to the very Thoughts, and Consciences of men, by Examination, and Inquisition of what they Hold, notwithstanding the Conformity of their Speech and Actions.
>
> (*Lev.* IV: 46, 471)

---

[70] See Mitchell, "Thomas Hobbes: On Religious Liberty and Sovereignty," 131–4. Also see Tuck, "The Civil Religion of Thomas Hobbes."

[71] Hobbes, *De Cive*, 13:5, 158.

[72] As Kevin Sharpe has shown, Charles emphasized the king's private conscience, and the extension of its authority over the kingdom. *Remapping Early Modern England*, 172–98. The sovereignty of Charles's conscience is a main target in Milton's *Eikonoklastes*, where he mocks the idea that "all Britain was to be ty'd and chain'd to the conscience, judgement, and reason of one Man," and declares, "For certainly a privat conscience sorts not with a public Calling." *CPW* III:359, 369.

Law wields power only over actions, and so has no power over the inward life of conscience. Hobbes values conformity, and goes on to say that a civil magistrate, when hiring a minister, can exert control over what doctrines are taught (*Lev.* IV: 46, 471). So he has not admitted into the commonwealth the liberties sought by Independents and tolerationists. But in carving out a sovereign space within each individual, one that is protected from the considerable force of the law, Hobbes preserves the fundamentally antinomian center of the Protestant conscience.

This leads to a remarkable passage in the ecclesiastical history of the next chapter, in which a clearly antinomian conscience plays a key role in the Reformation. Hobbes tells a story of the tying and untying of three knots. Primitive Christianity under the apostles was subject to civil but not ecclesiastical power, and as a result, "Their Consciences were free, and their Words and Actions subject to none but the Civill Power." But then Presbyters and their assemblies began to police doctrine through excommunication – "And this was the first knot upon their Liberty." The Presbyters' power increased, and they became Bishops, which was "the second knot on Christian Liberty." And the "third and last knot" was the creation of papal power. Hobbes then describes the untying of these knots in reverse order, through the English Reformation. First the power of the Popes was undone by Elizabeth. Then the English Presbyterians put down Episcopacy – "and so was the second knot dissolved." And then the third knot is untied by the recent rise of the Independents:

> And almost at the same time, the Power was taken also from the Presbyterians: And so we are reduced to the Independency of the Primitive Christians to follow Paul, or Cephas, or Apollos, every man as he liketh best: Which, if it be without contention, and without measuring the Doctrine of Christ, by our affection to the Person of his Minister, (the fault which the Apostle reprehended in the Corinthians) is perhaps the best: First, because there ought to be no Power over the Consciences of men, but of the Word it selfe, working Faith in every one, not always according to the purpose of them that Plant and Water, but of God himself, that giveth Increase: and secondly, because it is unreasonable in them, who teach there is such danger in every little Errour, to require of a man endued with Reason of his own, to follow the Reason of any other man, or of the most voices of many other men; Which is little better, then to venture his Salvation at crosse and pile.
>
> (*Lev.* IV: 47, 479–80)

Most surprising here is Hobbes suggesting that Independency "is perhaps the best" form of religion. He aligns it with primitive Christianity, a sure marker of approval in Protestant discourse, and defends it with a seemingly revolutionary call, that "there ought to be no Power over the Consciences of men, but of the Word it selfe." He considers contemporary England to be the turning point in liberty, echoing the millenarianism of many radicals. Hobbes does qualify his judgment of Independency with "if it be without contention," which with the Civil War in mind can quickly reinstate Erastian controls over religion. But this is a rather subordinated qualification, and the surprising assertion of liberty of conscience is otherwise left to stand. Hobbes turns to a chapter on Catholicism and fairies, and then *Leviathan* comes to a close.

That Independency "is perhaps the best," and that "there ought to be no Power over the Consciences of men," opens a door to the sovereignty of private conscience even in the public realm of the commonwealth. In this way the passage is contrary to Hobbes's repeated dismissals of personal inspiration and private judgment. Early in *Leviathan* Hobbes is quite categorical in his assertions of public over private conscience, and this has generally won the attention of readers.[73] But private conscience lingers. It is instrumental to Hobbesian contract, serving as a conduit from natural law to the commonwealth; it remains entirely intact in the sovereign; it is present even in the commonwealth's subjects, though walled off from public discourse and action; and it survives as a key to the revolutions of ecclesiastical history.

Recognizing the surprising endurance of the private conscience, Olivier Feltham has observed that the faculty is continuously present in the commonwealth, and suggests that it has an active function as a kind of "switch" in which the individual repeatedly makes and remakes a commitment to the social contract. According to Feltham, "Conscience is thus not merely the inward and opaque site of private beliefs but rather a source of action, switching allegiance on or off. This is a permanent possibility: it is coextensive with the existence of the commonwealth."[74] Feltham's reading is based on the insight that Hobbesian contract, as many readers have noticed, is not something that happens once, but must happen again and again in the commonwealth. Contract is not just how the commonwealth is made, but also how it is maintained, as it must be reenacted in each generation and in the life of each subject.[75]

---

[73] E.g. Fish, "How Hobbes Works."
[74] Feltham, *Anatomy of Failure*, 209.
[75] E.g. Giorgio Agamben: "The state of nature is, in truth, a state of exception, in which the city appears for an instant (which is at the same time a chronological interval and a nontemporal

The movement from private to public conscience, closely bound up in the formation of contract, is similarly not a single event in history, but rather creates the necessary conditions for the commonwealth in each individual. The movement from private to public conscience, then, is part of the construction of a subject that can take part in contract and Hobbesian obligation.

This process can be better understood in light of Carole Pateman's analysis of the problem of political obligation. Pateman takes Hobbes as an exemplar of liberal obligation, an extreme example of the liberal reliance on voluntarism, the process by which subjects "voluntarily oblige themselves."[76] Such "self-assumed obligation" depends upon a radically independent subject, the self who can be the sole origin of the contract – what Michael Sandel calls the Archimedean point of the liberal subject. So in Hobbes, and throughout liberalism, self-assumed obligation has been entangled with the wholly autonomous subject of possessive individualism. But inevitably, Pateman argues, the possessive individual becomes "radically abstract."[77] The problem is that liberal obligation cannot function in a purely voluntarist mode, but necessarily relies on an increasingly "hypothetical voluntarism." Individuals do not directly promise: their obligations "are not explicit undertakings, but the implicit or tacit consequences of actions" such as voting, or, in Locke's example, simply walking down the highway. Consent is inferred by theorists and understood to take place hypothetically, rather than explicitly willed by each individual.[78] In private, self-assumed obligation may remain intact, but publicly it becomes hypothetical and abstract.

In making conscience public, Hobbes constructs Pateman's hypothetical self-assumed obligation. The strong and expanding power of the sovereign conscience is quieted by its abstraction from the individual, leading to consent that fits into the public sphere universally, and without possibility of retraction. Just as Cromwell's move toward a public conscience reasserts the obligation of past engagements for the New Model Army, so Hobbes's translation of private conscience into a public faculty establishes the totalizing political obligation of his

---

moment) *tanquam dissoluta*. The foundation is thus not an event achieved once and for all but is continually operative in the civil state in the form of the sovereign decision." *Homo Sacer*, 109.

[76] Pateman, *The Problem of Political Obligation*, 49.

[77] *Ibid.*, 24, 38.

[78] *Ibid.*, 16. Or Pateman points to the simple fact that a first generation could agree to a social contract, but each successive generation must consent only hypothetically or by implication. *Ibid.*, 22.

commonwealth.[79] Hobbes does not entirely banish private conscience, though, because the move from private to public cannot be a one-time event, but must take place in each individual. Hobbes's political subject requires both: the judgment and consent of a private conscience establishes self-assumed obligation, driving the basic voluntarism of Hobbes's political system; this powerful but unruly force then is abstracted in order to take part in the public sphere.

The movement from private to public conscience, then, is what brings each individual fully into line with the needs of the commonwealth. It is key to the creation of the liberal subject of contract theory. Pateman does not name it as such, but her observations about the abstraction of the voluntarist individual serve as an account of the formation of the "thin subject" that communitarians have noticed in classic liberal theory. Reading Rawls, Sandel focuses on liberalism's reliance on a deontological self, "the human subject as a sovereign agent of choice."[80] This voluntarist subject is made thin through a process of abstraction: "the self, shorn of all contingently given attributes, assumes a kind of supra-empirical status, essentially unencumbered, bounded in advance and given prior to its ends, a pure subject of agency and possession, ultimately thin."[81] The thin subject is necessary to a pure voluntarism, though in the communitarian critique it is at the expense of an understanding of the self that is more widely and more thickly intertwined with others. The subject of Hobbes's commonwealth is just such a thin subject. It becomes so when it moves from the robust sovereignty of private conscience to the artificial and abstract subject of public conscience.

In this light, the early modern conscience detailed in this book can be seen as some of the thickness ususally missing from the liberal subject.[82]

---

[79] Pateman recognizes that conscience, in its typical modern sense of private and sovereign, cannot lead to a strong sense of obligation: "The last thing that Hobbes would want is that 'conscience' in the conventional sense should be enshrined at the heart of his political argument; he makes it very clear that conscience has no politically relevant place in civil society." *Ibid.*, 49.

[80] Sandel, *Liberalism and the Limits of Justice*, 22.

[81] *Ibid.*, 94. Stephen Mulhall and Adam Swift describe the thin subject as the liberal voluntarist claim that "when it comes to thinking about justice, people should be regarded as distinct from their particularity, both their particular natural endowments and social position and their particular conception of the good." *Liberals and Communitarians*, 11. In John Rawls's response to the communitarian critique, the liberal subject becomes political rather than metaphysical, which is to say it exists and does its work in a public sphere, driven by public reason. *Political Liberalism*, 212–54. Rawls makes the subject public, just as Hobbes does to conscience.

[82] Victoria Kahn makes the argument that the passions thicken the early modern subject: "the seventeenth-century subject of contract was not the thin modern subject of formal equality but rather, at one and the same time, a richly imagined 'aesthetic' subject of passion and interest, and an artifact of the creative powers of language." *Wayward Contracts*, 282–3.

The solidity of the scholastic structures, the destructuring of the reformed conscience, and all of the experiential texture that Protestant poets and theologians capture – all of these give remarkable thickness to the liberal subject. Similarly, the faculty's role in salvation and despair indicates the theological stakes of a thickly constituted being; self-reflection, consciousness, and the unconscious bespeak a complexity that is anything but thin; antinomian inspiration, and its clash with the public discursiveness of the casuistic stream, demonstrate an ambivalence that adds depth and dimension to the liberal subject. All of these form the early modern scene of conscience, a drama that allows the faculty to be discussed and experienced, and so allows it to give shape to the early modern political subject. If Hobbes's public conscience feels hard to imagine, it is because the conscience he inherits is so full of detail, so thick with contingencies and dramatic energies.

The voluntarist subject of Hobbes's commonwealth works because it has been thinned down and abstracted from the complex early modern conscience. Hobbes's etymology of conscience performs exactly this thinning, by shifting the faculty to mere metaphor, and stripping away the voices and visions that animate the scene of *knowing with*. As with Herbert of Cherbury's geometric faculty, it has been disenchanted – removed from the moralized universe, and largely secularized. This disenchanting is what prepares the subject to become the possessive individual of liberal voluntarism, as Sandel explains:

> Bound up with the notion of an independent self is a vision of the moral universe this self must inhabit. Unlike classical Greek and medieval Christian conceptions, the universe of the deontological ethic is a place devoid of inherent meaning, a world 'disenchanted' in Max Weber's phrase, a world without an objective moral order. Only in a universe empty of *telos*, such as seventeenth-century science and philosophy affirmed, is it possible to conceive a subject apart from and prior to its purposes and ends.[83]

The Archimedean point – the thin subject of liberalism – emerges in Hobbes's disenchanting of conscience. The lingering of the private conscience in *Leviathan*, then, can be described as uncanny, in the specific sense of when an enchanted world has been skeptically surmounted, but then returns to break in upon the skepticism. The private conscience, with its antinomian inspiration and thickly constituted scene of *knowing*

---

[83] Sandel, *Liberalism and the Limits of Justice*, 175.

with, returns to *Leviathan* in a ghostly manner, or as a kind of theoretical unconscious.

As liberal political theory helps to show, this ambivalent scene is highly productive, becoming the key site in which Hobbes forges his political subject. Hobbes reveals how conscience is ambivalently but continually operative in each liberal subject – just as the destructured Protestant faculty is experienced as again and again falling away from structure. In its theological context, conscience is experienced as continually destructuring; this thickness of conscience is then, in its political context, experienced as continually thinning. Such a chain reaction forms a continual justification for the deontological subject, and traces a continual movement from Christian liberty to liberalism. In this way conscience serves as a kind of hidden battery, powering the politics of revolutionary England with the energy of the Reformation.

Hobbes, in his devotion to a systematic philosophy, seems unaware of how contradictory his handling of conscience is. But John Milton, who thinks as a theologian and as a political philosopher, and who approaches both of these modes with the imaginative and synthetic resources of a poet, is uniquely positioned to capture the early modern conscience in all of its complexity.

6

Milton's Expansive Conscience

Paradise Lost

Paradise Lost surveys nearly every important scene of conscience in early
modern England. It invokes the faculty in a wide array of situations and
forms, an array that the preceding chapters of this book equip us to recognize. Coming late in the Reformation and writing his late works after the
radical politics of the mid century, Milton is in a position to understand the
faculty as both rational and inspirational, and as both private experience and
public discourse. He is, moreover, a poet, with a poet's linguistic resources
and syncretic imagination, and so he combines poetry, theology, and politics
in a uniquely expansive conscience. Early schemes for *Paradise Lost* included
an allegorical personification, "Conscience" (*CPW* VIII:554–5). Having left
behind that archaic figure for a more destructured faculty, Milton gathers
in the many different ways that conscience is understood in the period, to
form an exceptionally expansive and plural conscience.

Working backward through the poem, which means beginning near-
est to the reader in the fallen world of Book 12, conscience appears
in its 1640s context as an antinomian expression of individual liberty.
Describing the evolution of the church, when "grievous wolves" have
taken over, Michael foresees that:

> Spiritual laws by carnal power shall force
> On every conscience; laws which none shall find
> Left them enrolled, or what the Spirit within
> Shall on the heart engrave. What will they then
> But force the spirit of grace it self, and bind
> His consort liberty; what, but unbuild
> His living temples, built by faith to stand,
> Their own faith not another's: for on earth
> Who against faith and conscience can be heard
> Infallible?
>
> (12.521–30)

Catholic priests, like the Presbyterians of the toleration crisis, exert carnal, i.e. temporal or political, power over the spiritual realm. So conscience must be protected from forcing and binding – a vocabulary that constructs the faculty as continuously facing restriction and striving toward freedom. As it does for many Independents and Levellers, such a conscience borders on the antinomian. So in this passage conscience is aligned twice with the Spirit, as well as with Grace, liberty, and faith.[1]

A little earlier in Book 12, Milton places conscience in a more Lutheran context. Having heard about the tabernacle and Abraham's promised seed, Adam wonders at the profusion of laws in the world of the Old Testament. Michael explains that the Law "can discover sin, but not remove" (12.290), and that the ineffectiveness of the Law is meant to demonstrate the necessity of Grace in the New Testament, so that

> they may conclude
> Some blood more precious must be paid for man,
> Just for unjust, that in such righteousness
> To them by faith imputed, they may find
> Justification towards God, and peace
> Of conscience, which the law by ceremonies
> Cannot appease, nor man the moral part
> Perform, and not performing cannot live.
>
> (12.292–9)

As Luther laments in the tower conversion, the Law makes demands that are impossible to fulfill, so that a conception of righteousness based upon works and ceremonies leads only to the rage and suffering of a wounded conscience.[2] In Luther's archetypal conversion he turns from righteousness to faith, and there discovers a regenerate conscience that is identifiable by its peacefulness. So Michael uses "peace/Of conscience" as the familiar marker of justification. This does not contradict the 1640s vocabulary of liberty of conscience, but focuses instead on the inward theology of the whole person, and the private freedom of Christian liberty. Luther

---

[1] Similarly, in the opening paragraph of *The Doctrine and Discipline of Divorce*, conscience is persuasive "in the plain demonstration of the spirit." *CPW* II:222. This matches the later argument for divorce as a matter of conscience, and not a matter of the law or the magistrate. *CPW* II:343. This chapter is preceded by the dismissal of custom, in which "wee never leave subtilizing and casuisting till wee have straitn'd and par'd that liberal path into a razors edge to walk on." *CPW* II:343.

[2] Similarly, in *Of Reformation*, the superstitious man, "being scarr'd from thence by the pangs, and gripes of a boyling conscience, all in a pudder shuffles up to himselfe such a *God*, and such a *worship* as is most agreeable to remedy his feare, which feare of his, as also is his hope, fixt onely upon the Flesh." *CPW* I.522.

and Calvin both mention conscience almost exclusively in terms of the suffering caused by works, and as a portal to Christian liberty. They rarely mention conscience in terms of forcing or the political consequences of its liberty. But, as we have seen, the faculty evolves in England from its private, Lutheran scene to public and political scenes, and Milton, in his expansive conception, articulates both in the world of Book 12.

Moving to Book 10, conscience appears in the wake of the fall as a deeply despairing experience. Adam's long soliloquy begins "O miserable of happy!" (10.720), and ends in Calvinist terms:

> Thus what thou desirest
> And what thou fear'st, alike destroys all hope
> Of refuge, and concludes thee miserable
> Beyond all past example and future,
> To Satan only like both crime and doom.
> O conscience! into what abyss of fears
> And horrors hast thou driven me; out of which
> I find no way, from deep to deeper plunged!
>   Thus Adam to himself lamented loud
> Through the still night, not now, as ere man fell,
> Wholesome and cool, and mild, but with black air
> Accompanied, with damps and dreadful gloom,
> Which to his evil conscience represented
> All things with double terror.
>
>   (10.837–50)

Fallen and remorseful, but not yet privy to Michael's news of redemption, Adam is overwhelmed by the despairing sense that he is forever alienated from God. Here conscience is stuck in the painful logic of the Law, all sin and retribution, without the hope of Grace. Like Luther in the tower, Adam laments. And like a Calvinist anxious that he is one of the reprobate, Adam is overwhelmed by fears and horrors until melancholy sets in. Imagination takes over, as with Redcrosse or the Macbeths, as the night's gloom combines with conscience to create double terror.

Michael will serve as Adam's Una, so that the despairing conscience eventually functions as a step toward the regenerate and liberating conscience of Book 12. But Milton is also interested in capturing the pure experience of despair, in its psychological and imaginative dimensions. Adam says he resembles Satan, and he is partly right. The despairing

conscience finds rich expression in Satan's tragic soliloquy of Book 4, and
it too is full of horror:

> Horror and doubt distract
> His troubled thoughts, and from the bottom stir
> The hell within him, for within him hell
> He brings, and round about him, nor from hell
> One step no more than from himself can fly
> By change of place: now conscience wakes despair
> That slumbered, wakes the bitter memory
> Of what he was, what is, and what must be
> Worse; of worse deeds worse sufferings must ensue.
> (4.18–26)

This is indeed how Adam feels in the moment. But the difference is that
Satan's despair is fully accurate, since, as we have learned from God,
Satan will receive no Grace (3.132). Although the theology of *Paradise
Lost* is careful to give Satan free will before his fall, here Milton stages a
most Calvinist experience, with conscience darkened by the conviction
of irrevocable damnation. There is no way to say that his suffering is due
to false conceptions – Hell really is within Satan; his is the single worst
case of a despairing conscience in history. Satan and Adam's despairing
consciences enact in rich poetic detail the central theological drama of
salvation, reminding us that the early modern faculty is not just about
the political matters of revolution, but also about the theological striving
and psychological suffering that go along with salvation and damnation.[3]

Located between these fallen moments of despair is an ambiguously
prelapsarian experience of conscience, hinting at a self-consciousness
that feels out of place in Eden. Speaking to Raphael, Adam describes the
moment that Eve was first brought to him, guided by a voice. Adam calls
out, but she turns away:

> She heard me thus, and though divinely brought,
> Yet innocence and virgin modesty,
> Her virtue and the conscience of her worth,
> That would be wooed, and not unsought be won,
> Not obvious, not obtrusive, but retired,
> The more desirable, or to say all,

---

[3] Similarly, in *De Doctrina Christiana* Chapter 12, "Of the Punishment of Sin," "guiltiness is either
accompanied or followed by terrors of conscience . . . also by the loss of divine protection and
favor, which results in the lessening of the majesty of the human countenance, and the degradation
of the mind . . . Thus the whole man is defiled." *CPW* VI.394.

> Nature her self, though pure of sinful thought,
> Wrought in her so, that seeing me, she turned.
>
> (8.500–7)

Conscience here, as in Hamlet's soliloquy, signifies equivocally between the moral faculty and awareness – conscience and consciousness. Eve may simply be aware of her worth. Or, as an adjunct to virtue, this awareness may carry the theological weight of the moral faculty. Such ambiguity would seem to occur naturally and innocently in the prelapsarian condition. Given that Eve explicitly does not know what sin is, conscience modulates into mere awareness. Such an innocent conscience, a pure knowing, coincides with the way that unfallen reason operates instinctively, like that of the angels. In the only explicit appearance of conscience before the fall in *Paradise Lost*, we can glimpse the possibility of *synderesis*, which is often described as a remnant of unfallen knowledge.

And yet Eve's conscience is more ambivalent than that, as it also reads as an unstable moment of subjectivity. Her conscience becomes consciousness, betraying a Hamlet-like mode of being which is entirely out of place in the Garden. Raphael is alarmed when, moments later, Adam says of Eve,

> so absolute she seems
> And in her self complete, so well to know
> Her own, that what she wills to do or say,
> Seems wisest, virtuousest, discreetest, best;
> All higher knowledge in her presence falls
> Degraded.
>
> (8.547–52)

Eve has a self-knowledge that appears synonymous with the self-reflective conscience: "so well to know/ Her own." She turns away from Adam, and we know from Book 4 that she is turning back to seek her own reflection. This kind of self-possession and reflexive awareness enacts a movement from conscience as mere awareness to conscience as reflexive knowledge and consciousness. It is disturbing because it feels too much like the psychology and subjectivity of fallen humanity. In fact it precipitates a fall in Adam, degrading higher knowledge as if this lower way of reflexive knowing was contagious. In this way, "conscience" may operate like "wanton," as one of those words which can be read in either a fallen or unfallen sense. If Eve has a conscience, a complex inner life of knowledge and moral judgment, then she is already in some sense fallen. Of course, it is important to recognize that Eve's conscience, with all of these implications, is not something we know at first hand, but is rather assumed by Adam. His Book 8 account of Eve's turn is at variance with Eve's account in Book 4, where no mention is made of conscience (4.449–91). Frustratingly, but typically, Adam uses "conscience" to stand in for an experience in Eve which eludes description and understanding. As the faculty becomes hard to define or even locate, we can see that *Paradise Lost* has included the Protestant conscience's tendency to become inchoate. Eve's conscience brings the destructured energies of subjectivity and self-reflection to the poem's expansive conception.[4]

Last in this survey of the appearances of conscience is the first and most famous in the poem, the "umpire conscience" decreed by God. As part of the long theological exposition of Book 3, the umpire conscience is essential to Milton's theology of free will, and is cast in rational terms:

> Some I have chosen of peculiar grace
> Elect above the rest; so is my will:
> The rest shall hear me call, and oft be warned
> Their sinful state, and to appease betimes
> The incensed Deity, while offered grace
> Invites; for I will clear their senses dark,
> What may suffice, and soften stony hearts
> To pray, repent, and bring obedience due.
> To prayer, repentance, and obedience due,
> Though but endeavoured with sincere intent,
> Mine ear shall not be slow, mine eye not shut.
> And I will place within them as a guide
> My umpire conscience, whom if they will hear,
> Light after light well used they shall attain,
> And to the end persisting, safe arrive.
> (3.183–97)

Merritt Hughes and Alastair Fowler both gloss the umpire conscience as equivalent to reason. Maurice Kelley aligns it with the "gift of reason" that Milton says in *De Doctrina* is "implanted in all."[5] As an umpire, conscience is authoritative: etymologically descending from "non" and "peer,"

---

[4] Similarly, in *De Doctrina* the evil conscience "should really be called a consciousness of evil." *CPW* VI:653.

[5] Kelley, *This Great Argument*, 18. Here Kelley uses the Sumner translation. When he translates *De Doctrina* in the *CPW*, he renders the passage as "everyone is provided with a sufficient degree of innate reason," and in a footnote points to the umpire conscience. *CPW* VI:186. Also see Low, "'Umpire Conscience,'" 356.

an umpire is peerless, a figure that stands above all others.[6] At the same time, the umpire works in the service of the law, as the word has several legal connotations, including arbitrator. In the vocabulary of Chapter 4, the umpire conscience is casuistic: rational, at home in the public discourse of rules and laws, and a practical guide.

These practical and rational qualities are reinforced by the Arminian context of God's larger exposition, which knits together free will and reason with the assertions that "reason also is choice" (3.108), and that humans are "authors to themselves in all/ Both what they judge and what they choose" (3.122–3). Judgment and choice together construct the authoritative place humans have in free will theology; the instrument that enables this entire Arminian system, guiding the rational work of judging and choosing, turns out to be the umpire conscience.[7]

Such a rational and practical conscience is quite opposite to the faculty of Book 12, when the temporal powers forcing conscience are said to "force the spirit of grace it self." An antinomian conscience of political sovereignty and a casuistic conscience of practical reason stand at either end of *Paradise Lost*, marking Milton's ability to think about the faculty in flexible and expansive ways. Meanwhile, in between these is a catalog of the various scenes of the inward conscience. These invoke Lutheran angst, Calvinist despair, and the reflexive consciousness of Hamlet or Perkins. Expansiveness in conscience does not simply allow for the inclusion of reason and inspiration; it calls forth another, related polarity, that of private and public. Milton feels intimately what this book has been demonstrating, that conscience is where the public and the private, as well as the rational and the inspired, blend and separate.

Milton is particularly inclined to think about these problems – to look at them and experiment with them. As was seen in the last chapter, Hobbes's effort to dismiss the private conscience only leads to a

---

[6] OED, s.v. "umpire."

[7] When Arminius makes room for free will in the process of salvation, he brings free will and conscience close together. One of his most important statements on soteriology is a response to a William Perkins treatise on predestination. In arguing against the perseverance of the saints, conscience becomes a key to the human activity that leads to salvation:

> A conscience accusing, and truly accusing, cannot consist with the grace or gratuitous favour of God to eternal life: for so the conscience would not accuse truly. For God will not bestow eternal life upon him whom his conscience testifies, and with truth, to be unworthy of eternal life; unless repentance intervene, which takes away the unworthiness by the gracious mercy of God.

Arminius, *Examination of Dr. Perkins's Pamphlet*, III:460. In contrast, Perkins says that a saint may feel "accusantem conscientiam, et testantem" but that "paternum affectum non exuit Deus: et propositum de adoptione vitaque aeterna non commutat." *De Praedestinationis*, 129.

commonwealth that is ambivalent about how private conscience enters into public discourse. Private conscience cannot be fully banished, but ambivalence relegates it to a kind of unconscious, outside of the direct gaze of his system. In contrast, Milton is capable of paying attention to the early modern conscience in all of its complexity. An expansive conception of the inward scene of conscience quite naturally allows for an expansive conception in public discourse: the ability to understand conscience as both rational and inspired goes hand in hand with the ability to understand it as both public and private. In this way Milton gets to know the problems of conscience as it enters into public discourse, and he begins to take on the habits of conscientious – emerging liberal – politics.

Such an expansive understanding of the conscience must be partly due to Milton's historical vantage, as he writes his late poetry after Luther, after Perkins, after Shakespeare, Calvinism, casuistry, and the emergence of conscience in the public discourses of toleration and the Civil War. It must also be due to Milton's achievements not only in theology and political theory, but also poetry. He is well attuned to the theological concerns of conscience as it navigates through works, faith, despair, and salvation. He is also deeply experienced in the political battles around liberty of conscience, toleration, obligation, and sovereignty. And, lending a fine-grained insight into the inward scene of conscience, Milton approaches all of these with his poetic imagination. As a result, there is a syncretic quality to Milton's conscience, which feels less like the ambivalence found in Hobbes, and more like inclusiveness and pluralism.

Areopagitica

The expansive quality of Milton's conscience gains early expression in *Areopagitica*. Conscience is clearly at the heart of the argument. Milton imagines a free society in which the faculty directs and legitimizes authorship:

> What can be more fair, then when a man judicious, learned, and of a conscience, for ought we know, as good as theirs that taught us what we know, shall not privily from house to house, which is more dangerous, but openly by writing publish to the world what his opinion is, what his reasons, and wherefore that which is now thought cannot be sound.
>
> (*CPW* II.547–8)

Learning is important, but conscience more so, trumping even the authority of teacher over pupil. Conscience guides not only the author, but also the reader, for "To the pure all things are pure, not only meats and drinks, but all kinde of knowledge whether of good or evill; the knowledge cannot defile, nor consequently the books, if the will and conscience be not defil'd" (*CPW* II:512). The faculty is at the center of an entire ecosystem of reading, writing, and knowledge, so that Milton declares: "Give me the liberty to know, to utter, and to argue freely according to conscience, above all liberties" (*CPW* II:560).

At the same time, *Areopagitica* has often been read as taking part in the formation of a politics that is newly public. Sharon Achinstein describes it as a "significant moment in the conceptualization of the public sphere"; David Norbrook calls it "Milton's major contribution toward the celebration of the public sphere."[8] This is part of a larger argument for Milton's republicanism.[9] And it engages with an even longer argument for *Areopagitica* as a landmark in the history of liberalism.[10] What I want to suggest here is that republicanism captures only part of how conscience operates in *Areopagitica*. As in Habermas's account, arguments for the emergence of the public sphere in *Areopagitica* emphasize reason. Achinstein describes how Milton envisions a revolutionary reading public that is "worthy to exercise their reasoning abilities amid a barrage of conflicting opinions."[11] Such a reading public is aligned with conscience, but it is a conscience functioning with "inner reason," "individual reason," and "reasoning capabilities."[12] Given how regularly and persuasively Milton invokes reason in *Areopagitica*, and given a more general critical assumption that conscience and reason are synonymous, this is an understandable generalization. But it does not sufficiently notice the antinomian tones that appear in the text's latter pages.[13]

In what Ernst Sirluck calls the "national digression" (*CPW* II.171), Milton directly asserts a vigorous public sphere for England, "a Nation not slow and dull, but of a quick, ingenious and piercing spirit" (*CPW* II.551). He first pictures the piercing spirit as a product of reason and its pursuits. The image of London defending truth involves not the use

---

[8] Achinstein, *Milton and the Revolutionary Reader*, 58. Norbrook, *Writing the English Republic*, 118–19. Also see Norbrook, "Areopagitica, Censorship, and the Early Modern Public Sphere."

[9] In addition to Achinstein and Norbrook, see Worden, "Milton's Republicanism"; Armitage et al., eds., *Milton and Republicanism*.

[10] See Kolbrenner, *Milton's Warring Angels*, 11–27; Fulton, "Areopagitica and the Roots of Liberal Epistemology."

[11] Achinstein, *Milton and the Revolutionary Reader*, 61.

[12] *Ibid.*, 67, 69.

[13] Nigel Smith notices echoes of radical puritanism, but sees republicanism and rationalism as more central, radical puritanism being merely "a set of tropes which are to be deployed when necessary." "*Areopagitica*: Voicing Contexts," 113–14.

of weapons, but writing and reading: "then there be pens and heads there, sitting by their studious lamps, musing searching, revolving new notions and ideas," and "others as fast reading, trying all things, assenting to the force of reason and convincement" (*CPW* II.554). But then Milton shifts to an argument that pictures a public sphere that is also authorized by inspiration. The nation is not merely learned, but becomes prophetic:

> What could a man require more from a Nation so pliant and so prone to seek after knowledge. What wants there to such a towardly and pregnant soile, but wise and faithfull labourers, to make a knowing people, a Nation of Prophets, of Sages, and of Worthies.
>
> (*CPW* II.554)

The "knowing" that the English people might achieve can indicate reason, but just as well consciousness and conscientiousness, all of which fit into Milton's complex idea of prophecy. Knowledge comes from reason, but in turning to prophecy Milton asserts that it also comes from the Spirit. He then pictures these citizen-prophets able to unite "into one generall and brotherly search after Truth; could we but forgoe this Prelaticall tradition of crowding free consciences and Christian liberties into canons and precepts of men" (*CPW* II.554).

The image of a "Nation of Prophets" derives from Numbers 11: 26–9, which tells how Moses explicitly allowed private individuals to express prophetic knowledge. In this episode Moses gathers the seventy elders at the tabernacle, where they are visited by the Spirit of God and prophesy. But the Spirit inspires more democratically:

> But there remained two of the men in the camp, the name of the one was Eldad, and the name of the other Medad: and the spirit rested upon them; and they were of them that were written, but went not out unto the tabernacle: and they prophesied in the camp. And there ran a young man, and told Moses, and said, Eldad and Medad do prophesy in the camp. And Joshua the son of Nun, the servant of Moses, one of his young men, answered and said, My lord Moses, forbid them. And Moses said unto him, Enviest thou for my sake? would God that all the Lord's people were prophets, and that the Lord would put his spirit upon them!

Numbers dramatizes *Areopagitica*'s argument against censorship, with inspiration rather than books. Moses is leading a limited prophetic gathering, of the seventy elders, in a limited space, the tabernacle. But he emphatically sanctions a more public form of prophecy, which authorizes a Spirit that visits private individuals. It turns out that not just the elders (regularly equated in the tolerationist discourse with Presbyterians) can be prophets, and that speech can take place not just in the tabernacle but in the public square: Eldad and Medad get to prophesy in the camp. Joshua sounds like a magistrate when he assumes that such an occurrence should be forbidden – Moses checks him, and further wishes that all people would be inspired, making the Israelites a nation of prophets.

The story is important enough to Milton that he returns to it twice more in *Areopagitica*. Continuing his description of the ascendant English nation, he declares, "For now the time seems come, wherein Moses the great Prophet may sit in heav'n, rejoycing to see that memorable and glorious wish of his fulfill'd, when not only our sev'nty Elders, but all the Lords people are become Prophets" (*CPW* II.555–6). What Moses wishes for the Israelites, Milton demands for England. And then in the conclusion, Milton returns to Joshua's suggestion, and how it was rejected by Moses, and sees it as analogous to the current censorship: "But if neither the check that Moses gave to young Joshua, nor the countermand which our Saviour gave to young John, who was so ready to prohibit those whom he thought unlicenc't, be not anough to admonish our Elders how unacceptable to God their testy mood of prohibiting is . . ." (*CPW* II.568). What is allowed by the Nation of Prophets is a politics like that of the Israelites' camp, which is to say, a public sphere with discourse authorized by the presence of the Spirit.

In its ecstatic tone, the national digression of *Areopagitica* reminds William Kerrigan of Cromwell, waiting "for some extraordinary dispensations."[14] Indeed, Numbers 11: 27 was a favorite of Cromwell's.[15] It was also a common text for separatists. Lord Brooke, in *Discourse of Episcopacie* (1642), says that separatist preachers often claim that they "have read of *Moses*, wishing all the Lords People were Prophets; and that God would poure out his Spirit on them all."[16] Brooke laments that the separatists are "stained with a taint of *Madnesse*, and I know not what *Enthusiasme*," for such a prophet, he says approvingly, will give up everything "rather than to breake his Peace, wound his Conscience, sinne against God."[17] In his argument for liberty of conscience, Brooke prefaces

---

[14] Kerrigan, *The Prophetic Milton*, 174. In contrast, Achinstein sees the nation of prophets as a figure for a "capable public." *Milton and the Revolutionary Reader*, 61. On *Areopagitica* as taking part in sectarian discourse, see Wilding, "Milton's *Areopagitica*: Liberty for the Sects."

[15] Morrow, "How Oliver Cromwell Thought," 109. Also see Corns, "Milton, Roger Williams, and the Limits of Toleration," 82.

[16] Greville, *A Discourse*, 111.

[17] *Ibid.*, 23.

his sympathetic account of the radicals by saying he is simply giving "the world an account, what Those men say for themselves," not reporting his own conviction.[18] Brooke's argument ventriloquizes Moses's wish for a Nation of Prophets. Milton, who celebrates Brooke in the midst of the national digression (*CPW* II:560–1) goes further and cites the biblical passage in his own enthusiastic voice.

Such an antinomian strain does not replace the strong reliance in *Areopagitica* on reason. Rather, it blends with it.[19] As Milton first describes the Nation of Prophets, it seems to function through the exercise of reason: "Where there is much desire to learn, there of necessity will be much arguing, much writing, many opinions" (*CPW* II:554). And just after his second reference to the story in Numbers, he pictures the people of London, even under the pressures of the Civil War, "disputing, reasoning, reading, inventing, discoursing" (*CPW* II:557). His picture of the English nation is of a citizenry both rational and inspired.

It is precisely this blending of inspiration and reason, I would speculate, that is most productive. As can be seen in the antinomian discourse discussed in Chapter 4, a key effect of the Spirit is to create the political energy of the sovereign conscience. It authorizes the individual to act ideologically, and revolutionarily. Milton's Nation of Prophets is a body politic made up of just such political subjects, energized individuals guided by a conscience that claims powerful sovereignty. At the same time, however, Milton has an unusual degree of confidence that all these individual prophets will be able to come together in shared discourse. His sense of how things would actually work is free of the concerns more conservative voices typically express about liberty of conscience. Adam Steuart declares, Independency "could not but prove the root of all sort of Schisms, and Heresie, and consequently the utter overthrow of Christs Universall Militant Church here upon Earth."[20] Or Hobbes says that "men, vehemently in love with their own new opinions" use the name of conscience metaphorically, "and so pretend to know they are true, when they know at most, but that they think so" (*Lev.* I.7, 48). Milton's

---

[18] *Ibid.*, 109, 114.

[19] As it does in Brooke's thinking. *A Discourse* argues for liberty of conscience mainly through right reason and offers a sympathetic account of separatists and their claims for prophetic inspiration. Brooke's right reason anticipates that of the Cambridge Platonist Nathaniel Culverwell, when Brooke calls it "the Candle of God, which He hath lighted in Man," *A Discourse*, 27. Both Brooke and Culverwell derive much of their rational religion from Cherbury. See Greville, *The Nature of Truth*, 40; Culverwell, *An Elegant and Learned Discourse*, 56–8, 93–6, 160.

[20] Steuart, *Some Observations*, "To the Divines."

Nation of Prophets, in contrast, is made stronger by the multiplication of opinions: "Where there is much desire to learn there of necessity will be much arguing, much writing, many opinions; for opinion in good men is but knowledge in the making" (*CPW* II:554).[21] For Milton, opinion is energetically authorized by inspiration, and it can simultaneously be communicable in rational discourse. This is how reason compliments inspiration: it suggests that the ideas held by each individual, even as they are vehemently held by the inspired subject, can be communicated to others, and submitted to a discursive process. Inspiration is not tamed or limited by blending with reason, but rather is harnessed and set in the path of vigorous communication. Few texts in the period express so much faith in public discourse as *Areopagitica*, and few portray reading, writing, and talking as such powerful and energetic, even inspired, activities.

Milton does not solve the toleration controversy; *Areopagitica* has little real effect on Parliament and does not make the case for absolute toleration. But the productiveness of the blending of reason and inspiration is recognizable within his own oratory. The prophetic energy of the Spirit blends with communicable rationality to inform Milton's voice, which ascends to sublime heights in contemplation of the Nation of Prophets. He imagines England as a body "when the blood is fresh, the spirits pure and vigorous," as having a cheerfulness that is "so sprightly up" as to "bestow upon the solidest and sublimest points of controversy," so that it will "wax young again" (*CPW* II:557). Freed from the limits of censorship, the body politic becomes so energized by Spirit that Milton himself is hurtled into a prophetic vision: "Methinks I see in my mind a noble and puissant Nation rousing herself like a strong man after sleep, and shaking her invincible locks" (*CPW* II:557–8). The Nation of Prophets is now spectacularly like Samson, who in Judges regularly experiences the "spirit of God" upon him before launching into his feats of strength.

This image of Samson, with strength and hair intact, is determinedly sanguine, presenting a confidence in the efficacy of action that comes from the Spirit. In *Samson Agonistes* Milton will develop a more ambivalent figure, one who is weak and isolated from his people, and whose return to strength is bound up in the Spirit in highly complicated ways. *Areopagitica*'s vision of Samson is not of an individual tragically separated from nation and God, but one embodying the nation with divine strength, a kind of antinomian Leviathan, figuring forth a prophetic public sphere. This successful nation full of prophets expresses a fundamental optimism about conscience, that it is expansive enough to be both replete with the potency of inspiration, and successfully communicable within public discourse.

Milton's aspirations in *Areopagitica*, and his sanguine conception of the role of conscience in the public sphere, are in keeping with the revolutionary hopes of the text's moment. But his most detailed theorization of conscience, which occurs significantly later, develops a more skeptical, and more nuanced, account. In his return to the problem of liberty of conscience in *A Treatise of Civil Power*, and in the detailed inward dynamics of inspiration in *De Doctrina Christiana*, Milton develops a rich understanding of how conscience fits, and fails to fit, into public discourse. Paying close attention to both the private and the public dynamics of conscience, he constructs a scene of conscience in which can be felt tolerant and quite self-aware habits of thought.

De Doctrina and *Of Civil Power*

Milton's most sustained discussions of conscience are to be found in *De Doctrina Christiana*, Chapter 30, and *A Treatise of Civil Power*, two texts that are likely written in the same period.[22] In their handling of conscience they intersect significantly, and can be seen as companions. *De Doctrina* adopts Milton's most explicitly antinomian position, articulating a conscience that is deeply imbued with the Spirit. This is a very private theology, both in the sense that *De Doctrina* is not a public document, and in that inspiration functions as an isolated and inward scene of knowledge. *Of Civil Power* shares the focus on the Spirit, but brings the private, inspired conscience into contact with political discourse and its demands for reason and communicability. Reading these texts together, we see Milton's expansive scene of conscience at work traversing the divide between inspiration and reason, and the related divide between private and public conscience.

In *De Doctrina* Milton looks his most antinomian in Chapter 30, 'Of the Holy Scripture.' The chapter is largely concerned with arguing for the ethic of *sola scriptura* – "The rule and canon of faith, therefore, is scripture alone" (*CPW* VI:585). But interpretation specifically depends

---

[22] Milton is often assumed to have begun *De Doctrina* about 1655. *CPW* II.23. *Of Civil Power* was written in 1658–9, and may refer to *De Doctrina* in its conclusion, *CPW* VII.230, 271.

on the Spirit: "In controversies there is no arbitrator except scripture, or rather, each man is his own arbitrator, so long as he follows scripture and the Spirit of God" (*CPW* VI:585). In this way Biblical interpretation becomes prophetic. The scriptures "must not be interpreted by the intellect of a particular individual, that is to say, not by merely human intellect, but with the help of the Holy Spirit. Hence the gift of prophecy" (*CPW* VI:579–80). Matching the ideal of the Nation of Prophets, Biblical interpretation is everyone's prerogative: "Every believer is entitled to interpret the scriptures; and by that I mean interpret them for himself. He has the spirit, who guides truth, and he has the mind of Christ" (*CPW* VI:583).

This is a strong but still fairly standard Protestant assertion of *sola scriptura*. As the chapter progresses, however, the Spirit does not simply function as a guide to the reader, but sets up as an authority that exists outside of Scripture. The Spirit becomes a second scripture:

> We have, particularly under the gospel, a double scripture. There is the external scripture of the written word and the internal scripture of the Holy Spirit which he, according to God's promise, has engraved upon the hearts of believers, and which is certainly not to be neglected.
>
> (*CPW* VI:587)

It is not a parallel text, but rather is preeminent:

> Nowadays the external authority for our faith, in other words the scriptures, is of very considerable importance and, generally speaking, it is the authority of which we first have experience. The pre-eminent and supreme authority, however, is the authority of the Spirit, which is internal, and the individual possession of each man.
>
> (*CPW* VI:587)

Here Milton moves beyond standard notions, drawing very near to the antinomianism that Geoffrey Nuttall documents. The necessity of the Spirit's influence for the reading of the Bible is doubted by none, Nuttall says. But radical voices raised further questions: "can the Spirit save, or even speak to, man apart from the Word in Scripture? Or is the Spirit tied to Scripture? Is the Word to be interpreted by the Spirit? Or should the Spirit's leadings, rather, be tested by the Word?"[23] Milton succinctly summarizes: "Thus, too, on the evidence of scripture itself,

---

[23] Nuttall, *The Holy Spirit*, 23.

all things are eventually to be referred to the Spirit and the unwritten word" (*CPW* VI:590). In these moments, he sides with the antinomian answers to such questions.

A case can be made that Milton's Spirit often guides the biblical interpreter in ways that are more rational than enthusiastic. *De Doctrina* is built out of Milton's own highly rational approach to Scripture, beginning with the initial decision "to puzzle out a religious creed for myself by my own exertions" (*CPW* VI:118). His systematic method calls for the reader of the Bible to "withold his consent from those opinions about which he does not feel fully convinced, until the evidence of the Bible convinces him and induces his reason to assent and to believe" (*CPW* VI:122). And this reasoning depends in no small part on the philology of humanism and rational biblical hermeneutics. Milton's command of original languages shapes all of *De Doctrina*, and although he rarely cites outside sources, he often turns to the bibles of Erasmus and Beza, in ways that bear comparison in particular to Socinian texts (*CPW* VI:221, 242, 244, 245, 412). And yet these rational hermeneutics end up serving as evidence of the Spirit. Reflecting in Chapter 30 on the textual corruption of the New Testament, Milton concludes:

> Thus Erasmus, Beza, and other learned men have edited from the various manuscripts what seems to them to be the most authentic text. I do not know why God's Providence should have committed the contents of the New Testament to such wayward and uncertain guardians, unless it was so that this very fact might convince us that the Spirit which is given to us is a more certain guide than scripture, and that we ought to follow it.
>
> (*CPW* VI: 589)

In a remarkable example of Milton's eclectic theology, scholarship itself becomes proof of an antinomian Spirit.[24] This syncretic fastening reveals in close detail Milton's ability to entertain reason and the Spirit simultaneously. Milton's ethic of *sola scriptura*, and the functioning of the Spirit within that, blend inspiration and reason.

Rational hermeneutics and the prophetic Spirit come together particularly in Milton's expansive conscience. Insisting on the prime authority of the individual reading Scripture, Milton describes the Spirit working in conjunction with conscience:

> Every believer is entitled to interpret the scriptures; and by that I mean interpret them for himself. He has the spirit, who guides truth, and he has

---

[24] Debora Shuger suggests that "the rhetoric of biblical scholarship does not demystify; it demythologizes sacred history." *The Renaissance Bible*, 47.

the mind of Christ. Indeed, no one else can usefully interpret them for him, unless that person's interpretation coincides with the one he makes for himself and his own conscience.

(*CPW* VI:583–4)

In this complex scene of biblical interpretation, conscience plays a central hermeneutic role. Working in tandem with the Spirit it assists in the discovery of knowledge from Scripture. The scene begins with the Spirit "who guides truth," enabling the individual to interpret scriptures "for himself." But it ends with that interpretation submitted to the individual's "own conscience."[25] What the relationship is between Spirit and conscience is obscured in the ambiguity of the Latin, "sibi conscientiaeque suae." Possibly, inspired interpretation is made *for* conscience, as John Carey's translation has it. This implies, it seems, that the Spirit plays the primary interpretive role, and then secondarily supplies the conscience, enabling a broader set of political determinations. Or possibly conscience has a more complimentary relationship to the Spirit, so that interpretation is "confirmed" by the faculty, as Charles Sumner's translation goes. It is impossible to parse what is clearly handled unsystematically, especially given Milton's insistence elsewhere that we cannot know much about the Spirit.[26] But clearly Spirit and conscience blend into each other in some manner, just as occurs in the antinomian stream. This blending helps make sense of the way that Milton's Spirit accommodates both rational and antinomian tendencies: by involving conscience with Spirit, Milton creates a scene of blended reason and inspiration at the center of his biblical hermeneutics.

The very same conjunction, of conscience with Spirit and with biblical interpretation, is also essential to *Of Civil Power*. Milton's most sustained argument for liberty of conscience, the treatise proceeds largely through readings of the toleration debate's key scriptural passages. In preparation,

[25] "Ius interpretandi scripturas, sibimet inquam interpretandi, habet unusquisque fidelium: habet enim spiritum, veritatis ducem; habet mentem Christi: immo alius nemo interpretari cum fructu potest, nisi ipse quoque sibi conscientiaeque suae idem interpretetur." ["Every believer has a right to interpret the Scriptures for himself, inasmuch as he has the Spirit for his guide, and the mind of Christ is in him; nay the expositions of the public interpreter can be of no use to him, except so far as they are confirmed by his own conscience."] *The Works of John Milton*, XVI:264–6.

[26] In the discussion of the Spirit in Chapter 6, Milton stresses how little Scripture clarifies about the Holy Spirit. It "says nothing about what the Holy Spirit is like, how it exists, or where it comes from – a warning to us not to be too hasty in our conclusions." *CPW* VI:281.

Milton establishes his methodology in the opening pages. As in *De Doctrina*, his argument depends on *sola scriptura*, and on the expansive conscience in the interpretation of Scripture.

Milton begins his methodology with a definition:

> Whence I here mean by conscience or religion, that full perswasion whereby we are assur'd that our beleef and practise, as far as we are able to apprehend and probably make appeer, is according to the will of God & his Holy Spirit within us, which we ought to follow much rather then any law of man, as not only his word every where bids us, but the very dictate of reason tells us.
>
> (*CPW* VII:242)

Conscience extends so broadly as even to become synonymous with religion itself – "conscience or religion" are simply interchangeable. It is, moreover, expansive in its inclusion of both reason and Spirit. In fact reason offers the dictate that we ought to follow the Holy Spirit over all human law.

This scene of conscience has a strong antinomian current. The authority of the Spirit is capable of "full perswasion" and assurance regarding belief and practice. It is so authoritative as to take precedence over all human law. William Hunter glosses this opening by underlining Milton's emphasis on the Holy Spirit, which "leads to concurrence with such diverse groups as the Quakers, the Baptists, and the radical Arminians (*CPW* VII:242 n.10).[27] The political force of the conscience, however, depends on more than the private apprehension of inspiration. Milton recognizes the need to go public when he qualifies full persuasion with "as far as we are able to apprehend and probably make appeer." First there is inward apprehension, then a making apparent through probability, which is to say, through rational and communicative discourse. As conscience becomes synonymous with not only belief but the practice of religion, which is external and inevitably public, there is a clear need for it to become communicable.

An individual may be inwardly persuaded, but in the functioning of civic and religious life that knowledge has to be made known to others. In the next paragraph Milton addresses this need when, exactly as in *De Doctrina*, he turns to *sola scriptura* and Biblical interpretation:

> First, it cannot be deni'd, being the main foundions of our protestant religion, that we of these ages, having no other divine rule or autoritie

---

[27] Also see Hunter, "John Milton: Autobiographer," 101–4.

> from without us warrantable to one another as a common ground but the
> holy scripture, and no other within us but the illumination of the Holy
> Spirit so interpreting that scripture as warrantable only to our selves and to
> such whose conscience we can so perswade, can have no other ground in
> matters of religion but only from the scriptures.
>
> (*CPW* VII:242)

With the force of *sola scriptura*, the Bible becomes "common ground"
between individuals, and so serves as the only external authority that
can be "warrantable to one another." As a result, when the Holy Spirit
illuminates the Bible it is explicitly not "warrantable only to our selves,"
but also to others who can be persuaded in conscience. Inspiration does
not remain entirely private, but becomes knowledge that can be put into
communicable terms. This knowing, it is easy to extrapolate, can take the
shape of sermons or disputations, or be the product of Erasmian philology and the kind of close textual argument that Milton practices in both
De Doctrina and *Of Civil Power*. In these, private inspiration stands a
chance at persuading another person's conscience. Inspired knowledge
transforms into the kind of rational and communicable discourse that
can take part in a public scene of conscience.

This work of the conscience occurs not only after the fact of the Spirit's
illumination, but as an integral part of it. Repeatedly, Milton describes
conscience as playing a role alongside the Spirit in creating meaning from
the Bible. For example:

> With good cause therfore it is the general consent of all sound protestant
> writers, that neither traditions, councels nor canons of any visible church,
> much less edicts of any magistrate or civil session, but the scripture only
> can be the final judge of rule in matters of religion, and that only in the
> conscience of every Christian to himself.
>
> (*CPW* VII:243)

All biblical interpretations, in the case of the individual as well as in more
collective acts of discourse, go through the conscience. So Milton takes
it to be a fundamental Protestant doctrine, "which preferrs the scripture before the church, and acknowledges none but the Scripture sole
intepreter of it self to the conscience" (*CPW* VII:243). And so he argues
against standard notions of heresy, since "ought we to beleeve what in our
conscience we apprehend the scripture to say" (*CPW* VII:248), and since
the heretic's opinions, "whatever they be, can hurt no protestant, whose
rule is not to receive them but from the scripture: which to interpret con-
vincingly to his own conscience none is able but himself guided by the

Holy Spirit" (*CPW* VII:249). Interpretation is guided by the Spirit and variously unfolds "in" or "to" the conscience. Just as in *De Doctrina*, the pronouns resist a precise mapping of how Spirit and conscience function. But they clearly do function together to shape both private interpretation of the Bible and the public discourse that follows.[28]

It is worth briefly observing how uncommon it is to find conscience playing such an active role in biblical hermeneutics. Major Protestant dogmatics do not typically say so. Tyndale does not include the faculty in his account of Biblical interpretation in *The Obedience of a Christian Man*. Neither does Calvin in the *Institutes*, nor Peter Martyr in his *Commonplaces*, Ursinus in the *Summe of Christian Religion*, or Bullinger in his *Decades*. William Whitaker does say that "In order, therefore that we should be internally in our consciences persuaded of the authority of scripture, it is needful that the testimony of the Holy Ghost should be added."[29] But Chillingsworth, who most famously articulates the ethic of *sola scriptura* in seventeenth-century England, never connects interpretation to conscience. Neither do Wolleb or Ames, main sources for Milton's *De Doctrina*. It is not in the Westminster Confession or the Savoy Declaration, key impetuses for Milton's writing *Of Civil Power*.

This innovative role makes conscience instrumental to the ethic of *sola scriptura* – which is to say it puts the faculty at the center of Milton's theology and helps to make it synonymous with religion. Operating in this center, the expansive conscience is part of the powerful private hermeneutics of inspiration. And at the same time, it is part of the public discourse of persuasion. Thus conscience can be the name for, and the location in which, Spirit becomes reason, and inspiration becomes communicable. It can bridge the gap between private and public, serving as the engine of Milton's argument for the sovereignty of individual belief and practice against the forcing of magistrate or law or church. So far in *Of Civil Power*, conscience establishes the sanguine conditions necessary for a nation of prophets.

But Milton also weaves into his methodology a surprisingly skeptical position, a hesitation about the Holy Spirit, which complicates the functioning of conscience. Returning to the assertion that Scripture is

---

[28] Theodore Huguelet speculates that conscience assists in exegesis "not by justifying subjective interpretations but by matching the teaching of Scripture with the natural laws of conduct engraved upon the mind of man." For Huguelet conscience is synonymous with right reason. *Milton's Hermeneutics*, 182–3.

[29] Whitaker, *A Disputation of Holy Scripture*, 295. "Ut ergo conscientiis nostris intus de Scripturae authoritate persuadeatur, accedat Spiritus sancti testimonium necesse est." Whitaker, *Disputatio De Sacra Scriptura*, 213. John Owen makes brief mention of conscience in his Biblical hermeneutics. *Of the Divine Original*, 70, 81.

the only common ground, and continuing in the quotation to the next step of the argument, we see Milton introducing into his methodology a moment of doubt about inspiration. This is surely the most difficult passage in *Of Civil Power*:

> First it cannot be deni'd, being the main foundation of our protestant religion, that we of these ages, having no other divine rule or autoritie from without us warrantable to one another as a common ground but the holy scripture, and no other within us but the illumination of the Holy Spirit so interpreting that scripture as warrantable only to our selves and to such whose consciences we can so perswade, can have no other ground in matters of religion but only from the scriptures. And these being not possible to be understood without this divine illumination, which no man can know at all times to be in himself, much less to be at any time for certain in any other, it follows clearly, that no man or body of men in these times can be infallible judges or determiners in matters of religion to any other mens consciences but thir own.
>
> (*CPW* VII:242–3)

In the first sentence Milton establishes his strongly antinomian version of conscience and *sola scriptura*, which, as has just been argued, promises the public communicability of inspiration. In the second sentence, though, inspiration becomes a slippery kind of knowledge when he asserts that divine illumination "no man can know at all times to be in himself." We should resist the more radical reading that Milton is saying that *at all times* no one can truly know inspiration, for the more moderate reading that even for the most prophetic, there will always be *some times* when he or she cannot know inspiration for sure. But even here a space of uncertainty and hesitation opens up in the experience of inspiration. Humans have a hard time knowing when they are inspired. No one can rely on the Spirit to be consistently present, authorizing every biblical interpretation; everybody must admit to the limits of inspiration.

Then, precisely from this space of uncertainty, follows Milton's claim for liberty of conscience. If inspiration is sometimes not even warrantable in ourselves, it is therefore not possible for another, at any time, to be certain about the biblical interpretation we have put forward. For all they know, this time may be one of those times of uncertainty. There is therefore very little persuading of others, let alone forcing another's conscience. What prevents forcing, in Milton's argument, is this limit to the communicability of inspired knowledge. A breakdown of communication would seem to undermine the confidence that antinomianism breeds, and undo the optimism that enables the Nation of Prophets.

But this hesitation is also precisely what clinches the argument against civil power. Christian liberty is won through an awareness of its own incommunicability, and a sensitivity to the political complexity that such awareness generates.

This passage is a close-up of the key matter of how conscience enters into politics. It draws our gaze to the dramatic moment in which private conscience is heading toward public discourse, but has not yet entered that sphere. The argument goes back and forth, first suggesting that inspiration and Scripture can warrant the persuasion of another's conscience, then that they cannot infallibly do so, then that they therefore should not determine public matters of religion at all. Milton's close attention to these opposing motions creates a reflexive scene of conscience. The political subject experiences important second thoughts, born of the awareness of the limits of even an inspired conscience. These are essentially pluralistic thoughts, aware of others and the values authorized by their consciences. In this scene of conscience the political subject hesitates, and in doing so, exercises the habits of a more communal and tolerant politics, checking the sovereign conscience. In this scene, not only is negative freedom protected, but positive freedom is scrutinized – Milton conceives of conscience not just as a faculty that must be protected from forcing by others, but as one which must limit itself, lest it force another.

With this recursive argument and this skeptical hesitation, conscience begins to feel like the "reflecting" faculty of Perkins, and even the uncanny conscience of *Macbeth*. Matching this inner scene of self-awareness is a heightened awareness of other subjects and their consciences – an awareness of how complex a thing it is for an individual conscience to function in a world full of other individual consciences. The limits of the sovereign conscience become themselves a matter of conscience: "But if any man shall pretend, that the scripture judges to his conscience for other men, he makes himself greater not only then the church, but also then the scripture, then the consiences of other men; a presumption too high for any mortal" (VII: 243–4). Liberty of conscience comes only from such awareness of the self in its communal setting.

In returning to the toleration debate fifteen years after *Areopagitica*, Milton articulates a more self-aware and self-controlled version of liberty of conscience. It still expresses the energy of the sovereign conscience, thanks to its antinomian reliance on the Holy Spirit. But it knows limitations in the move into public discourse. This maturity could be the fruit of the 1650s, when Milton's idealism was severely stretched. It could, for example, be a response to the moderation of magisterial Independents such as John Owen, whose support of an established church leads Milton to urge Cromwell to "Help us save free conscience from the paw/Of hireling wolves whose gospel is their maw."[30] It could be that Milton's time in government, including working as a censor, pulled him away from the idealism of the Nation of Prophets. It could be the ongoing religious settlement, as multiple attempts at a new confession eventually led to the establishmentarian Savoy Declaration, instigating *Of Civil Power*.[31] It could be the unspooling of the Grand Old Cause itself. The 1650s, and then the Restoration on its heels, pull Milton into real-world matters of governance. In effect they pull his conception of conscience further into the practical considerations of the casuistic stream – another way of noticing his expansive conscience.

Reason and Inspiration

In these readings of *Areopagitica, De Doctrina*, and *Of Civil Power*, Milton is revealed as ambivalently camped between reason and inspiration. Conscience plays an important role in this ambivalence, but the issue is a broader and more fundamental feature in Milton's thought, and an enduring problem for his readers. Milton criticism has long struggled to determine to what degree Milton is a rationalist who eschews the enthusiasm of private inspiration, and to what degree he valorizes the inward working of the Spirit. William Riley Parker describes Milton in *De Doctrina Christiana* as ultimately dependent on the Holy Spirit for guidance, suggesting that "he believes, with George Fox and other Quakers, in the efficacy of the 'inner light.'"[32] On the other hand, Herbert McLachlan groups Milton with Locke and Newton as pioneers of rational religion, and argues that "it is more than doubtful whether Milton understood by the Holy Spirit any immediate revelation in the Quaker sense."[33] The evidence is conflicting, and very different versions of Milton have emerged in the reception, from a radical Puritan with antinomian tendencies to a rational theologian leaning toward deism, and these versions establish a number of political, philosophical,

[30] "To The Lord General Cromwell," 13–14. In the same year, 1652, Milton writes a sonnet to Henry Vane, a strong voice for disestablishment, celebrating his ability "to know/ Both spiritual power and civil." "To Sir Henry Vane the Younger," 9–10.
[31] See William Hunter, "Introduction," CPW VII:41–5. Also see Coffey, "John Owen and the Puritan Toleration Controversy."
[32] Parker, *Milton: A Biography*, 497.
[33] McLachlan, *The Religious Opinions*, 39. Also see Conklin, *Biblical Criticism and Heresy in Milton*.

and theological filiations, such as Milton as skeptic, as revolutionary, as republican, or as prophet. This is one of the great unsettled matters in Milton studies.

Christopher Hill stresses the biographical connections to Quakers, and finds Milton in extensive dialogue with them, as well as with many radicals of the 1640s and 1650s, leading him to see a generally antinomian figure.[34] David Loewenstein argues for a Milton deeply enmeshed in "the radical religious politics of the Spirit."[35] The clearest support for these views lies in *De Doctrina*, where, as we have seen, Milton draws near to the antinomian position, described by Geoffrey Nuttall, in which "the Word is to be tried by the Spirit."[36] As Hill observes, if Milton's contemporaries had read *De Doctrina*, they would not have hesitated to classify him as antinomian.[37] But much of the poetry is susceptible to the same reading. The invocation in *Paradise Lost* of the heavenly Muse who "didst inspire/That shepherd" (I.7–8) and who is likely the "Spirit" of line 17, operates through the conceit that the Spirit who inspired Moses might also visit a seventeenth-century poet. James Holly Hanford takes the conceit seriously, arguing that Milton truly considered himself inspired.[38] Much of the early poetry suggests as much, particularly "Il Penseroso" and "Lycidas." And the prose often makes claims to the prophetic, particularly in *The Reason of Church Government*, where Milton aligns himself with Isaiah and Jeremiah. Stressing such moments, William Kerrigan recovers a prophetic Milton whose "bets were absolute" – who really asserts his divine inspiration.[39] William Haller reads Milton's career as spiritual autobiography, aligning him with Puritan preachers and reformers, rather than Bacon, in that for them knowledge "was to be sought by observation of the operations of the Holy Spirit in their own breasts." He suggests that Milton resembles "those enthusiasts of lesser calibre who were already asserting the sole sufficiency of the spirit's teaching."[40]

But on the other hand, there has been good reason for seeing Milton as a rationalist, and there is a strong line in the reception that refines the Puritan Milton so as to exclude extreme moments of inspiration.

---

[34] Hill, *Milton and the English Revolution*, 100–7, 311–16.
[35] Loewenstein, *Representing Revolution*, 5. Also see Wilding, *Dragons Teeth*, 242–9; Fixler, *Milton and the Kingdoms of God*.
[36] Nuttall, *The Holy Spirit*, 28.
[37] Hill, *Milton and the English Revolution*, 315.
[38] Hanford, "'That Shepherd.'"
[39] Kerrigan, *The Prophetic Milton*, 186.
[40] Haller, *The Rise of Puritanism*, 301–2, 350. Also see Wolfe, *Milton in the Puritan Revolution*, 62.

E. M. Tillyard argues for "flexible" beliefs, in which "miracles are distasteful to his nature."[41] Arthur Barker argues that Milton

> thought of divine inspiration in terms of heavenly light; but he never had the profoundly-moving religious experience, the sense of mystical rebirth and miraculous enlightenment, at once supernatural in its origins and enrapturing in its effects, which provided the Puritan extremists with their energetic and fiery zeal.[42]

Without evidence of direct divine revelation, it is not easy to sustain the sense of an enthusiastic and literal alignment with the prophetic. Catherine Gimelli Martin's argument against calling Milton a Puritan enacts this long-standing tension between reason and inspiration. Arguing for rationalism as much as against the Puritan label, Martin demonstrates an array of skeptical, scientific, and rational associations, from Bacon and Hooker, to republicanism and humanism, to Socinianism and Deism. Milton is not a Puritan, according to Martin, but one who "migrated toward religious rationalism rather than Antinomian mysticism."[43] Milton's devotion to reason has probably garnered more attention than his devotion to the Spirit. For many readers, Arminianism ties Milton to a logical humanist temperament.[44] Republican theory accounts for Milton's political radicalism without recourse to the more enthusiastic strains of Puritan revolution.[45] Milton's anti-Trinitarianism has highlighted his affinities with Socinianism, which is the period's most assertive school of rational religion.[46] Suggestive of even more extreme rationalism is the fact that Charles Blount, John

---

[41] Tillyard, *Milton*, 190. Maurice Kelley responds to Tillyard, however, by asserting that, "It seems hardly reasonable, therefore, to assume that in the matter of miracles Milton differed with the Puritans of his age, or that he embraced a scepticism that is characteristic of a more recent *Weltanschauung*." Kelley, "Milton and Miracles," 172. In *Paradise Lost* Michael easily ascribes miracles to the apostles (12.501). But they look far less certain in the only other appearance of the word, when Eve is so impressed by the serpent's ability to speak that she calls it a miracle (9.562). The one extended discussion of miracles in *De Doctrina* considers them irrelevant or even debasing: "Miracles are no more able to produce belief than, in itself, doctrine is: that is to say, they cannot produce it at all"; and "They are blessed who believe without miracles." *CPW* VI:565.

[42] Barker, *Milton and the Puritan Dilemma*, 81. Stephen Fallon points to "The absence of a narrative of an overwhelming inner experience of light or of God's presence." *Milton's Peculiar Grace*, 38.

[43] Martin, *Milton among the Puritans*, 22, 103–4.

[44] Danielson, *Milton's Good God*; Burden, *The Logical Epic*.

[45] Worden, "Milton's Republicanism," 229. Also see Dzelzainis, "Republicanism"; Armitage et al., *Milton and Republicanism*.

[46] See Kelley, *This Great Argument*, 84–122; Stoll, *Milton and Monotheism*, 183–263. On Socinianism and rational religion, see Mortimer, *Reason and Religion in the English Revolution*.

Toland, and Anthony Collins admired and appropriated Milton, suggesting an affinity with deism.[47]

A deist Milton is a long way from a Quaker Milton, and yet both can be persuasive. Criticism disagrees over what to do with inspiration and reason because both are essential to Milton's mature theology. Barker concludes as much, discerning a thinker whose evolution "resulted largely from a combination of rationalism and Puritan principles."[48] Joan Bennet describes this same blending of reason and inspiration when she aligns Milton with the seemingly contradictory category of "humanist antinomianism."[49] Milton finds a way to have things both ways. The highly eclectic political theology of his late writings manages to be both rational and inspired, and is in fact well described by this contradiction.

At stake in these competing readings is how modern we think Milton is. Do we see in his works a trajectory of disenchantment and a move toward a scientific temper? Do we see a waning of a religious orientation, and the great outline of the emerging secular Enlightenment? And the particular problem raised by the politics of conscience is, do we see in Milton the rise of modern liberalism? Whiggish readings have been a contested tendency in Milton studies.[50] But from our inevitable vantage, which is looking backward, history does move forward. So it should not be an embarrassment to discern the early modern conscience anticipating modern liberalism. Milton's conscience does so, although its expansive quality, inclusive of reason and inspiration, anticipates liberalism in complex ways. It does not lead Milton to absolute toleration or absolute freedom of the press, nor does it build a rational public sphere, or establish a secular contract theory. Rather, to make a less assertive historical claim than those, Milton's close attention to conscience brings him to understand, better than most in the period, what it means to exercise the individual conscience in the political sphere. Milton enacts a fully developed scene of conscience, one that is expansive in its inclusion of reason and inspiration, and full of care in its movement between private and public spheres. Particularly conscious and imaginative, Milton's scene of

---

[47] Frank, "Milton's Movement toward Deism"; Kolbrenner, *Milton's Warring Angels*, 118. Stoll, *Milton and Monotheism*, 143–215.

[48] Barker, *Milton and the Puritan Dilemma*, xxiii.

[49] Bennet, *Reviving Liberty*, 94–118.

[50] Sensabaugh, *That Grand Whig, Milton*. In response, see Ernst Sirluck's review, "*That Grand Whig*"; Kolbrenner, *Milton's Warring Angels*. Achinstein reads for a "postrevisionist generation." *Milton and the Revolutionary Reader*, 21. Patterson argues for a liberal, not Whig, Milton. *Early Modern Liberalism*, 64–6.

conscience stages habits that later are demanded of the liberal subject in a modern pluralist society.

One way to put this is to say that Milton's political subject is both thin and thick. As described in Chapter 5, Hobbes's subject is disenchanted and abstracted, made thin in order to facilitate liberal contract. Milton's more complex subject, shaped by a conscience that is both rational and inspired, can be both thickly constituted in its theological inwardness, and thinly constituted in its political discursiveness. A predominantly rational conscience, enmeshed in practical discourse rather than the Holy Spirit, leans toward the secularized political subject of C. B. Macpherson's possessive individualism. For Macpherson, the innovation of "deducing political obligation from the supposed or observed facts of man's nature" makes the individual, rather than God, into the foundation of political legitimacy.[51] As Michael Sandel argues, such a liberal subject is disenchanted, and abstracted for the purpose of forming a deontological subject that serves as an Archimedean point. The liberal subject can only be fully deontological, can only put the right before the good, if there are no ideologies or contingencies prior to it that could be said to be shaping it. In the seventeenth century, the most salient contingency is the divine. So Hobbes rejects the conception of conscience as a *knowing with* God, reducing it to mere metaphor. Similarly if the Miltonic conscience was understood as functioning rationally, with a minimized foundation in divine inspiration, it would construct a thinner liberal subject.

An antinomian conscience, on the other hand, explicitly takes its authority from God, and is overwhelmingly enmeshed in a divine antecedent. A conscience connected to the divine through the Spirit is one that therefore becomes more thickly constituted. The joint testimonies of conscience and Spirit give form to the scene of *knowing with*. Taking part in the theology of the whole man, this scene of conscience can send the subject into the depths of despair or the heights of Christian liberty, depending on the individual's relationship to God. The very opposite of an Archimedean point, such a political subject would be an embarrassment to liberalism, and would need to be suppressed, as it is in *Leviathan*. In addition, the psychological valences of the destructured Protestant conscience, the way it slides away from *knowing with* God into a self-reflective conscience, as William Perkins theorizes, can

---

[51] Macpherson, *The Political Theory of Possessive Individualism*, 15.

be understood as thickening subjectivity.[52] Milton's expansive conscience suggests that his political subject is inclusive of both of these possibilities – it is capable of functioning both as a possessive individual and as thickly enmeshed in divine influence. In this way Milton's political subject can take part in liberal contract, with the qualities and obligations that it entails, but can do so without giving up a thick entanglement in divinity.[53]

Being thick and thin, Milton's subject is dynamically located between private and public spheres. The thin subject of liberalism is raised mainly by communitarian critiques, which ask us to consider how isolated or how communal a political subject is. Michael Walzer argues that social contract cannot be made with discrete individuals, but rather that "the processes through which men incur obligations are unavoidably pluralistic."[54] Rather than the asocial subject of possessive individualism, Sandel describes the communitarian subject as based on "'intersubjective' or 'intrasubjective' forms of self-understanding."[55] Such a subject, unlike the possessive individual, is constitutively conscious of others, and understands itself as inseparable from the larger public.

In *Of Civil Power*, as argued above, Milton's conscientious subject takes form in just this way. The treatise, as is typical in the toleration controversy, argues for a sovereign conscience that must not be forced. This would construct a strongly isolated and voluntarist subject. But hesitation concerning divine illumination softens the outward, public-directed trajectory of such sovereignty, and insists upon a more social perspective. His political subject does not simply assert itself in unforced liberty of conscience; it turns its gaze back on itself in self-reflection, and then does the remarkable work of thinking about what other subjects might know. This is a subject hesitating over the complexities of communal relations. It is precisely this sympathetic investigation of knowledge, and the limits it encounters, that clinch Milton's argument for liberty of conscience in the commonwealth. So the larger argument for liberty of conscience issues from a subject that is not thinly isolated or an Archimedean point, but rather is thickly shaped by an awareness of other subjects.

---

[52] In a thin subject, Sandel argues, genuine self-reflection would be impossible. Sandel, *Liberalism and the Limits of Justice*, 153–9. Also see Mulhall and Swift, *Liberals and Communitarians*, 57.

[53] This unique situation is made explicit in Milton's theory of contract, which centers on the Fall, in *Tenure of Kings and Magistrates*. *CPW* III:198–200.

[54] Walzer, *Obligations*, 15.

[55] Sandel, *Liberalism and the Limits of Justice*, 62. Also see Mulhall and Swift, *Liberals and Communitarians*, 62–3.

As Milton's conscience expands across the private–public divide, it engages with the socialized conscience that Walzer articulates in defense of conscientious objection. In his account, the modern, liberal conscience is unfortunately isolated: "For what is lost when morality becomes 'merely personal' is surely not piety or fervor, but the sharing of knowledge, the sense of Another's presence, the connection of the individual to a universal order."[56] Walzer instead argues for a conscience that is communal, in that it is shaped by membership in the various groups that surround the individual. As a result, the subject is not abstracted from contingencies, but is rather thickly constituted by those groups. Conscience and obligations, and the conscientious objection to obligations, arise through socialization. Here Walzer's communitarian conscience reaches back to the discourse that prevails in the early modern period: "the very word 'conscience' implies a shared moral knowledge, and it is probably fair to argue not only that the individual's understanding of God or the higher law is always acquired within a group but also that his obligation to either is at the same time an obligation to the group and to its members."[57] The Miltonic scene of conscience is careful to stage this lively awareness of other consciences. It insists on a powerfully sovereign conscience. But it is only free and sovereign to the extent that it is part of a plurality of consciences that are also in themselves sovereign.

Communitarian critiques of the thin subject are particularly aimed at supporting pluralism in a liberal society. A thin subject readily conforms to the abstract voluntarism of contract theory, but abstraction from particularity and from connections to other groups means that all thin subjects are the same.[58] The thick and thin subject, then, can be recognized as opening itself to pluralism. This is not to deny Milton's incomplete tolerance, especially of Catholics. But neither should we deny that, throughout his writings, intolerance appears within remarkably pluralizing understandings of truth, things indifferent, heresy, and liberty of conscience. In *Of Civil Power* the papist is "the only heretic," and

---

[56] Walzer, *Obligations*, 129.

[57] *Ibid.*, 5.

[58] As Stephen Macedo summarizes, "Traditional liberalism – with its demand that political power should be guided by public reasons and standards of justice that can be shared by all – is increasingly regarded as unfairly homogenizing." *Diversity and Distrust*, 1. Carole Pateman points to "the naturally free and equal (masculine) individuals who people the pages of the social contract theorists." *The Sexual Contract*, 41. John Rawls's answer to the communitarian critique is to posit a "reasonable pluralism" in *Political Liberalism*. But this is not the intra-subjective subject of communitarian theorizing, but an add-on to the thin subject that continues the work that Hobbes does when he makes a public conscience.

not to be tolerated; but just before this, heresy is recovered for pluralism as "choise only of one opinion before another, which may bee without discord" (*CPW* VII:249, 247).[59] The liberal narrative of toleration tends to see its achievement as a victory for reason over revelation, which is to say, in the construction of a secularized and deontological subject that is thin because based on rights that are prior to the goods of the theological sphere. *Of Civil Power*, in contrast, advances a strong antinomianism, continuing to assert a pre-secular subject. And then it arrives at liberty of conscience by layering in a skeptical hesitation. In Milton, what opens toward pluralism is not secularism and rationalism, but rather those things together with a commitment to antinomian inspiration.[60]

When Milton finds room for both thin and thick subjectivity, both reason and inspiration, he is feeling his way through the basic liberal problems of individual and plural subjects. How it is that thick and thin fit together can perhaps be understood by returning to the dynamic of the destructured conscience. Destructuring is not a one-time event, but rather a continuous process. Each Protestant conscience is perpetually turning from works to faith, slipping from structured conceptions into more inchoate and dynamic forms, so that an authentic conscience emerges in the repeated turn away from structure. Similarly, we might speculate, Milton's expansive conscience repeatedly turns from thickness to abstract thinness, as it shuttles between inwardness and the public sphere. In this way Milton's expansive conscience is not a fixed thing, but rather a dynamic scene of exploration and rehearsal. It is not so much a political theory, such as Hobbes develops, as an attempt to capture a scene, with all of its tendencies and habits. In his capacity as a poet, it therefore turns out, the late Milton is best positioned to stage conscience in its most expansive and challenging forms.

Samson Agonistes

The Samson of *Areopagitica* offers an image of triumph, as Milton sees the Nation of Prophets "rousing herself like a strong man after sleep, and shaking her invincible locks" (*CPW* II:557–8). But in the Book

---

[59] See Mueller, "Milton on Heresy."

[60] This draws Milton near to Richard Flathman's conception of "willful liberalism," which seeks to avoid liberalism's tendency to see individualism and pluralism as oppositional by turning to a more robust understanding of will: "that robust and widely distributed individualities are productive of group and associational life, and that the latter support and stimulate individualities." Flathman, *Willful Liberalism*, 8.

of Judges, Samson wakes from sleep and shakes himself, only to discover that everything has changed: "he awoke out of his sleep, and said,
I will go out as at other times before, and shake myself. And he wist not
that the Lord was departed from him" (16:19–20). As constructed in
Areopagitica, this is a sanguine moment of antinomian strength, invincible because directly from God. But it is only that because Milton edits
the story to remove the great irony of the moment: Samson is shaking
locks that are not there, and planning to use a divine strength that is
already departed from him. In *Samson Agonistes* Milton faces what he
had ignored, picking up the story just after Judges 16:20, and telling of
the tragic collapse of Samson's strength. If the earlier treatise somewhat
naively asserts the efficacy of inspiration in the public sphere, the later
poem stages Milton's most penetrating and mature investigation of how
inspiration enters into politics. This hinges upon conscience.

At the crucial moment of decision, when Samson refuses to perform
at the Philistian festival, the Officer warns him, "Regard thyself, this will
offend them highly." Samson answers, "Myself? my conscience and internal peace," declaring that his refusal to cooperate with the authorities is a
matter of conscience (1333–4). He backs up his resistance to obligation
with a string of well-reasoned arguments, suggesting that his conscience
is operating in meticulous fashion. But then Samson changes his mind,
taking the very opposite course. He announces to the Chorus,

> Be of good courage, I begin to feel
> Some rousing motions in me which dispose
> To something extraordinary my thoughts.
> I with this messenger will go along.
>
> (1381–4)

Abandoning his previous resolve, Samson decides to go to the festival.
There are two ways to read this change of mind. One, Samson's choice
appears to be against conscience: the faculty says not to go, but he chooses
to ignore it. Either that, or two, Samson's change of mind is also guided
by conscience: the faculty has reevaluated its prior arguments, and arrived
at a new judgment. Whether or not conscience continues to be a guide to
Samson is the same problem as whether he dies "with God not parted from
him" (1719). If Samson's declaration, "I with this messenger will go along,"
is against conscience, then the destruction of the temple would be, as many
readers have suspected, entirely unconscientious. On the other hand, if
Samson continues to follow conscience, the play arguably ends redemptively, in that it issues from a conscientious decision guided by God.

Samson's conscience reaches its crisis with the Officer, but unfolds across the entire agon of the play. Samson is plagued from the beginning by thoughts which, like conscience, are figured by pricks and stings. Samson complains of

> restless thoughts, that like a deadly swarm
> Of hornets armed, no sooner found alone,
> But rush upon me thronging, and present
> Times past, what once I was, and what am now.
>
> (19–22)

And then again, as the pricks lead to wounds,

> Thoughts my tormentors armed with deadly stings
> Mangle my apprehensive tenderest parts,
> Exasperate, exulcerate, and raise
> Dire inflammation which no cooling herb
> Or med'cinal liquor can assuage,
> Nor breath of vernal air from snowy alp.
>
> (623–8)

This wounded conscience leads Samson to "swoonings of despair,/And sense of heaven's desertion" (631–2), suggesting the kind of despair at a righteous God that vexes Luther and so many Calvinists. In the crisis with the Officer, at issue is whether Samson's wounded conscience is cured, like Redcrosse's. Does Samson attain a regenerate and free conscience, which would assure us that God has not deserted him? Or does he, like Macbeth, sink into distempered thought and tragically excessive violence? As with Richard and Launcelot Gobbo and Hamlet, we are watching Samson in the throes of conscience. Moving from the Officer's command, to Samson's "Myself? my conscience and internal peace," to his ultimate decision to go to the temple, Milton stages Samson's experience of conscience in real time.

But what kind of conscience is guiding Samson proves hard to say. Camille Wells Slights celebrates Samson as "Milton's hero of conscience" for his adherence to the "casuistical paradigm."[61] Norman Burns, on the other hand, argues for Samson as an "antinomian hero of faith."[62] The casuistic Samson resolves his doubtful conscience through practical reason, as seen in the many legalistic debates he has with himself

---

[61] Slights, *The Casuistical Tradition*, 247–96.
[62] Burns, "'Then stood up Phinehas,'" 28.

and his interlocutors. Slights details Samson's consideration of typical subjects of casuistry, such as law, marriage, religious practice, and suicide, so that "The central action of the tragedy is the process by which Samson decides what to do next, or, in the terminology of casuistry, the resolving of a doubtful conscience."[63] This is the Samson that Mary Ann Radzinowicz sees growing dialectically toward "intellectual control," and that Joan Bennet sees ultimately dying into "the restoration of his right reason."[64] Such casuistic reliance on law and reason is most apparent in Samson's initial resistance to the Officer's command: "Thou know'st I am an Hebrew, therefore tell them,/Our law forbids at their religious rites/ My presence" (1319–21). And it continues as he meticulously argues that he must not abuse his Nazarite vows, and that voluntarily serving in the temple differs from labor in the mill (1354–79). These arguments surround Samson's invocation of conscience.

An antinomian Samson, in contrast, is anything but rational, depending on the way the "Spirit of God" comes upon Samson in the Book of Judges (13:25, 14:6, 14:19, 15:14) and the "intimate impulse," "divine impulsion," "divine instinct," and "rousing motions" that seem to guide Milton's Samson (223, 422, 526, 1382). William Kerrigan sees Milton "replacing the conventional alliance between conscience and reason" with extraordinary moments of inspiration.[65] Inspiration makes Samson a serial lawbreaker, according to Burns, marrying outside his tribe and breaking his Nazarite vows.[66] Such antinomianism elicits comparisons to radical Puritan saints, and to the Nonconformists of the Restoration.[67]

The crux in this question of casuistic or antinomian conscience fittingly turns out to be the problem that has vexed most readings of the play, Samson's rousing motions. Samson's declaration, "I with this messenger will go along" (1384), comes immediately after "Be of good courage, I begin to feel/Some rousing motions in me which dispose/ To something extraordinary my thoughts" (1381–3). His new choice issues directly from the inspiration. If this is a conscientious choice, then Samson's conscience must, in antinomian fashion, include inspiration. In fact, since they suddenly reverse all the carefully articulated reasons

---

[63] Slights, *Casuistical Tradition*, 262.
[64] Radzinowicz, *Toward Samson Agonistes*, xx; Bennett, *Reviving Liberty*, 137.
[65] Kerrigan, "The Irrational Coherence," 217.
[66] Burns, "'Then stood up Phinehas,'" 34–43. Stanley Fish seconds Samson and Milton as antinomian. "'There is Nothing He Cannot Ask,'" 259.
[67] Worden, "Milton, *Samson Agonistes*, and the Restoration"; Loewenstein, *Representing Revolution*, 269–91; Achinstein, *Literature and Dissent*, 138–53.

for not going, the rousing motions would essentially become Samson's conscience, forming its inner workings. Conversely, if Samson's going is a departure from conscience, then it is precisely the rousing motions that enthusiastically and tragically stomp on Samson's casuistry.[68]

A great many critics have tried to sort out Samson's rousing motions, and they are consistently at the heart of disagreement over how to interpret the end of the poem.[69] To this extensive debate, I would add the context of conscience. Doing so will not define rousing motions or resolve whether the play ends redemptively. Rather, rousing motions help indicate Milton's expansive conscience at work in the poem, with its political consequences. In the crux of rousing motions, Samson's conscience could operate in an antinomian fashion, shaped by divine inspiration, or it could just as well operate in a casuistic fashion, shaped by the rational arguments that first told him not to go with the officer. The ongoing critical debate only emphasizes what Stanley Fish has most pointedly argued, that the rousing motions and the end of the play remain radically indeterminate, so that "God and Samson unite only in being inaccessible."[70] If Samson's rousing motions have become the greatest interpretive crux in Milton criticism, then Samson's conscience takes part in the identical complexity.

This complexity constructs in *Samson Agonistes* what I have been calling Milton's expansive conscience. The denouement is a scene of conscience that locates the political subject in the public sphere with the same mature reflection found in *Of Civil Power*. In the midst of the scene, Samson enunciates this key context: the Officer and the Philistines, he notes, "have me in their civil power" (1367). Describing this very moment in the poem's "Argument," Milton adopts the language of the treatise when he says that Samson "at first refuses, dismissing the public officer with absolute denial to come; at length persuaded inwardly that this was from God, he yields to go along with him" (71–4). In *Of Civil Power*, it will be recalled, "conscience or religion" is "that full

---

[68] Casuistic readings have to defuse the antinomian power of rousing motions. According to Slights, "Samson's sudden inspiration results from the careful analysis that precedes it." *The Casuistical Tradition*, 283–4. Radzinowicz identifies "the reasonableness of Samson's 'rouzing motions.'" *Toward Samson Agonistes*, 349. Bennett argues that "The 'motions' are divine inspiration, to be sure, but Milton's God inspires rational creatures with reason." *Reviving Liberty*, 137.

[69] For a survey of critical responses to the rousing motions see Wood, '*Exiled from Light*,' 129–39. For a survey from the other side, see Rudrum, "Milton Scholarship." On what rousing motions are, see DuRocher, "Samson's 'Rousing Motions.'"

[70] Fish, "Spectacle and Evidence," 586. Joseph Wittreich's two books, *Interpreting Samson Agonistes* and *Shifting Contexts*, state the skeptical case most thoroughly.

perswasion whereby we are assur'd that our beleef and practise, as far as we are able to apprehend and probably make appeer, is according to the will of God & his Holy Spirit within us" (*CPW* VII:242). At this turning point Milton stages what he investigates in the treatise: how the inward persuasions of the private conscience interact with the larger obligations of the public sphere.

Rousing motions, rather than the surrounding casuistry, are what supply Samson's full persuasion in the "Argument," bringing it in line with the antinomian tone that largely informs *Of Civil Power*. But in the treatise, as discussed above, Milton backs off from an unlimited sovereign conscience, when he hesitates over the Holy Spirit, "which no man can know at all times to be in himself, much less to be at any time for certain in any other" (*CPW* VII:242). Paralleling this moment of self-reflection is the indeterminacy that surrounds the rousing motions in the poem. Although the "Argument" asserts full persuasion, the poem never does. Just as in the treatise, Samson struggles to know that divine illumination is in him "at all times." Indeed this issue dominates the poem: Samson was at one time full of divine instinct but now is blind and despairing, with "sense of heaven's desertion"; the possibility of inspiration at one moment, as with the Bride of Timna, may or may not guarantee inspiration at a later moment, as with Dalila. Given this history, at the turning point of his rousing motions Samson must be determining, in some way or another, that *this time* the inspiration is true. He may be fully persuaded, but, as the treatise tells us, much less can anyone else in the public sphere be certain "at any time" of this fact.

That includes Milton's readers. The indeterminacy of rousing motions has left criticism uncertain how Samson's final action fits with conscience. Arguments against revisionist readings generally turn on the persuasion that for Samson and Milton idolators simply do not come within the compass of their consciences, which is well supported in *Of Civil Power*, where he says about idolatry, "a magistrate can hardly err in prohibiting and quite removing at least the publick and scandalous use thereof" (*CPW* VII:254–5).[71] Feisal Mohamed says that "it is quite clear that Samson's divinely inspired massacre of the Philistines was much more a source of comfort than distress for the poet."[72] Yet many readers find a real exploration of pluralism in the poem. This is particularly evident in

[71] See *De Doctrina Christiana*, *CPW* VI:690–6; Lewalski, "Milton and Idolatry."
[72] Mohamad, *Milton and the Post-Secular Present*, 9.

responses to Dalila, who, since William Empson, has elicited sympathy.[73] Such sympathy has been read as a poetic challenge to include Dalila, and by extension her tribe, in a pluralistic reckoning. So Linda Gregerson has recently argued that Dalila pushes us to see the play "not, or not only, as the triumph or tragedy of a chosen nation and its representative hero but as the tragedy of two nations fighting over a single geographic place."[74] Here the Philistines have value within the poem's political and ethical calculus. Killing them is not a conscientious action. Whether the poem calls forth such a pluralizing scene of conscience has been at the heart of the debate over Samson as suicide bomber, and at the heart of the question whether the Philistines are near Milton's conscience.

The intensity of critical disagreement over the poem's ending indicates how inconclusive the expansive conscience is. But, as *Of Civil Power* shows, for Milton the indeterminacy that accompanies conscience actually *is* the argument for liberty of conscience and its value pluralism. By keeping us on the outside of Samson's rousing motions, by constructing the poem with the strong indeterminacy that Fish stresses, Milton is inserting his readers into the scene he theorizes in the treatise, where the strong privacy of the antinomian conscience implies the necessity of accepting the sovereignty of other conscientious judgments in the public sphere. Precisely because we cannot fully understand Samson's experience of conscience, his inward persuasion and final action must be admitted into public toleration.

What is so challenging about this situation is that we are asked to tolerate exactly what is most difficult to tolerate. Milton brings in conscience, and makes his case for toleration, at the very moment that Samson decides to inflict overwhelming religious violence on another tribe. These two things happen together and conflict impossibly, testing the liberty of conscience. In such an ironic scene, Milton is asking the reader to experience tolerance at its hardest moment. Something like the case in which we contemplate free speech for Nazis, we must decide whether to tolerate the intolerant. In Samson's remarkable end, Milton makes the argument for liberty of conscience – but he does so precisely as he stages a violence that must prick our consciences, must bite like a worm. The poem does not necessarily arrive at modern liberal conclusions, but it stages dynamics that are familiar from modern

---

[73] Empson, *Milton's God*, 211–28.
[74] Gregerson, "Milton and the Tragedy of Nations," 675. Also see Achinstein, "*Samson Agonistes* and the Politics of Memory"; Sauer, *Milton, Toleration, and Nationhood*, 136–58.

pluralism. It rehearses key habits of liberalism, and for this reason its scene of conscience continues to resonate powerfully among modern liberal readers.[75]

When Samson declares "Myself? my conscience," he sets aside mere self-interest, operating instead according to the complex subjectivity of Milton's expansive conscience. Samson sounds the kind of confident theological and political cry that is heard from Luther to the Civil War. But when rousing motions render conscience indeterminate, when, in this unfolding scene, private conscience becomes publicly unpersuasive, we are brought back to the profoundly destructured nature of the Protestant faculty. It is the same in *Samson Agonistes* as it is in *Hamlet*, and throughout the early modern period, conscience has become increasingly inchoate as it has become increasingly important.

---

[75] Sharon Achinstein says *Samson Agonistes* "may be the most brilliant piece of political theory created in the seventeenth century if we think about political theory not only in terms of a discourse of abstraction, but also of contemplation, experience and subjective experience. "*Samson Agonistes* and the Drama of Dissent," 137. Sanford Budick argues for *Samson Agonistes* as crucial to the formation of deontological moral decision-making in Kant's categorical imperative. Budick, *Kant and Milton*, 209–52.

Bibliography

Because *Early English Books Online* (EEBO) is the most precise and readily available resource, whenever possible I quote from texts available on EEBO and cite the Short Title Catalogue (STC) or Wing number.

Achinstein, Sharon. *Milton and the Revolutionary Reader*. Princeton: Princeton University Press, 1994.
  "*Samson Agonistes* and the Drama of Dissent." *Milton Studies* 33 (1996). 133–58.
  "*Samson Agonistes* and the Politics of Memory." *Altering Eyes: New Perspectives on Samson Agonistes*. Ed. Mark R. Kelley, Joseph Wittreich. Newark: University of Delaware Press, 2002. 168–91.
  Literature and Dissent in Milton's England. Cambridge: Cambridge University Press, 2003.
Agamben, Giorgio. *Homo Sacer: Sovereign Power and Bare Life*. Trans. Daniel Heller-Roazen. Stanford: Stanford University Press, 1998.
Althaus, Paul. *The Ethics of Martin Luther*. Trans. Robert Schultz. Philadelphia: Fortress Press, 1972.
Altman, Joel. "Justice and Equity." *The Spenser Encyclopedia*. Ed. A. C. Hamilton. Toronto: University of Toronto Press, 1990. 413–15.
Ames, William. *Conscience with the Power and Cases Thereof*. London, 1643. Wing A2995A.
Anderson, Judith. "'Nor Man It Is': The Knight of Justice in Book V of Spenser's *Faerie Queene*." *PMLA* 85 (1970). 65–77.
  The Growth of a Personal Voice. New Haven: Yale University Press, 1975.
  "Britomart." *The Spenser Encyclopedia*. Ed. A. C. Hamilton. Toronto: University of Toronto Press, 1990. 113–15.
Andrew, Edward. *Conscience and Its Critics: Protestant Conscience, Enlightenment Reason, and Modern Subjectivity*. Toronto: University of Toronto Press, 2012.
Anon. *The World and the Child*. London, 1522. STC 25982.
  A Newe Interlude of Impacyente Poverte. London, 1560. STC 141125.
  A True and Perfect Relation of the Procedings at the Several Arraignments of the Late most Barbarous Traitors. London, 1606. STC 11619.
  Anti-Toleration. London, 1646. Wing A3515.

The Humble Advice of the Assembly of Divines. London, 1647. Wing W1429.

The Assembly of Gods. Ed. Jane Chance. Kalamazoo: Medieval Institute Publications, 1999.

Antoninus, *Summa Theologica.* Strassburg: Reynard, 1490.

Aptekar, Jane. *Icons of Justice: Iconography and Thematic Imagery in Book V of The Faerie Queene.* New York: Columbia University Press, 1969.

Aquinas, Thomas. *Summa Theologiae.* 60 vols. Trans. Timothy Suttor. New York: Blackfriars, 1970. Latin and English.

Arendt, Hannah. *The Life of the Mind.* New York: Harcourt, Brace, Jovanovich, 1978.

Aristotle. *The Nicomachean Ethics.* Trans. H. Rackham. Cambridge: Harvard University Press, 1982.

The Art of Rhetoric. Trans. John Henry Freese. Cambridge: Harvard University Press, 1994.

Arminius, *Examination of Dr. Perkins's Pamphlet on Predestination. The Works of James Arminius.* 3 vols. Trans. James Nichols and William Nichols. Repr. Grand Rapids: Baker, 1986.

Armitage, David, Armand Himy, and Quentin Skinner, eds. *Milton and Republicanism.* Cambridge: Cambridge University Press, 1995.

Azor, Joannes. *Institutionum Moralium.* Paris, 1612.

Barker, Arthur. *Milton and the Puritan Dilemma: 1641–1660.* Toronto: University of Toronto Press, 1971.

Baylor, Michael. *Action and Person: Conscience in Late Scholasticism and the Young Luther.* Leiden: Brill, 1977.

Bear, Edmond. *An Agreement of the People.* London, 1647. Wing A780.

Beckwith, Sarah. *Shakespeare and the Grammar of Forgiveness.* Ithaca: Cornell University Press, 2011.

Belsey, Catherine. "The Case of Hamlet's Conscience." *Studies in Philology* 76 (1979). 127–48.

Benjamin, Walter. *The Origin of German Tragic Drama.* Trans. John Osborne. London: New Left Books, 1977.

Bennet, Joan. *Reviving Liberty: Radical Christian Humanism in Milton's Great Poem.* Cambridge: Harvard University Press, 1989.

Berlin, Isaiah. "Two Concepts of Liberty." *Four Essays on Liberty.* Oxford: Oxford University Press, 1984.

Bolton, Robert. *Instructions for a Right Comforting Afflicted Consciences.* London, 1631. STC 3238.

Bourne, Immanuel. *The Anatomie of Conscience.* London, 1623. STC 3416.

Bradley, A. C. *Shakespearean Tragedy.* 2nd edition. New York: St. Martin's, 1978.

Braun, Harald and Edward Vallance, eds. *Contexts of Conscience in Early Modern Europe, 1500–1700.* New York: Palgrave Macmillan, 2004.

Bright, Timothy. *A Treatise of Melancholy.* London, 1586. STC 3747.

Brown, Meg Lota. *Donne and the Politics of Conscience in Early Modern England.* New York: Brill, 1995.

Budick, Sanford. *Kant and Milton.* Cambridge: Harvard University Press, 2010.

Bullough, Geoffrey. *Narrative and Dramatic Sources of Shakespeare.* 8 vols. New York: Columbia University Press, 1957–75.

Burden, Dennis. *The Logical Epic: A Study of the Argument of Paradise Lost.* London: Routledge & Kegan Paul, 1967.

Burns, Norman. "'Then Stood Up Phinehas': Milton's Antinomianism, and Samson's." *Milton Studies* 33 (1996). 27–46.

Burton, Robert. *The Anatomy of Melancholy.* New York: New York Review of Books, 2001.

Busher, Leonard. *Religions Peace.* Amsterdam, 1614. STC 4189.

Butler, Judith. *The Psychic Life of Power: Theories in Subjection.* Stanford: Stanford University Press, 1997.

Calvin, John. *The Institution of Christian Religion.* Trans. Thomas Norton. London, 1578. STC 4418.

Carletti, Angelo. *Summa Angelica.* Mantua, 1492.

Carlin, Norah. "Toleration for Catholics in the Puritan Revolution." *Tolerance and Intolerance in the European Reformation.* Ed. Ole Peter Grell and Bob Scribner. New York: Cambridge University Press, 1996. 216–30.

Carpenter, Frederic Ives. "Spenser's Cave of Despair." *Modern Language Notes* 12:5 (1897). 129–37.

Cascardi, Anthony. *The Subject of Modernity.* Cambridge: Cambridge University Press, 1992.

Castellio, Sebastian. *Concerning Heretics.* Trans. Roland H. Bainton. New York: Octagon, 1965.

Champion, Justin A. I. "Willing to Suffer: Law and Religious Conscience in Seventeenth-Century England." *Religious Conscience, the State, and the Law: Historical Contexts and Contemporary Significance.* Ed. John and Harold Coward. Albany: SUNY Press, 1999. 13–28.

Clarke, Elizabeth. *Theory and Theology in George Herbert's Poetry: "Divinitie and Poesie Met."* New York: Oxford University Press, 1997.

Coffey, John. *Persecution and Toleration in Protestant England: 1558–1689.* Essex: Longman, 2000.

   "The Toleration Controversy." *Religion in Revolutionary England.* Ed. Christopher Durston and Judith Maltby. Manchester: Manchester University Press, 2006. 42–68.

   "John Owen and the Puritan Toleration Controversy, 1646–59." *The Ashgate Research Companion to John Owen's Theology.* Ed. Kelly Kapic and Mark Jones. Burlington: Ashgate, 2012. 227–48.

   "The Language of Liberty in Calvinist Political Thought." *Freedom and the Construction of Europe.* Ed. Quentin Skinner and Martin van Gelderen. Vol. I. Cambridge: Cambridge University Press, 2013. 296–316.

Como, David. *Blown by the Spirit: Puritanism and the Emergence of an Antinomian Underground in Pre-Civil-War England.* Stanford: Stanford University Press, 2004.

Conklin, George Newton. *Biblical Criticism and Heresy in Milton.* New York: King's Crown, 1949.

Cooper, Anthony Ashley, Third Earl of Shaftesbury. *Characteristics of Men, Manners, Opinions, Times*. Ed. Lawrence Klein. Cambridge: Cambridge University Press, 2004.

Coornhert, D. V. *Synod on the Freedom of Conscience*. Trans. Gerrit Voogt. Amsterdam: Amsterdam University Press, 2008.

Cormack, Bradin. *A Power to Do Justice: Jurisdiction, English Literature, and the Rise of Common Law, 1509–1625*. Chicago: University of Chicago Press, 2007.

Corns, Thomas. "Milton, Roger Williams, and the Limits of Toleration." *Milton and Toleration*. Ed. Sharon Achinstein and Elizabeth Sauer. New York: Oxford University Press, 2007. 72–85.

Craddock, Walter. *Gospel-Holinesse, or The Saving Sight of God*. London, 1651. Wing C6760.

Cudworth, Ralph. *The True Intellectual System of the Universe*. London, 1678. Wing C7471.

Culverwell, Nathaniel. *An Elegant and Learned Discourse of the Light of Nature*. London, 1652. Wing C7569.

Cummings, Brian. "Conscience and the Law in Thomas More." *Journal of the Society for Renaissance Studies* 23:4 (2009). 463–85.

Danielson, Dennis. *Milton's Good God: A Study in Literary Theodicy*. Cambridge: Cambridge University Press, 1982.

de Azpilcueta, Martín. *Enchiridion, sive manuale confessiorum, et poenitentium*. Antwerp, 1592.

Delhaye, Philippe. *The Christian Conscience*. Trans. Charles Underhill Quinn. New York: Desclee, 1968.

Denne, Henry. *The Man of Sin Discovered*. London, 1646. Wing D1023.

Doerksen, Daniel. "Nicholas Ferrar, Arthur Woodnoth, and the Publication of George Herbert's *The Temple*, 1633." *George Herbert Journal* 3:1–2 (1979). 22–44.

"'All the Good Is God's': Predestination in Spenser's *Faerie Queene*, Book I." *Christianity and Literature* 32:3 (1983). 11–18.

"Show and Tell: George Herbert, Richard Sibbes, and Communings with God." *Christianity and Literature* 51:2 (2002). 175–90.

Downame, John. *The Christian Warfare*. London, 1604. STC 7133.

Drury, John. *Music at Midnight: The Life and Poetry of George Herbert*. Chicago: University of Chicago Press, 2013.

DuRocher, Richard. "Samson's 'Rousing Motions': What They Are, How They Work, and Why They Matter." *Literature Compass* 3 (2006). 453–69. doi: 10.1111/j.1741-4113.2006.00340.x.

Dzelzainis, Martin. "Republicanism." *A Companion to Milton*. Ed. Thomas Corns. Oxford: Blackwell, 2001. 294–308.

Eaton, John. *The Honeycombe of Free Justification by Christ Alone*. London, 1642. Wing E115.

Eggert, Katherine. *Showing Like a Queen: Female Authority and Literary Experiment in Spenser, Shakespeare, and Milton*. Philadelphia: University of Pennsylvania Press, 2000.

Eliot, T. S. "George Herbert." *George Herbert: The Critical Heritage*. Ed. C. A. Patrides. London: Routledge and Kegan Paul, 1983. 332–36.

Empson, William. *Milton's God*. London: Chatto and Windus, 1961.

Engelberg, Edward. *The Unknown Distance: From Consciousness to Conscience, Goethe to Camus*. Cambridge: Harvard University Press, 1972.

England and Wales Army. A Representation of the Army. In *A Declaration of the Engagements, Remonstrances, Representations, Proposals, Desires and Resolutions from His Excellency Sir Tho: Fairfax, and the Generall Councel of the Army*. London, 1647. Wing F152A. 36–46.

A Solemn Engagement of the Army. In *A Declaration of the Engagements, Remonstrances, Representations, Proposals, Desires and Resolutions from His Excellency Sir Tho: Fairfax, and the Generall Councel of the Army*. London, 1647. Wing F152A. 25–27.

English Historical Documents 1485–1558. Vol. 5. Ed. C. H. Williams. New York: Oxford University Press, 1971.

Escobedo, Andrew. *Volition's Face: Personification and the Will in Renaissance Literature*. Notre Dame: University of Notre Dame Press, 2017.

Fairfax, Thomas. *The Case of the Armie Truly Stated*. London, 1647. Wing W2168.

Fallon, Stephen. *Milton's Peculiar Grace: Self-Representation and Authority*. Ithaca: Cornell University Press, 2007.

Feltham, Olivier. *Anatomy of Failure: Philosophy and Political Action*. London: Bloomsbury, 2013.

Fenner, William. *A Treatise of Conscience*. In *The Soules Looking-glasse*. Cambridge, 1640. STC 10780.

Fish, Stanley. "Spectacle and Evidence in *Samson Agonistes*." *Critical Inquiry* 15 (1989). 556–86.

"'There Is Nothing He Cannot Ask': Milton, Liberalism, and Terrorism." *Milton in the Age of Fish: Essays on Authorship, Text, and Terrorism*. Ed. Michael Lieb and Albert Labriola. Pittsburgh: Duquesne University Press, 2006. 243–64.

"How Hobbes Works." *Visionary Milton: Essays on Prophecy and Violence*. Ed. Peter Medine, John Shawcross, David Urban. Pittsburgh: Duquesne University Press, 2010. 65–87.

Fixler, Michael. *Milton and the Kingdoms of God*. Chicago: Northwestern University Press, 1964.

Flathman, Richard. *Willful Liberalism: Voluntarism and Individuality in Political Theory and Practice*. Ithaca: Cornell University Press, 1992.

Fletcher, Angus. *Allegory: The Theory of a Symbolic Mode*. Ithaca: Cornell University Press, 1964, reprinted 1995.

Fletcher, Giles and Phineas. *Poetical Works*. Ed. Frederick Boas. 2 vols. Cambridge: Cambridge University Press, 1909, reprinted 1970.

Fortier, Mark. *The Culture of Equity in Early Modern England*. Burlington: Ashgate, 2005.

Foucault, Michel. "The Subject and Power." *Michel Foucault: Beyond Structuralism and Hermeneutics*. Ed. Hubert L. Dreyfus and Paul Rabinow. 2nd edition. Chicago: University of Chicago Press, 1982. 208–26.

Fowler, Elizabeth. "The Failure of Moral Philosophy in the Work of Edmund Spenser." *Representations* 51 (1995). 47–76.

Fox, George. *Journal of George Fox.* Ed. John Nickalls. Cambridge: Cambridge University Press, 1952.

Frank, Joseph. "Milton's Movement toward Deism." *Journal of British Studies* 1 (1961). 38–51.

Freud, Sigmund. *The Standard Edition of the Complete Psychological Works of Sigmund Freud.* Trans. James Strachey. 24 vols. London: The Hogarth Press, 1953–74.

Fulton, Thomas, "Areopagitica and the Roots of Liberal Epistemology." *English Literary Renaissance* 34:1 (2004). 42–82.

Gallagher, Lowell. *Medusa's Gaze: Casuistry and Conscience in the Renaissance.* Stanford: Stanford University Press, 1991.

Garber, Marjorie. *Dreams in Shakespeare: From Metaphor to Metamorphosis.* New Haven: Yale University Press, 1974.

Garnett, Henry. *A Treatise of Equivocation.* Ed. David Jardine. London: Longman, 1851.

Gentles, Ian. *The New Model Army in England, Ireland and Scotland: 1645–1653.* Oxford: Blackwell, 1992.

Gerson, Jean. *Opera.* Ed. Nicolaus Kesler. 3 vols. Basel, 1489.

Early Works. Trans. Brian Patrick McGuire. New York: Paulist Press, 1998.

Gless, Darryl. *Interpretation and Theology in Spenser.* Cambridge: Cambridge University Press, 1994.

Goodwin, Thomas. *A Childe of Light Walking in Darknesse.* London, 1636. STC 12037.

Goodwin, Thomas, Philip Nye, Sidrach Simpson, Jeremiah Burroughes, and William Bridge. *An Apologeticall Narration.* London, 1643. Wing G1225.

Gottlieb, Sidney. "Herbert's Case of 'Conscience': Public or Private Poem?" *SEL* 25 (1985). 109–26.

Gray, Jonathan. *Oaths and the English Reformation.* Oxford: Oxford University Press, 2013.

Graziani, René. "Elizabeth at Isis Church." *PMLA* 79:4 (1964). 376–89.

Greenblatt, Stephen. "Shakespeare Bewitched." *New Historical Literary Study: Essays on Reproducing Texts, Representing History.* Ed. Jeffrey Cox and Larry Reynolds. Princeton: Princeton University Press, 1993. 108–35.

Greene, Robert A. "Synderesis, the Spark of Conscience, in the English Renaissance." *Journal of the History of Ideas* 52:2 (1991). 195–219.

Greenham, Richard. *Paramythion: Two Treatises of the Comforting of an Afflicted Conscience.* London, 1598. STC 12322.

Gregerson, Linda. *The Reformation of the Subject: Spenser, Milton and the English Protestant Epic.* Cambridge: Cambridge University Press, 1995.

"Milton and the Tragedy of Nations." *PMLA* 129:4 (2014). 672–87.

Grell, Ole Peter, Jonathan Israel, and Nicholas Tyacke, eds. *From Persecution to Toleration: The Glorious Revolution and Religion in England.* Oxford: Clarendon Press, 1991.

Greville, Robert, Lord Brooke. *The Nature of Truth*. London, 1641. Wing B4913.

A Discourse Opening the Nature of Episcopacy. London, 1642. Wing B4911.

Guy, John. *Politics, Law and Counsel in Tudor and Early Stuart England*. Burlington: Ashgate, 2000.

Thomas More. London: Arnold, 2000.

Habermas, Jürgen. *The Structural Transformation of the Public Sphere: An Inquiry into a Category of Bourgeois Society*. Trans. Thomas Burger. Boston: Massachusetts Institute of Technology Press, 1991.

Hadfield, Andrew. *Edmund Spenser's Irish Experience: Wilde Fruit and Salvage Soyl*. Oxford: Clarendon Press, 1997.

Edmund Spenser: A Life. Oxford: Oxford University Press, 2012.

Hake, Edward. *Epieikeia: A Dialogue on Equity in Three Parts*. Ed. D. E. C. Yale. New Haven: Yale University Press, 1953.

Hall, Joseph. *Meditations and Vows, Divine and Moral*. London, 1616. STC 12683.

Haller, William. *The Rise of Puritanism*. New York: Harper, 1957.

Liberty and Reformation in the Puritan Revolution. New York: Columbia University Press, 1963.

Hammond, Henry. *Of Conscience*. London, 1644. Wing H548.

Hanford, James Holly. "That Shepherd, Who First Taught the Chosen Seed." *University of Toronto Quarterly* 8 (1939). 403–19.

Hanson, Donald. *From Kingdom to Commonwealth: The Development of Civic Consciousness in English Political Thought*. Cambridge: Harvard University Press, 1970.

Held, George. "Brother Poets: The Relationship between George and Edward Herbert." *Like Season'd Timber: New Essays on George Herbert*. Ed. Edmund Miller and Robert DiYanni. New York: P. Lang, 1987. 19–35.

Helwys, Thomas. *A Short Declaration of the Mistery of Iniquity*. London, 1612. STC 13056.

Obiections Answered by way of Dialogue. London, 1615. STC 13054.

Herbert, Edward, Lord of Cherbury. *De Veritate*. Trans. Meyrick Carré. Bristol: J. W. Arrowsmith, 1937.

Lord Herbert of Cherbury's De Religione Laici. Ed. Harold Hutchesen. New Haven: Yale University Press, 1944.

Herbert, George. *The Complete English Works*. Ed. Ann Pasternak Slater. New York: Everyman, 1995.

The English Poems of George Herbert. Ed. Helen Wilcox. Cambridge: Cambridge University Press, 2007.

Hill, Christopher. *Milton and the English Revolution*. New York: Penguin, 1978.

"Covenant Theology and the Concept of the Public Person." *Powers, Possessions and Freedom: Essays in Honour of C.B. Macpherson*. Ed. Alkis Kontos. Toronto: University of Toronto Press, 1979. 3–22.

Hobbes, Thomas. *De Cive*. Ed. Howard Warrender. Oxford: Clarendon, 1983.

Leviathan. Ed. Richard Tuck. Cambridge: Cambridge University Press, 1997.

Holl, Karl. *What Did Luther Understand by Religion?* Trans. Fred Meuser and Walter Wietzke. Ed. James Luther Adams and Walter Bense. Philadelphia: Fortress Press, 1977.

Holland, Peter. "'The Interpretation of Dreams' in the Renaissance." *Reading Dreams: The Interpretation of Dreams from Chaucer to Shakespeare.* Ed. Peter Brown. Oxford: Oxford University Press, 1999. 125–46.

Hoopes, Robert. *Right Reason in the English Renaissance.* Cambridge: Harvard University Press, 1962.

Huguelet, Theodore. *Milton's Hermeneutics: A Study of Scriptural Interpretation in the Divorce Tracts and in* De Doctrina Christiana. Unpublished PhD. Chapel Hill: University of North Carolina, 1959.

Huit, Ephraim. *The Anatomy of Conscience.* London, 1626. STC 13928.

Hume, Alexander. *Ane Treatise of Conscience.* Edinburgh, 1594. STC 13943.

Hume, Anthea. *Edmund Spenser: Protestant Poet.* Cambridge: Cambridge University Press, 1984.

Hunter, William B. Jr. "John Milton: Autobiographer." *Milton Quarterly* 8 (1974). 100–4.

Huntley, Frank. "Macbeth and the Background of Jesuitical Equivocation." *PMLA* 79:4 (1964). 390–400.

Hutchinson, F. E. *The Works of George Herbert.* Oxford: Clarendon Press, 1941.

Hutson, Lorna. "The 'Double Voice' of Renaissance Equity and the Literary Voices of Women." *'This Double Voice': Gendered Writing in Early Modern England.* Ed. Danielle Clarke and Elizabeth Clarke. New York: St. Martin's Press, 2000. 142–63.

"Not the King's Two Bodies: Reading the 'Body Politic' in Shakespeare's Henry IV, Parts 1 and 2." *Rhetoric and Law in Early Modern Europe.* Ed. Victoria Kahn and Lorna Hutson. New Haven: Yale University Press, 2001. 166–98.

Jones, David Martin. *Conscience and Allegiance in Seventeenth Century England: The Political Significance of Oaths and Engagements.* Rochester: University of Rochester Press, 1999.

Jonsen, Albert and Stephen Toulmin. *The Abuse of Casuistry: A History of Moral Reasoning.* Berkeley: University of California Press, 1988.

Jordan, W. K. *The Development of Religious Toleration in England.* 4 vols. Gloucester: Peter Smith, 1965.

Kahn, Victoria. *Wayward Contracts: The Crisis of Political Obligation in England, 1640–1674.* Princeton: Princeton University Press, 2004.

The Future of Illusion: Political Theology and Early Modern Texts. Chicago: University of Chicago Press, 2014.

Kant, Immanuel. *The Metaphysics of Morals.* Trans. Mary Gregor. Cambridge: Cambridge University Press, 1996.

Keenan, James. "William Perkins and the Birth of British Casuistry." *The Context of Casuistry.* Ed. James Keenan and Thomas Shannon. Georgetown, Washington, DC: Georgetown University Press, 1995. 105–30.

"Was William Perkins' *Whole Treatise of Cases of Conscience* Casuistry?: Hermeneutics and British Practical Divinity." *Contexts of Conscience in Early Modern Europe, 1500–1700*. Ed. Harald Braun and Edward Vallance. New York: Palgrave Macmillan, 2004. 17–31.

Keenan, James and Thomas Shannon, eds. *The Context of Casuistry*. Georgetown, Washington, DC: Georgetown University Press, 1995.

Kelley, Maurice. "Milton and Miracles." *Modern Language Notes* 53:3 (1938). 170–2.

This Great Argument: A Study of Milton's De Doctrina Christiana *as a Gloss upon* Paradise Lost. Gloucester: Peter Smith, 1962.

Kendall, R. T. *Calvin and English Calvinism to 1649*. Oxford: Oxford University Press, 1979.

Kerrigan, William. *The Prophetic Milton*. Charlottesville: University Press of Virginia, 1974.

"The Irrational Coherence of Samson Agonistes." *Milton Studies* 22 (1986). 217–32.

King, John. *Spenser's Poetry and the Reformation Tradition*. Princeton: Princeton University Press, 1990.

King, Martin Luther. "Letter from a Birmingham Jail." *Why We Can't Wait*. New York: Signet, 2000. 64–84.

Klinck, Dennis. *Conscience, Equity and the Court of Chancery in Early Modern England*. Burlington: Ashgate, 2010.

Knapp, Steven. *Personification and the Sublime: Milton to Coleridge*. Cambridge: Harvard University Press, 1985.

Kolbrenner, William. *Milton's Warring Angels: A Study of Critical Engagements*. Cambridge: Cambridge University Press, 1997.

Langland, William. *The Vision of Piers Plowman*. Ed. A. V. C. Schmidt. London: Everyman, 1995.

Langston, Douglas. *Conscience and Other Virtues: From Bonaventure to MacIntyre*. University Park: The Pennsylvania State University Press, 2001.

Leites, Edmund, ed. *Conscience and Casuistry in Early Modern Europe*. Cambridge: Cambridge University Press, 1988.

Letters and Papers Foreign and Domestic of the Reign of Henry VIII. 2nd edition. Gen. Ed. J. S. Brewer. 10 vols. London: Kraus, 1965.

Lewalski, Barbara. "Milton and Idolatry." *SEL Studies in English Literature 1500–1900* 43. 1 (2003). 213–32.

Lewis, C. S. *Studies in Words*. Cambridge: Cambridge University Press, 1996.

Lilburne, John. *Foundations of Freedom, or An Agreement of the People*. London, 1648. Wing L2110A.

Linaker, Robert. *A Comfortable Treatise for the Reliefe of Such As Are Afflicted in Conscience*. London, 1595. STC 15638.

Lobo, Giuseppina Iacono. "Early Quaker Writing, Oliver Cromwell, and the Nationalization of Conscience." *Exemplaria* 24:1–2 (2012). 112–26.

Locke, John. *An Essay Concerning Human Understanding*. Ed. Peter Nidditch. Oxford: Clarendon Press, 1979.

Lockey, Brian. "'Equitie to Measure': The Perils of Imperial Imitation in Edmund Spenser's *The Faerie Queene.*" *Journal for Early Modern Cultural Studies* 10:1 (2010). 52–70.

Loewenstein, David. *Representing Revolution in Milton and His Contemporaries: Religion, Politics, and Polemics in Radical Puritanism.* Cambridge: Cambridge University Press, 2001.

Lottin, Odon. *Psychologie et morale aux XIIe et XIIIe siècles.* 2 vols. Gembloux: J Ducolot, 1957.

Low, Anthony. "'Umpire Conscience': Freedom, Obedience, and the Cartesian Flight from Calvin in Paradise Lost." *Studies in Philology* 96:3 (1999). 348–65.

Lupton, Julia Reinhard. *Thinking with Shakespeare: Essays on Politics and Life.* Chicago: The University of Chicago Press, 2011.

Luther, Martin. *D. Martin Luthers Werke: Kritische Gesamtausgabe.* Weimar, 1883. 127 vols.

Luther's Works. Gen. Ed. Jaroslav Pelikan, Helmut T. Lehman, Joel W. Lundeen. 55 vols. Saint Louis: Concordia, Philadelphia: Fortress Press, 1958–86.

Macedo, Stephen. *Diversity and Distrust: Civic Education in a Multicultural Democracy.* Cambridge: Harvard University Press, 2000.

Macpherson, C. B. *The Political Theory of Possessive Individualism: Hobbes to Locke.* Oxford: Oxford University Press, 1962.

Majeske, Andrew. *Equity in English Renaissance Literature: Thomas More and Edmund Spenser.* New York: Routledge, 2006.

Maley, Willy. *A Spenser Chronology.* New York: Barnes and Noble, 1994.

Manning, Brian. "The Levellers and Religion." *Radical Religion in the English Revolution.* Ed. J. F. McGregor and B. Reay. Oxford: Oxford University Press, 1984. 65–90.

Martin, Catherine Gimelli. *Milton among the Puritans: The Case for Historical Revisionism.* Burlington: Ashgate, 2010.

McAdoo, H. R. *The Structure of Caroline Moral Theology.* London: Longman, 1946.

McCabe, Richard. "The Fate of Irena: Spenser and Political Violence." *Spenser and Ireland: An Interdisciplinary Perspective.* Ed. Patricia Coughlan. Cork: Cork University Press, 1989. 109–23.

McInerny, Ralph. *Ethica Thomistica: The Moral Philosophy of Thomas Aquinas.* Revised edition. Washington, DC: Catholic University of America Press, 1997.

McKim, Donald. "The Functions of Ramism in William Perkins' Theology." *The Sixteenth Century Journal* 16:4 (1985). 503–17.

McLachlan, Herbert. *The Religious Opinions of Milton, Locke, and Newton.* Manchester: Manchester University Press, 1941.

Michel, Dan of Northgate. *Ayenbite of Inwyt or Remorse of Conscience.* Ed. Richard Morris. London: Kegan Paul, 1866.

Milton, John. *The Works of John Milton.* Gen. Ed. Frank Allen Patterson. 18 vols. New York: Columbia University Press, 1931–8.

The Complete Prose Works of John Milton. Gen. Ed. Don M. Wolfe. 8 vols. New Haven: Yale University Press, 1953–82.

Complete Shorter Poems. Ed. John Carey. London: Longman, 1990.

Paradise Lost. Ed. Alastair Fowler. London: Longman, 1992.

Mitchell, Joshua. "Thomas Hobbes: On Religious Liberty and Sovereignty." *Religious Liberty in Western Thought*. Ed. Noel Reynolds and W. Cole Durham. Atlanta: Scholar's Press, 1996. 123–42.

Mohamad, Feisal. *Milton and the Post-Secular Present: Ethics, Politics, Terrorism*. Stanford: Stanford University Press, 2011.

Montaigne, Michel. "Of Freedom of Conscience." *The Complete Essays of Montaigne*. Trans. Donald Frame. Stanford: Stanford University Press, 1958. 506–9.

Moore, Rosemary. *The Light in Their Consciences: Early Quakers in Britain, 1646–1666*. University Park: Pennsylvania State University Press, 2000.

More, Thomas. *The Correspondence of Sir Thomas More*. Ed. Elizabeth Frances Rogers. Princeton: Princeton University Press, 1947.

Morrow, John. "How Oliver Cromwell Thought." *Liberty, Authority, Formality: Political Ideas and Culture, 1600–1900: Essays in Honour of Colin Davis*. Ed. John Morrow and Jonathan Scott. Charlottesville: Imprint Academic, 2008. 89–111.

Mortimer, Sarah. *Reason and Religion in the English Revolution: The Challenge of Socinianism*. Cambridge: Cambridge University Press, 2010.

Mueller, Janel. "Milton on Heresy." *Milton and Heresy*. Ed. Stephen Dobranski and John Rumrich. Cambridge: Cambridge University Press, 1998. 21–38.

Mulhall, Stephen and Adam Swift. *Liberals and Communitarians*. 2nd edition. Oxford: Blackwell, 1996.

Mullaney, Stephen. *The Place of the Stage: License, Play, and Power in Renaissance England*. Ann Arbor: University of Michigan Press, 1995.

New Catholic Encyclopedia. Washington, DC: Catholic University of America Press, 2003.

Nietzsche, Friedrich. *On the Genealogy of Morals*. Trans. Walter Kaufman. New York: Random House, 1967.

Nohrnberg, James. *The Analogy of* The Faerie Queene. Princeton: Princeton University Press, 1976.

Norbrook, David. "Areopagitica, Censorship, and the Early Modern Public Sphere." *The Administration of Aesthetics: Censorship, Political Criticism and the Public Sphere*. Ed. Richard Burt. Minneapolis: University of Minnesota Press, 1994. 3–33.

Writing the English Republic: Poetry, Rhetoric and Politics, 1627–1660. Cambridge: Cambridge University Press, 2000.

Nuttall, Geoffrey. *The Holy Spirit in Puritan Faith and Experience*. Chicago: University of Chicago Press, 1992.

Oberman, Heiko. *The Harvest of Medieval Theology: Gabriel Biel and Late Medieval Nominalism*. Grand Rapids: Eerdmans, 1967.

Overton, Richard and William Walwyn. *A Remonstrance of Many Thousand Citizens*. London, 1646. Wing O632B.

Owen, John. *Of the Divine Original*. London, 1659. Wing O784.

Ozment, Steven. *Homo Spiritualis*. Leiden: Brill, 1969.

"Martin Luther on Religious Liberty." *Religious Liberty in Western Thought*. Ed. Noel Reynolds and W. Cole Durham. Atlanta: Scholar's Press, 1996. 75–82.

Parker, Willam Riley. *Milton: A Biography*. Oxford: Clarendon Press, 1968.

Parsons, Robert. *A Treatise Tending to Mitigation Towardes Catholick Subiectes in England*. London, 1607. STC 19417.

Pateman, Carole. *The Problem of Political Obligation: A Critique of Liberal Theory*. Berkeley: University of California Press, 1985.

The Sexual Contract. Stanford: Stanford University Press, 1988.

Patterson, Annabel. *Early Modern Liberalism*. Cambridge: Cambridge University Press, 1997.

Perkins, William. *A Case of Conscience: The Greatest There Ever Was: How a Man May Know Whether He Be the Child of God or No*. London, 1592. STC 19666.

A Discourse of Conscience. London, 1596. STC 19696.

De Praedestinationis Mode et Ordine. Cambridge, 1598. STC 19682.

Works. London, 1603. STC 19647.

Hepieíkeia, or a Treatise of Christian Equity. London, 1604. STC 19699.

Works. London, 1605. STC 19648.

The Whole Treatise of the Cases of Conscience. London, 1606. STC 19669.

A Treatise of Man's Imagination. London, 1607. STC 19751.

Works. London, 1609. STC 19649.

William Perkins 1558–1602: English Puritanist. Ed. Thomas Merrill. Nieuwkoop: B. De Graaf, 1966.

The Work of William Perkins. Ed. Ian Breward. Appleford: Sutton Courtenay Press, 1970.

Petto, Samuel. *The Voice of the Spirit*. London, 1654. Wing P1903.

Pierce, C. A. *Conscience in the New Testament*. London: SCM Press, 1958.

Porter, H. C. *Reformation and Reaction in Tudor Cambridge*. Cambridge: Cambridge University Press, 1958.

Potts, Timothy. *Conscience in Medieval Philosophy*. Cambridge: Cambridge University Press, 1980.

Radzinowicz, Mary Ann. *Toward Samson Agonistes: The Growth of Milton's Mind*. Princeton: Princeton University Press, 1978.

Rawls, John. *Political Liberalism*. New York: Columbia University Press, 1993.

Records of the Churches of Christ Gathered at Fenstanton, Warboys, and Hexham, 1644–1720. Ed. Edward Bean Underhill. London: Hanserd Knollys, 1854.

Reynolds, Noel and W. Cole Durham Jr., eds. *Religious Liberty in Western Thought*. Atlanta: Scholar's Press, 1996.

Rittgers, Ronald. *The Reformation of the Keys: Confession, Conscience and Authority in Sixteenth-Century Germany*. Cambridge: Harvard University Press, 2004.

Rivius, Ioannes. *De Conscientia Libri III.* Leipzig, 1541.

Robinson, Henry. *Liberty of Conscience.* London, 1644. Wing R1675.

John the Baptist, Forerunner of Christ Jesus, or A Necessity for Liberty of Conscience. London: 1644. Wing R1673.

Rogers, G. A. J. "The Other-Worldly Philosophers and the Real World: The Cambridge Platonists, Theology and Politics." *The Cambridge Platonists in Philosophical Context: Politics, Metaphysics and Religion.* Ed. Rogers, J. M. Vienne, Y. C. Zarka. Dordrecht: Kluwer, 1997. 3–15.

Rudrum, Alan. "Milton Scholarship and the Agon over Samson Agonistes." *Huntington Library Quarterly* 65 (2002). 465–88.

Rupp, Gordon. *The Righteousness of God.* London: Hodder and Stoughton, 1968.

Rutherford, Samuel. *A Free Disputation against Pretended Liberty of Conscience.* London, 1649. Wing R2379.

Saltmarsh, John. *The Smoke in the Temple.* London, 1646. Wing S499.

Sandel, Michael. *Liberalism and the Limits of Justice.* 2nd edition. Cambridge: Cambridge University Press, 1998.

Sanderson, Robert. *Several Cases of Conscience, Discussed in Ten Lectures.* Trans. Robert Codrington. London, 1660. Wing S630.

Nine Cases of Conscience. London, 1678. Wing S618.

De Obligatione Conscientiae. London, 1682. Wing S594.

Sauer, Elizabeth. *Milton, Toleration, and Nationhood.* Cambridge: Cambridge University Press, 2014.

Schmitt, Carl. *Hamlet or Hecuba: The Intrusion of the Time in the Play.* Trans. David Pan and Jennifer Rust. New York: Telos Press, 2009.

Scot, Reginald. *The Discoverie of Witchcraft.* London, 1584. STC 21864.

Scribner, Robert. "The Reformation, Popular Magic, and the 'Disenchantment of the World.'" *The Journal of Interdisciplinary History* 23. 3 (1993). 475–494.

Seaton, A. A. *The Theory of Toleration under the Later Stuarts.* New York: Octagon, 1972.

Selden, John. *Table Talk of John Selden.* Ed. Frederick Pollock. London: Selden Society, 1927.

Sensabaugh, George. *That Grand Whig, Milton.* Stanford: Stanford University Press, 1952.

Shakespeare, William. *The Riverside Shakespeare.* 2nd edition. Ed. G. B. Evans, *et al.* Boston: Houghton Mifflin, 1997.

The Norton Shakespeare: Based on the Oxford Editions. Ed. Stephen Greenblatt, *et al.* 2nd edition. New York: Norton, 2008.

Sharp, Andrew, ed. *The English Levellers.* Cambridge: Cambridge University Press, 1998.

Sharpe, Kevin. *Remapping Early Modern England: The Culture of Seventeenth-Century Politics.* Cambridge: Cambridge University Press, 2000.

Shuger, Debora. *The Renaissance Bible: Scholarship, Sacrifice, and Subjectivity.* Berkeley: University of California Press, 1994.

Sibbes, Richard. *A Fountaine Sealed, or the Dutie of the Sealed to the Spirit.* London: 1638. STC 22496.

The Saints Priviledge (1638) in *The Returning Backslider*. London, 1639. STC 225005.

Sirluck, Ernst. "A Note on the Rhetoric of Spenser's Despair." *Modern Philology* 47 (1949). 8–11.

"That Grand Whig." *Modern Philology* 52:1 (1954). 63–67.

Skinner, Quentin and Martin van Gelderen, eds. *Freedom and the Construction of Europe*. 2 vols. Cambridge: Cambridge University Press, 2013.

Skulsky, Harold. "Revenge, Honor and Conscience in *Hamlet*." *PMLA* 85:1 (1970). 78–87.

"Spenser's Despair Episode and the Theology of Doubt." *Modern Philology* 78 (1981). 227–42.

Slights, Camille Wells. *The Casuistical Tradition in Shakespeare, Donne, Herbert, and Milton*. Princeton: Princeton University Press, 1981.

Smith, Nigel. "George Herbert in Defence of Antinomianism." *Notes and Queries* (1984). 334–35.

Perfection Proclaimed: Language and Literature in English Radical Religion. Oxford: Clarendon Press, 1989.

"Areopagitica: Voicing Contexts, 1643–5." *Politics, Poetics, and Hermeneutics in Milton's Prose*. Ed. David Loewenstein and James Grantham Turner. Cambridge: Cambridge University Press, 1990. 103–22.

Snyder, Susan. "The Left Hand of God: Despair in Medieval and Renaissance Tradition." *Studies in the Renaissance* 12 (1965). 18–59.

Solt, Leo. *Saints in Arms: Puritanism and Democracy in Cromwell's Army*. Stanford: Stanford University Press, 1959.

Sommerville, Johann. "'The New Art of Lying:' Equivocation, Mental Reservation, and Casuistry." *Conscience and Casuistry in Early Modern Europe*. Ed. Edmund Leites. Cambridge: Cambridge University Press, 1988. 159–84.

Spenser, Edmund. *The Works of Edmund Spenser: A Variorum Edition*. Ed. Edwin Greenlaw, *et al.* 9 vols. Repr. Baltimore: The Johns Hopkins Press, 1932–49.

The Faerie Queene. 5 vols. Gen. Ed. Abraham Stoll. Ed. Carol Kaske, Erik Gray, Dorothy Stephens, Abraham Stoll, and Andrew Hadfield. Indianapolis: Hackett Publishing, 2006–07.

Sprigge, Joshua. *The Ancient Bounds or Liberty of Conscience*. London, 1645. Wing R2011.

Sprunger, Keith. *The Learned Doctor William Ames: Dutch Backgrounds of English and American Puritanism*. Urbana: University of Illinois Press, 1972.

Spurr, John. "'The Strongest Bond of Conscience': Oaths and the Limits of Tolerance in Early Modern England." *Contexts of Conscience in Early Modern Europe*. Ed. Harald Braun and Edward Vallance. New York: Palgrave Macmillan, 2004. 151–66.

St. German, Christopher. *Doctor and Student*. Ed. T. F. T. Plucknett and J. L. Barton. London: Selden Society, 1974.

Stachniewski, John. *The Persecutory Imagination: English Puritanism and the Literature of Religious Despair*. Oxford: Clarendon Press, 1991.

Steuart, Adam. *Some Observations and Annotations upon the Apologeticall Narration*. London, 1643. Wing S5492.

Stoll, Abraham. *Milton and Monotheism*. Pittsburgh: Duquesne University Press, 2009.

Stone, E. M. W. "Scrupulosity and Conscience: Probabilism in Early Modern Scholastic Ethics." *Contexts of Conscience in Early Modern Europe*. Ed. Harald Braun and Edward Vallance. New York: Palgrave Macmillan, 2004. 1–16.

Strier, Richard. "Shakespeare and the Skeptics." *Religion and Literature* 32 (2000). 171–96.

Strohm, Paul. *Conscience: A Very Short Introduction*. Oxford: Oxford University Press, 2011.

Stump, Donald. "Isis Versus Mercilla: The Allegorical Shrines in Spenser's Legend of Justice." *Spenser Studies* 3 (1982). 87–98.

Suarez, Francisco. *De Anima* in *Opera Omnia*. 28 vols. Paris, 1856–78.

Sullivan, Ceri. *The Rhetoric of the Conscience in Donne, Herbert and Vaughan*. Oxford: Oxford University Press, 2008.

Summers, Joseph. *George Herbert: His Religion and Art*. Cambridge: Harvard University Press, 1968.

Symonds, Joseph. *The Case and Cure of a Deserted Soul*. London, 1642. Wing S6354.

Taylor, Jeremy. *Discourse of the Liberty of Prophesying*. London, 1647. Wing T400.
Ductor Dubitantium, or The Rule of Conscience. London, 1660. Wing T324.

Taylor, Thomas. *Regula Vitae*. London, 1631. STC 23851.
The Progresse of Saints to Full Holinesse. London, 1631. STC 23850a.

Tentler, Thomas. *Sin and Confession on the Eve of Reformation*. Princeton: Princeton University Press, 1977.

Thayer, Anne. "Judge and Doctor: Images of the Confessor in Printed Model Sermon Collections, 1450–1520." *Penitence in the Age of Reformations*. Ed. Katherine Jackson Lualdi and Anne Thayer. Boston: Ashgate, 2000. 10–29.

Thiel, Udo. *The Early Modern Subject: Self-Consciousness and Personal Identity from Descartes to Hume*. Oxford: Oxford University Press, 2011.

Thomas, Keith. *Religion and the Decline of Magic: Studies in Popular Beliefs in Sixteenth and Seventeenth Century England*. Oxford: Oxford University Press, 1971.

Thomason, W. D. J. Cargill. *The Political Thought of Martin Luther*. Sussex: Harvester Press, 1984.

Thoreau, Henry David. *Walden and Civil Disobedience*. Ed. Sherman Paul. Boston: Houghton Mifflin, 1960.

Tilley, Morris Palmer. *A Dictionary of the Proverbs in England in the Sixteenth and Seventeenth Centuries*. Ann Arbor: University of Michigan Press, 1950.

Tillich, Paul. "A Conscience above Moralism." *Conscience: Theological and Psychological Perspectives*. Ed. C. Ellis Nelson. New York: Newman Press, 1973. 46–61.

Tillyard, E. M. W. *Milton*. Revised edition. New York: Collier, 1966.

Tilmouth, Christopher. "Shakespeare's Open Consciences." *Journal of the Society for Renaissance Studies* 23:4 (2009). 501–15.

Tolmie, Murray. *The Triumph of the Saints: The Separate Churches of London, 1616–1649.* Cambridge: Cambridge University Press, 1977.

Trevor, Douglas. *The Poetics of Melancholy in Early Modern England.* Cambridge: Cambridge University Press, 2004.

Trovamala, Baptista. *Summa Casuum Conscientiae.* Venice, 1499.

Tuck, Richard. "The Civil Religion of Thomas Hobbes." *Political Discourse in Early Modern Britain.* Ed. Nicholas Phillipson and Quentin Skinner. Cambridge: Cambridge University Press, 1993. 120–38.

Van Til, L. John. *Liberty of Conscience: The History of a Puritan Idea.* Nutley: Craig Press, 1972.

Vane, Henry. *Zeal Examined, or a Discourse for Liberty of Conscience in Matters of Religion.* London, 1652. Wing Z8.

Veith, Gene Edward. "The Religious Wars in George Herbert Criticism: Reinterpreting Seventeenth-Century Anglicanism." *George Herbert Journal* 11 (1988). 19–35.

Vendler, Helen. *The Poetry of George Herbert.* Cambridge: Harvard University Press, 1975.

Vermigli, Pietro. *The Common Places of the Most Famous and Renowmed Diuine Doctor Peter Martyr.* Trans. Anthonie Marten. London, 1583. STC 24669.

Wallace, John. *Destiny His Choice: The Loyalism of Andrew Marvell.* Cambridge: Cambridge University Press, 1968.

Walwyn, William. *The Compassionate Samaritan.* London, 1644. Wing W681A.

Walwyn's Just Defence against Aspertions. London, 1649. Wing W685.

Walzer, Michael. *The Revolution of the Saints: A Study in the Origins of Radical Politics.* Cambridge: Harvard University Press, 1965.

Obligations. Cambridge: Harvard University Press, 1970.

Warminski, Andrzej. *Readings in Interpretation: Hölderlin, Hegel, Heidegger.* Minneapolis: University of Minnesota Press, 1987.

Weber, Max. "Science as Vocation." *From Max Weber: Essays in Sociology.* Trans. H. H. Gerth and C. Wright Mills. Oxford: Oxford University Press, 1953.

Weber, Samuel. "Taking Exception to Decision: Walter Benjamin and Carl Schmitt." *Diacritics* 22 (1992). 5–18.

Webster, Tom. *Godly Clergy in Early Stuart England: The Caroline Puritan Movement c. 1620–43.* Cambridge: Cambridge University Press, 1997.

Whitaker, Virgil. *The Religious Basis of Spenser's Thought.* Stanford: Stanford University Press, 1950.

Whitaker, William. *A Disputation of Holy Scripture.* Trans. William Fitzgerald. Cambridge: Cambridge University Press, 1849.

Disputatio De Sacra Scriptura. London, 1588. STC 25366.

Wilding, Michael. *Dragons Teeth: Literature in the English Revolution.* Oxford: Clarendon Press, 1987.

"Milton's *Areopagitica*: Liberty for the Sects." *The Literature of Controversy: Polemical Strategy from Milton to Junius.* Ed. Thomas Corns. London: Frank Cass, 1987. 7–38.

Wildman, John. *Putney Projects, Or the Old Serpent in a New Forme*. London, December 1647. Wing W2171.

Wilkerson, Robert. *The Saints Travel to the Land of Canaan*. London, 1648. Wing 2251B.

Wilks, John. *The Idea of Conscience in Renaissance Tragedy*. London and New York: Routledge, 1990.

Williams, Roger. *The Bloudy Tenent of Persecution, for Cause of Conscience*. London, 1644. Wing W2758.

Wills, Gary. *Witches and Jesuits: Shakespeare's Macbeth*. Oxford: Oxford University Press, 1995.

Wilson, Luke. "*Hamlet*: Equity, Intention, Performance." *Studies in the Literary Imagination* 24 (1991). 91–113.

Wilson, Robert. *Three Ladies of London*. London, 1584. STC 25784.

The Three Lords and Three Ladies of London. London, 1590. STC 25783.

Witte, John Jr., "Moderate Religious Liberty in the Theology of John Calvin." *Religious Liberty in Western Thought*. Ed. Noel Reynolds and W. Cole Durham. Atlanta: Scholar's Press, 1996. 83–122.

Wittreich, Joseph. *Interpreting* Samson Agonistes. Princeton: Princeton University Press, 1986.

Shifting Contexts: Reinterpreting Samson Agonistes. Pittsburgh: Duquesne University Press, 2002.

Wolfe, Don. *Milton in the Puritan Revolution*. New York: Thomas Nelson, 1941.

Wood, Derek. *'Exiled from Light': Divine Law, Morality, and Violence in Milton's Samson Agonistes*. Toronto: University of Toronto Press, 2001.

Wood, Thomas. *English Casuistical Divinity during the Seventeenth Century, with Special Reference to Jeremy Taylor*. London: S.P.C.K., 1952.

Woodes, Nathaniel. *The Conflict of Conscience*. London, 1581. STC 25966.5.

Woodhouse, A. S. P., ed. *Puritanism and Liberty: Being the Army Debates (1647–9) from the Clarke Manuscripts with Supplementary Documents*. Chicago: University of Chicago Press, 1951.

Woolton, John. *Of the Conscience*. London, 1574. STC 25978.

Wooten, David. *Divine Right and Democracy*. New York: Penguin, 1986.

"Leveller Democracy and the Puritan Revolution." *The Cambridge History of Political Thought, 1450–1700*. Ed. J. H. Burns. Cambridge: Cambridge University Press, 1991. 412–42.

Worden, Blair. "Toleration and the Cromwellian Protectorate." *Persecution and Toleration*. Ed. W. J. Sheils. Oxford: Basil Blackwell, 1984. 199–233.

"Milton's Republicanism and the Tyranny of Heaven." *Machiavelli and Republicanism*. Ed. Gisela Bock, Quentin Skinner, and Maurizio Viroli. Cambridge: Cambridge University Press, 1990. 225–45.

"Milton, *Samson Agonistes*, and the Restoration." *Culture and Society in the Stuart Restoration: Literature, Drama, History*. Ed. Gerald MacLean. Cambridge: Cambridge University Press, 1995. 111–36.

God's Instruments: Political Conduct in the England of Oliver Cromwell. Oxford: Oxford University Press, 2012.

Wright, Louis B. "William Perkins: Elizabethan Apostle of 'Practical Divinity.'" *Huntington Library Quarterly* 3:2 (1940). 171–96.

Zachman, Randall. *The Assurance of Faith: Conscience in the Theology of Martin Luther and John Calvin*. Minneapolis: Fortress Press, 1993.

Zagorin, Perez. *Ways of Lying: Dissimulation, Persecution, and Conformity in Early Modern Europe*. Cambridge: Harvard University Press, 1990.

Hobbes and the Law of Nature. Princeton: Princeton University Press, 2009.

Zurcher, Andrew. *Spenser's Legal Language: Law and Poetry in Early Modern England*. Cambridge: D. S. Brewer, 2007.

Index